ROI OF SOFTWARE PROCESS IMPROVEMENT

Metrics for
Project Managers and Software Engineers

DAVID F. RICO

Foreword by Dr. Roger S. Pressman

ISBN 1-932159-24-X

Printed and bound in the U.S.A. Printed on acid-free paper
10 9 8 7 6 5 4 3 2 1

Capability Maturity Model® and CMM® are registered in the U.S. Patent and Trademark Office. Capability Maturity Model Integration® and CMMI® are registered in the U.S. Patent and Trademark Office. Personal Software Process℠ and PSP℠ are service marks of Carnegie Mellon University. Team Software Process℠ and TSP℠ are service marks of Carnegie Mellon University.

Library of Congress Cataloging-in-Publication Data

Rico, David F., 1964–
  ROI of software process improvement : metrics for project managers and software engineers / David F. Rico.
      p. cm.
    ISBN 1-932159-24-X
  1. Computer software—Development. I. Title.
  QA76.76.D47 R56 2004
  005.1—dc22   2003019248

Direct all inquiries to J. Ross Publishing, Inc., 6501 Park of Commerce Blvd., Suite 200, Boca Raton, Florida 33487.

Phone: (561) 869-3900
Fax: (561) 892-0700
Web: www.jrosspub.com

DEDICATION

This book is dedicated to my loving wife, Celia. She is the rock of my life, my guiding light, and my inspiration. This book is also dedicated to my children, David, Serena, Faith, and Christian. May they overcome the obstacles of this world and easily obtain the desires of their hearts. And, of course, to countless generations of my family, who laid an ever so gradual foundation for future success.

CONTENTS

FOREWORD

There are three important rules that everyone should follow when using metrics to assess a software process: (1) be sure that you define your goals before you begin measuring, (2) identify meaningful metrics that will help you to achieve your goals, and (3) keep it simple — very simple. Over the years, most software engineering organizations have struggled as they attempt to implement these rules. First, it has been difficult to establish well-defined goals that are meaningful to senior management and at the same time consequential to technical managers and practitioners. Second, it has been challenging to define a set of metrics that truly reflect the efficacy of a software process. And last, we refuse to keep it simple — defining metrics that sometimes do more to confuse than to illuminate.

But now we have help. With the publication of this book, David Rico cuts through the complexity and confusion associated with the measurement of the software process and provides us with a road map for understanding its costs and benefits. At the core of Rico's approach is an age-old business metric — *return-on-investment* (ROI) — a common-sense method for evaluating whether the costs associated with any business activity are justified based on the return (benefit) accrued as the business activity is applied over time. It seems pretty obvious that this measure is the one to apply. After all, we spend money (sometimes lots of it) to implement a software process. It seems only reasonable that we should justify these expenditures with more than arm waving.

Then why haven't more software organizations used ROI as a primary metric in the evaluation of software process models? The reason, I think, is that most software organizations don't really understand how to measure ROI in a software context. There has been no cohesive information source that delineates (1) the data that should be collected as the software process is instantiated and applied, (2) the models that must be developed to understand cost and benefit, and (3) the mechanisms that should be applied to interpret and act upon the results derived from application of the ROI metric.

ROI of Software Process Improvement changes all of this by providing concrete, quantitative guidelines for determining process improvement costs, benefits, ROI, net present value, and the breakeven point. Rather than doing this for an abstract "process," Rico selects today's major software process models and process improvement strategies — the Software Inspection Process, the Personal Software Process[SM], Team Software Process[SM], Software Capability Maturity Model®, ISO 9001, and Capability Maturity Model Integration® — and defines a methodology for computing ROI for each.

This book will help you in your efforts to improve the software process within your organization. Why? It will show you how to characterize the problem and your efforts to solve it in terms that senior management can appreciate using metrics that every senior manager understands. And as a result, it will provide you with the ammunition you'll need to convince senior management to adequately fund software process improvement efforts and to continue funding over the long haul. The end result is a better software process and, as a consequence, higher quality software, better time to market, and controlled development costs.

Dr. Roger S. Pressman

PREFACE

The purpose of this book is to teach useful concepts in return on investment of software process improvement or ROI of SPI. The title was carefully chosen to convey its meaning and purpose. "Return on investment" was selected because this book teaches software practitioners how to measure the value of their work. "Software process improvement" is used to emphasize the highly specialized field of increasing productivity and quality. "Metrics for project managers and software engineers" also has a very special meaning, which is to emphasize software measurement.

This book is designed to realize several objectives. The basic objective is to introduce ROI concepts, briefly describe the field of SPI, and highlight important approaches to SPI. The second objective is to explain the relevance of ROI measurement. ROI is explained for commercial firms as well as large, nonprofit organizations. The overriding objective is to show software practitioners how to measure software processes and determine their value. The final objective is to point out that SPI is extremely difficult, expensive, and risk intensive. Yet, the reader is taught how to overcome all too typical resistance to change using the ROI of SPI.

ROI is a basic but powerful tool for evaluating costs and benefits. Costs and benefits are expressed in economic or monetary terms. That is, ROI is all about measuring value in dollars and cents. First, the benefits are converted into monetary terms and accumulated. Then the costs are accounted for in great detail. Once the benefits and costs have been determined, ROI is a rather elementary matter. ROI is simply the ratio of benefits to costs, less the costs of course. The notion of net present value and breakeven point analysis is introduced, and all of these concepts are related to software project and quality management.

SPI, on the other hand, presents a rather ominous challenge. SPI is a controversial and even much maligned subdiscipline of software engineering. SPI is the application of organizational change for software engineers and software engineering. That is, SPI is the act of changing and improving software engineering processes. The software engineering processes are changed for a reason. That reason is usually increased productivity, faster cycle times, better product quality, and happier customers. However, SPI is often performed for the sake of SPI. Software engineering processes are usually changed for the sake of changing them. Rarely is their performance measured, analyzed, and used as a basis for improvement. This book covers the field of SPI in enough depth to sort through some of the more challenging aspects of change.

However, this book goes beyond the field of SPI. It takes the reader on a journey through SPI measurement. That is, this book shows the reader how to measure software process performance. It also shows how to transform process performance into monetary or economic terms.

Several pervasive issues are addressed in this book. One is to solve seemingly difficult problems in software measurement. The harder part of ROI of SPI is not counting the costs but counting the benefits. A major contribution is teaching practitioners how to identify benefits, quantify them, and express them in economic terms. This book also emphasizes the importance of counting the costs. Many software practitioners avoid costs, because they may be embarrassingly high.

Finally, this book is not designed to promote SPI. It is designed to show how difficult SPI can be, how expensive it is, and how to be successful with SPI in the long run. Software engineering is a difficult problem, but it is not an impossible one.

ABOUT THE AUTHOR

 **David F. Rico** is an itinerant technical leader for software process and quality improvement. He is internationally recognized for helping prestigious organizations become accredited and compliant with CMMI®, SW-CMM®, and ISO 9001, 15288, and 12207. His strength is helping fiercely resistant and resource-constrained organizations achieve fast and measurable benefits and accreditation.

Mr. Rico has advanced skills with state-of-the-art methods and tools for designing software engineering policies, procedures, standards, and processes. His capabilities include motivational lectures, program diagnosis, economic justification, strategic planning, program management, appraisals, life cycle design, compliance analysis, training, software metrics and models, quality assurance, and configuration management. His expertise consists of using earned value management and reliability models to design quantitative project and quality management systems.

Mr. Rico specializes in cost and benefit, return on investment, net present value, and breakeven point analysis for software process improvement and project portfolio management. He designed a cost and benefit study of eight major software process improvement methods which was distributed by the European Software Institute, Netherlands Software Engineering Research Center, and the U.S. DTIC/AFRL-IF Data and Analysis Center for Software. He authored an e-book on return on investment which was downloaded over 30,000 times in its first few weeks, and he has published numerous articles on return on investment which have been published in *TickIT,* SEPG, ICSPI, *SPIder*

Koerier, Software TechNews, and ISPA/SCEA. His Web site (http://
davidfrico.com) attracts 250,000 visitors a month from 75 countries.

Mr. Rico has led, managed, and participated in over 15 SW-CMM® Level
2, 3, 4, and 5 initiatives for NASA, U.S. Air Force, U.S. Navy, DISA, DARPA,
Japanese firms, and some of the most prestigious U.S. high-technology corporations. He helped capture a $250 million software engineering modernization
contract for NASA, design the spacecraft software for NASA's $20 billion
space station, and achieve SW-CMM® and ISO 9001 accreditation for Japan's
largest computer company at $40 billion. He helped modernize a family of U.S.
Air Force static radar ranges, reengineer 36 military logistics depots in Cairo,
Egypt, and design a $30 billion constellation of U.S. Air Force satellites. He
helped conduct a $42 million U.S. Navy source selection, design a cost model
for distributing $70 million to 37 U.S. Navy aircraft programs including F-18
and F-14, and implement engineering management practices for leading-edge
DISA and DARPA high-technology initiatives. He helped the U.S. Space and
Naval Warfare Center, an $87 million U.S. General Services Administration
(GSA) information technology center, and a $25 million electrical engineering
center of excellence to achieve SW-CMM® accreditation. He recently managed
a multimillion-dollar software engineering training curriculum for hundreds of
computer programmers, spearheaded an initiative to measure the return on
investment of institutional software engineering training, and is helping integrate multiple families of enterprise architectures for a multibillion-dollar U.S.
government agency.

Mr. Rico has been an international keynote speaker, published numerous
articles, and completed SW-CMM® and CMMI® introductory and intermediate
training. He holds a B.S. in Computer Science and an M.S.A. in Software
Engineering and has been in the field of computer programming since 1983.

ACKNOWLEDGMENTS

I want to personally thank Jason Handy, Byon Williams, and Julie Garrard of Knowledge Based Systems, Inc. (http://www.kbsi.com) for donating the world's best IDEF0 modeling tool to support this project, AI0 WIN®. I would also like to thank Thomas McGibbon, whose works have been inspirational and whose personal support and encouragement have been critical to the formation of the concepts in this book. Last, but not least, I want to thank Kyle Y. Rone for introducing me to quantitative concepts in software process improvement and framing the context for my entire professional career.

™Web Added Value

Value-added materials available from
the Download Resource Center at www.jrosspub.com

At J. Ross Publishing we are committed to providing today's professional with practical, hands-on tools that enhance the learning experience and give readers an opportunity to apply what they have learned. That is why we offer free ancillary materials available for download on this book and all participating Web Added Value™ publications. These online resources may include interactive versions of material that appears in the book or supplemental templates, worksheets, models, plans, case studies, proposals, spreadsheets, and assessment tools, among other things. Whenever you see the WAV™ symbol in any of our publications, it means bonus materials accompany the book and are available from the Web Added Value Download Resource Center at www.jrosspub.com/wav.

The free downloads available for *ROI of Software Process Improvement* consist of valuable detailed software process improvement (SPI) cost models for SW-CMM®, ISO 9001:2000, and CMMI®. They include spreadsheets with metrics and models to calculate costs, benefits, benefit/cost ratio, net present value, return on investment, and breakeven point. These documents are available from the Web Added Value™ Download Resource Center at www.jrosspub.com/wav.

The *ROI Model* is a comprehensive spreadsheet and data source for estimating the ROI of the Software Inspection Process, Personal Software Process℠, Team Software Process℠, Software Capability Maturity Model®, ISO 9001, and Capability Maturity Model Integration®. It contains detailed analytical worksheets for estimating the costs, benefits, B/CR, ROI%, NPV, and breakeven point of inspections, PSP℠, TSP℠, SW-CMM®, ISO 9001, and CMMI®. As an educational instrument, it will help readers master SPI ROI concepts and validate results presented in the book. It is also an excellent tool for large organizations, mid-sized firms, and small enterprises to conduct unprecedented ROI simulations using their own data.

The *CMMI® Cost Model* is the first cost model ever created for the CMMI® or SW-CMM® community since the debut of CMMI®. It provides an unprecedented glimpse into the economics of CMMI® and is a comprehensive, highly scalable cost estimation model and budgeting spreadsheet for accurately estimating CMMI® implementation costs. It is based on the author's practical real-world experience developing CMMI® and SW-CMM® strategic plans for multiple international clients in the Far East, Europe, and United States. The *CMMI® Cost Model* is based on a highly sophisticated, yet powerfully simplistic spreadsheet that consists of a work breakdown structure which quantitatively mirrors the architecture of CMMI®.

It is also based on real-world Delphi techniques and input data for accurately estimating the complete costs of implementing CMMI® policies, procedures, and evidence-of-use. The model is completely scalable for organizations of all shapes and sizes and can be easily tailored using simple Visual Basic macros.

The *SW-CMM® Cost Model* is a common-sense cost model that provides a rare glimpse into the economics of SW-CMM® for performing strategic planning of SW-CMM® initiatives. It consists of a streamlined bottom-up cost estimation model and budgeting spreadsheet for rapidly estimating SW-CMM® implementation costs. It can be used to produce highly scalable SW-CMM® cost estimates and timelines for organizations of all shapes and sizes in a matter of minutes. This model has been successfully used by small, medium, and large high-tech firms to achieve SW-CMM® accreditation in record time.

The *ISO 9001 Cost Model* is a bottom-up budgeting spreadsheet for accurately estimating the costs of implementing ISO 9001 and quantitatively mirrors the architecture of ISO 9001:2000. It was painstakingly, meticulously, and conscientiously designed and calibrated using data from the author's own firsthand experience implementing ISO 9001. It was validated using multiple international parametric cost models for accuracy and analytically compared to comprehensive North American ISO 9001 surveys. It is comprised of a simple one-page spreadsheet, which yields highly accurate ISO 9001 cost estimates in minutes, and can be easily tailored to productivity levels for almost any organization.

If you are interested in obtaining a more comprehensive package in support of the book and free downloads, a complete 169-page *IDEF0 Methodology* is available for sale in PDF® and AI0 Win® formats at www.jrosspub.com.

This document is an interconnected enterprise model for rapidly, easily, and authoritatively estimating the ROI of SPI methods such as the Software Inspection Process, Personal Software Process℠, Team Software Process℠, Software Capability Maturity Model®, ISO 9001 and Capability Maturity Model Integration®.

The *IDEF0 Methodology* is a watershed download for large corporations and nonprofit organizations, which spend millions of dollars on SPI annually. It is also very useful to small- to medium-sized high-tech firms for optimizing the value of their investments in SPI. It will help these companies effectively compete with large blue-chip firms, without having to spend millions of dollars on SPI. It also serves as the perfect tool for the academic community by helping scientists conduct state-of-the-art research in ROI, SPI, and software metrics and deliver just-in-time learning modules to further the education of 21st century students.

This groundbreaking *IDEF0 Methodology*, in conjunction with the book and the free downloads available from the WAV section of the J. Ross Publishing Web site, will save the high-technology community thousands of hours of development time. *The IDEF0 Methodology* establishes a highly extensible and adaptable framework, foundation, and blueprint for creating automated commercial ROI tools, enterprise policies and procedures for ROI, and just-in-time training and educational programs, curricula, and modules in ROI.

INTRODUCTION

The return on investment (ROI) of software process improvement (SPI) is an indispensable tool for determining how effective an organization is at computer programming. The ROI of SPI also extends to the fields of software engineering, information technology, and commercial shrink-wrapped software. The ROI of SPI is useful for providers of high-technology products and services. ROI is not limited to a single market sector, but rather applies equally to the commercial, government, and military sectors. ROI of SPI is useful for ensuring the peak operating efficiency of large, nonprofit organizations in terms of dollars and cents.

The ROI of SPI involves determining how much money a new software tool, process, or methodology yields. ROI reveals how much money a software engineering standard yields on the bottom-line corporate balance sheet. It can also reveal how much money a training program, improvement initiative, or new organizational design yields. The ROI of SPI is an invaluable measurement instrument for stakeholders at all levels of a corporation and organization. ROI enables stakeholders to design the most effective strategies to achieve the maximum benefits. The benefits are often expressed in terms of productivity, quality, profits, and peak operating efficiency.

The ROI of SPI answers the basic question, "How effective is my software engineering in economic or monetary terms?" Gone are the days when processes were improved for the sake of merely changing. Instead, we now ask the question, "What is the economic impact of changing the software process?"

1.1 WHAT IS ROI OF SPI?

The ROI of SPI is the amount of money gained from a new and improved software process. That is, the ROI of SPI refers to a new and improved software process which results in more money than is spent to improve it. For example, ROI is 10 to 1 or 1,000% if a new process requires 100 hours to create and use, versus 1,100 hours for an old one.

The ROI of SPI is generally a ratio of benefits to costs for creating a new and improved software process. The benefits are first adjusted by removing all of the costs before calculating the ratio of benefits to costs. The ROI of SPI or ratio of adjusted benefits to costs indicates the economic value of a new and improved software process. The ROI of SPI is used for determining the value of a new and improved software process. It is also used to decide whether to use a new process, revert to an old one, or begin seeking an even better software process.

ROI of SPI is a tool for teaching people, ranging from executives to the technical staff, that processes have economic value. Software processes affect economic performance and should be evaluated for the purpose of improving cost and quality efficiency. Cost and quality are inseparably linked in often surprising ways.

1.2 WHY IS ROI OF SPI IMPORTANT?

The ROI of SPI is important because it is a process of determining the amount of money to be gained from a new process. It can even be used to determine how much money is lost from creating and using a new and improved software process. The ROI of SPI for a new software process can be astonishingly large, disinterestingly negligible, or soberingly negative. The ROI of SPI is an indispensable everyday tool for aggressively profit-driven corporations. Oftentimes their rise and fall hinges on the ability to successfully steward their assets through many economic obstacle courses. The market is often fraught with dangerous fluctuations, conditions, and confusing indicators. Corporations can avert financial catastrophe and seize their rightful titles as captains of industry by applying the ROI of SPI.

The ROI of SPI is quite useful for large nonprofit organizations and government institutions. The ROI of SPI helps them manage their hard-won resources, capitalization, and funding. It does this by helping to steer them clear of a new software process that has negligible effects on peak operating efficiency. Minimally, the ROI of SPI has a sobering effect on unbridled enthusiasm for a new software process with a negative ROI.

However, it is important to note that the ROI of SPI is merely one of many tools to support critical decision-making processes. There are many tools to support decision making when it comes to selecting a new and improved software process. In fact, it may be necessary for a corporation or organization to create a new process that has a negligible or even negative ROI. This is often done because it is sociopolitically correct or part of a mandatory government regulation or industrial trade agreement. Sometimes, inefficient processes are tied to other forms of economic incentives, motivations, or gains.

For instance, a new and improved software process may have an acceptably negative ROI. However, this process may be part of an industrial trade agreement, resulting in long-term economic gains in place of short-term loss. This, of course, doesn't mean that the ROI of SPI is unimportant, invalid, or fails under certain conditions. It simply means that long-term economic gains should be factored into the equation for ROI of SPI if they can be reliably quantified. Doing this helps to overcome the effects of negligible or even negative impacts on short-term economic performance.

1.3 HOW IS ROI OF SPI DETERMINED?

The ROI of SPI is determined by calculating the ratio of benefits to costs for creating a new and improved software process. The ROI of SPI is a simple ratio of all of the benefits to all of the costs for a new and improved software process. The exact formulas for the ROI of SPI involve subtracting the costs from the benefits before stating the ratio of benefits to costs. The formulas are nonetheless very simple, easy to use, and indispensable.

The benefits for a new and improved software process are usually increases in product variety, portfolio size, and market share. The benefits also include increases in customer satisfaction, productivity, efficiency, quality, and reliability. Decreases in costs, cycle times, and process complexity are important benefits too.

The costs of a new and improved software process include strategic planning, education, and designing new processes. Additional costs include process and development tools, consultants, training, travel, facilities, lost productivity, and project simulation. Costs also include salaries, actual project effort, sociopolitical resistance, and preparation for appraisals and external audits. Don't forget the costs of appraisals and audits, action plans, reaudits and re-certification, and software process maintenance. The benefits of some SPI methods are quite large, so do not be discouraged by the overwhelming costs.

1.4 WHAT ARE KEY METHODS FOR ROI OF SPI?

The key methods for ROI of SPI include analyzing SPI studies, conducting literature surveys, and collecting cost–benefit data. This also includes researching ROI studies and data, examining the cost of quality, and performing cost modeling. Studying defect models, conducting benchmarking studies, using pilots, and collecting long-term data are also key methods.

The key methods have been purposely arranged in order of increasing complexity. They have been arranged from the easiest and most cost-effective means to the most difficult and expensive approaches. It is ironic that the most effective methods for ROI of SPI are often the simplest and least expensive. Conversely, the most difficult and cost-prohibitive methods for ROI of SPI are often the most risk intensive. The difficult methods are generally not worth the time and trouble. They can be hazardous to a person's political career and undermine one's power and status.

It is ironic that some people would insist that you place your hand in a fire for a long time to determine its temperature. That only results in a trip to the hospital and a long and painful recovery. In other words, you don't have to burn yourself to learn that a fire can be very hot. The same principle applies here. Use your head, or your brain to be more specific. Apply a small and inexpensive amount of effort to learning what others have spent millions of dollars to learn firsthand. Use reliable sources of data to help you zero in and focus on the methods that will offer the greatest ROI of SPI. Then, when you have collected some convincing hard data, begin with small-scale piloting and experimentation.

1.5 WHAT ARE KEY PRINCIPLES OF ROI OF SPI?

Key principles of ROI of SPI include application of basic ROI formulas, analysis of ROI inputs, and focusing on benefits of SPI. Key principles also include analysis of simple defect models, cost of quality, total life cycle costs, and pervasive defect prevention. Key principles of ROI of SPI do not require a postgraduate degree in design of mathematically analyzable attitudinal surveys, and they do not include the derivation of indecipherable ROI equations or the application of complex discounting methods. Mastery of Nobel laureate economics, collecting reams of data, and performing years of software measurement are not necessary. ROI of SPI also does not require a personal 15-year SPI journey.

ROI formulas contain only two fundamental terms: benefits and costs. How hard is that? Cost is by far the easiest of the terms to grasp, so focus on the benefits. If you can master the benefits, then you're almost there. Where does information on benefits come from? Benefit data come from analyzing SPI studies, conducting literature surveys, and collecting cost–benefit data. Information also comes from ROI studies, examining the cost of quality, performing cost modeling, and studying defect models.

The benefits of SPI come from two basic sources, increased revenue and profits and decreased costs and cost savings. The benefits of SPI originating from increased revenue and profits are primarily due to increased productivity. That is, increased output or work products per unit time. The benefits of SPI originating from decreased costs and cost savings are due to less maintenance, rework, and testing. This often leads to shorter cycle times and faster schedules.

1.6 WHAT ARE PITFALLS OF ROI OF SPI?

The pitfalls of ROI of SPI are quite numerous. It is easy to believe that ROI is more than just the application of a few basic equations if you haven't done your homework. Unfortunately, many believe that the ROI of SPI and SPI economics are a nonessential part of their continuing SPI journey. Similarly, some people feel that ROI does not apply to them, their situation, or to the field of SPI. A few well-placed individuals think that there is no room for ROI principles in an ad hoc, immature organization. Oftentimes, key SPI leaders believe that their software organization has to be performing at world-class levels before using ROI principles. Too many people think ROI is a farce, all ROI studies are a bunch of lies, and ROI authors are snake oil salesmen. SPI is often perceived as too difficult and immeasurable, but SPI is worthy in spite of its impossibility. Some believe organizations must embark on a multiyear, multimillion-dollar ROI study by itinerant measurement scholars. Some feel that organizations cannot perform an early, top-down ROI analysis of their portfolio of software assets due to immaturity.

The exact opposite of these common pitfalls for the ROI of SPI is remarkably true. The formulas for SPI are amazingly simple. SPI economics should be your first concern, not your last. ROI is an indispensable tool in the field of SPI. ROI is the perfect tool for low-maturity organizations. ROI is a stepping-stone to high maturity, not vice versa. ROI of SPI is a simple fact. SPI without ROI is not SPI. ROI can and should be a quick, easy, and cost-effective exercise. Performing an early, top-down ROI analysis of your portfolio of software assets is the ideal approach to strategic planning.

1.7 WHO CARES ABOUT ROI OF SPI?

Computer programmers, software engineers, supervisors, and software engineering managers care about the ROI of SPI. Software quality assurance analysts, test analysts, support group leads, and functional area managers care about the ROI of SPI. Software process improvement analysts, software process improvement managers, and directors care about the ROI of SPI. Software engineering managers and directors and business unit managers and vice presidents also care about the ROI of SPI.

Computer programmers and software engineers often carry the bulk of the responsibility and workload in the field of technology. They are constantly seeking ways to ease the burden of poor management and get the job done successfully. Supervisors and software leaders are often asked to manage overly ambitious projects without the necessary resources. They often seek ways to overcome the productivity paradox.

Software quality assurance and testing analysts are saddled with the impossibility of building in product quality after the fact. They desperately seek ways to educate managers that the only way to build high-quality products is to do it right the first time. Support group leads and functional area managers are usually given the job of Atlas, to support the world on their shoulders. They welcome the idea that front-line engineers and managers should seize responsibility for quality, productivity, and reliability.

SPI analysts are responsible for coaching engineers and managers to simplify their processes. They also coach engineers to measure their results and constantly improve productivity and quality. They have no excuse for ignoring the ROI of SPI. Software process improvement managers and directors have the authority and responsibility to create and enforce a vision for SPI. It is their job to form strategies to realize their vision and establish tactical plans to implement a strong and pervasive vision for SPI. Doing so ultimately ensures the success of their software-producing organizations.

Senior software engineering managers and directors are responsible for ensuring peak levels of operating efficiency. They should be the primary stakeholders and customers for performing studies involving the ROI of SPI. Business unit managers, directors, and vice presidents are responsible for economic performance and business growth. They do this by expanding the customer base, reorganizing the infrastructure, and hiring productive workers at fair market prices. They also view their job as getting rid of the bad apples. However, they need to realize that the ROI of SPI is an indispensable tool for achieving near-term profitability. In addition, the ROI of SPI is a good tool for responding to ever-changing and constantly fluctuating market conditions.

2

SOFTWARE PROCESS IMPROVEMENT

Software process improvement (SPI) is an approach to designing and defining a new and improved software process to achieve basic business goals and objectives. Examples include increased revenues and profitability and decreased operating costs. The benefits of SPI are numerous. Major benefits include increased customer satisfaction, productivity, quality, cost savings, and cycle time reduction.

SPI is used to increase revenues or profits and decrease operating costs by manipulating or changing software processes. SPI is accomplished by measuring the performance of an old software process, improving the process, and then trying it out. SPI also consists of measuring the performance of new software processes and institutionalizing them if they have improved.

Key methods for SPI consist of process improvement cycles, process improvement criteria, and software process notations. Key methods also include software standards, software life cycles, software methodologies, and software notations. Software processes, software tools, software metrics, and programming languages are also key methods for SPI.

SPI is often performed to improve effort, cost, cycle time, productivity, quality, reliability, precision, and predictability. Goals also include improving efficiency, simplicity, customer satisfaction, degree of automation, consistency, and repeatability. Improving measurability, variety, and innovation are also popular goals.

SPI is the means by which software organizations can achieve significant increases in profitability and peak operating efficiency. The benefits of SPI form the basis for calculating the return on investment (ROI) of SPI. Thus, SPI and the ROI of SPI are intimately, intricately, and inseparably linked by basic origin, purpose, and function.

2.1 WHAT IS SPI?

SPI is the act of creating a new and improved software process in order to obtain a benefit. In other words, SPI is used to create a new and improved software process to achieve some level of benefits. The benefits are often increased revenues or profits, decreased costs, and significant cost savings. It is somewhat ironic that the field of SPI has evolved to include cost savings. Early attempts at SPI were designed to improve quality and reliability at any cost.

SPI is simply the act of changing the software development and maintenance process. The goals are usually to increase efficiency, decrease costs, and increase profitability. For instance, SPI can be used to create a new and improved process for software project management.

This may result in faster cycle times, shorter time to market, higher customer satisfaction, and alignment with strategic goals. Improved project management also leads to accurate time and budget accounting and better cost and schedule performance. Lower defect rates, smaller module sizes, increased verification and validation efficiency, and increased productivity also result. Improvement certainly leads to better cost, quality, and reliability estimation and higher software quality and reliability.

SPI is used to create a new and improved software process. First, the performance of an old software process is measured using statistical process control. Then, a new and simplified software process is formed to improve performance. Oftentimes, the new and improved software process is piloted to measure its new performance. Finally, the new software process which exhibits the desired performance level may be institutionalized.

SPI is used to create new software processes for strategic software activities. Software project management and software quality management are certainly strategic activities. However, software design management is a very strategic software activity.

SPI of processes for software quality management is a proven discipline which yields orders-of-magnitude improvement. SPI of processes for software project management is starting to achieve international recognition. It is fueled by emerging data and hard economic justification for this discipline. SPI of processes for software design management is a fledgling discipline. Its economic underpinnings are anchored in the fields of software reuse and product line management.

2.2 WHY IS SPI IMPORTANT?

SPI is important because it is the primary means by which a new and improved software process is created. This is done in order to achieve significant economic benefits at the least possible costs. Notice that benefits and costs are mentioned yet again. Aren't these the terms of the ROI equation? Indeed they are. ROI of SPI is the ratio of benefits to costs. In fact, higher benefits and lower costs increase the ratio of benefits to costs. This helps realize a greater ROI of SPI. SPI is important because it maximizes the ROI of SPI.

A well-designed software process has a positive effect on the bottom-line economic performance of a software enterprise. Performance is often measured in terms of productivity and cost efficiency. This applies to commercial and nonprofit organizations.

Conversely, poorly designed software processes have negative consequences on the economic performance of an enterprise. Poor software processes result in high cost of operations, inefficient use of resources, and lost market opportunities. Lack of quality and reliability, poor customer satisfaction, and poor internal morale are the results of poorly designed processes.

It is important to remember that ROI is just one tool for evaluating the performance of a new and improved software process. SPI is used to create a new and improved software process for a variety of reasons, not just ROI. At a very basic level, SPI can be used to increase productivity, quality, cycle time reduction, and cost reduction.

However, SPI can also be used to create a new and improved software process to respond to a new industry standard. SPI is often performed to adhere to a new customer standard, lower operating capital, and changing skill requirements. Technological innovations, changes to organizational structures, and increased competition are also reasons to perform SPI. Unprecedented and ambitious product and service offerings usually result in broad sweeping SPI initiatives. SPI may be performed to effect incremental changes in operating efficiency.

SPI is even performed in support of aggressively new market maneuvers that require radically new software processes. SPI is the primary means by which operating performance is deliberately measured and manipulated. This is done to achieve basic business goals, leading to improved economic performance.

Getting new customers doesn't satisfy them, entering markets doesn't capture them, and cutting costs doesn't lower them. Hiring and firing people doesn't improve productivity, and reorganizing doesn't implicitly increase operating efficiency. However, SPI can result in higher customer satisfaction, lower costs, increased productivity, and greater operating efficiency.

2.3 HOW IS SPI DETERMINED?

SPI is determined by measuring the performance of a new and improved process using tools such as statistical process control. First, the attributes or characteristics of an old software process are measured and analyzed to determine its performance. Then, the attributes or characteristics of a new software process are measured and analyzed to determine its performance. Classes of attributes or characteristics include effort, cost, and cycle time. Productivity, quality, reliability, precision, predictability, efficiency, simplicity, and customer satisfaction are also key attributes. Significant characteristics include degree of automation, consistency, repeatability, measurability, variety, and innovation.

Effort is a measure of how many hours a process requires. Cost is a measure of how much money a process requires. Cycle time is a measure of how long a process takes. Productivity is a measure of how many units a process yields. Quality is a measure of how many defects a process yields. Reliability is a measure of the frequency of failures encountered. Precision is a measure of exactness and conciseness. Predictability is a measure of statistical accuracy. Efficiency is a measure of resources consumed relative to process output. Simplicity is a measure of process complexity. Customer satisfaction is a measure of how well clients are served. Degree of automation is a measure of eliminating the causes of human variation. Consistency is a measure of minimal performance variation. Repeatability is also a measure of minimum performance variation. Measurability is a quantitative and often tangible or physical characteristic of a process or product. Variety is a measure of process flexibility to satisfy multiple diverse customer requirements. Innovation is a measure of the range and creativity of products and services.

2.4 WHAT ARE KEY METHODS FOR SPI?

Key methods consist of general-purpose process improvement cycles and general-purpose process improvement criteria. Methods include software process modeling notations, software engineering standards, and software engineering life cycles. Software engineering methodologies, software engineering notations, and software engineering processes are key methods. Software engineering tools, software engineering measurement, and computer programming languages are also key SPI methods.

General-Purpose Process Improvement Cycles

General-purpose process improvement cycles are used in conjunction with general-purpose process improvement criteria. These are very popular and are the preferred methods for many. Software engineering methodologies tend to integrate many of the SPI methods into a single unified approach.

General-purpose process improvement cycles are designed to be the basic frameworks necessary to begin the process of SPI. However, these frameworks tend to be diluted and ineffective at best, with little overall direction for improving software processes. These methods are not recommended for novices who need specific help to identify high-impact and high-ROI SPI methods. Examples include Six Sigma, statistical process control, plan-do-check-act, and initiating-diagnosing-establishing-acting-learning. Total quality management, total productivity management, and total cost management are also popular examples. Total resource management, total technology management, and total business management are part of this family of methods.

General-Purpose Process Improvement Criteria

General-purpose process improvement criteria are used in conjunction with general purpose process improvement cycles. General-purpose process improvement cycles tend to have an appraisal stage. This stage is used to leverage the specific requirements of general-purpose process improvement criteria. These criteria have built-in mechanisms to help organizations identify high-leverage areas for improvement. They also have mechanisms to prioritize process improvements and steward resources toward high-priority areas.

They tend to be more specific than general-purpose process improvement cycles and minimize some confusion for the novice. However, they tend to have so many criteria as to confuse and dilute the overall effectiveness of using them. Examples of general-purpose process improvement criteria include ISO 9001, TL 9000, BOOTSTRAP, and TRILLIUM. The Malcolm Baldrige National Quality Award and Software Process Improvement and Capability Determination are popular examples.

And who can forget the host of capability maturity models? There are the Software Capability Maturity Model® and Capability Maturity Model Integration®. There are the Systems Engineering Capability Maturity Model and Integrated Product Team Capability Maturity Model. There are the Systems Security Engineering Capability Maturity Model and System Acquisition Capability Maturity Model. The Trusted Capability Maturity Model, People Capability Maturity Model, and Integrated Capability Maturity Model are unique models. The Network Engineering Capability Maturity Model and Testing Capability Maturity Model are good examples. And don't forget the E-Commerce Capability Maturity Model.

Software Process Modeling Notations

Software process modeling notations are textual or visual aids designed to define and document software processes. These notations are also used to communicate, facilitate, and even use a new and improved software process. Software process modeling notations can be confusing for a variety of reasons. First, many are inadequate for expressing the depth of detail necessary to describe software processes. This can hinder the use, exploitation, and consistency of software processes. Second, choice of which notation to use can lead to debilitating politics. This results in little progress toward the creation and use of a new and improved software process. Third, only one or two of these notations are effective. Few are recommended for defining new and improved software processes. These methods provide little direction for novices on what software processes to define and at what depth to define them. They also lack guidance on how to define software processes to achieve peak operating efficiency. In many cases, definition of software processes is a task for highly trained experts, not arbitrary novices.

Examples of software process modeling notations include short checklists, textual descriptions, flowcharts, and ETVX diagrams. IDEF0 diagrams, information mapping, input/output charts, and professional policy and procedure formats are good examples. Proprietary notations built into workflow automation tools are also prime examples of software process modeling notations.

Software Engineering Standards

Software engineering standards are basic but well-rounded minimum requirements for designing new software processes. They, too, have their strengths and weaknesses. Software engineering standards have greater breadth than general-purpose process improvement criteria. Therefore, they tend to offer better priorities for SPI. However, software engineering standards have much less depth than general-purpose process improvement criteria. Without depth, their guidance can be ineffective to achieve their purpose. An ideal approach may be to blend general-purpose process improvement criteria and software engineering standards. This would seem to achieve a balance of both breadth and depth. But this too is futile, quite confusing, and amounts to attempting to save the Titanic with Scotch tape and bailing wire. Examples of software engineering standards include MIL-STD-1521B, MIL-STD-973, MIL-HDBK-61, and MIL-STD-2549. MIL-HDBK-881, DO-178B, DOD-STD-2167A, MIL-STD-498, J-STD-016, ISO 12207, and ISO 15288 are good examples.

Software Engineering Life Cycles

Software engineering life cycles add integration, workflow, and tactical execution to software engineering processes. Tactical execution is intended to help organizations manage the design and development of software products and services. They sometimes have activities for software quality and reliability. Unfortunately, software engineering life cycles lack the breadth of software engineering standards. They also lack the depth of general-purpose process improvement criteria. With a few rare exceptions, they lack critical activities for successfully performing software project and quality management. Software engineering life cycles tend to offer much tactical guidance for novices. Once again, however, they do not provide enough guidance in software project and quality management. Without these skills, novices simply cannot succeed. Examples include waterfall, Spiral, evolutionary, prototyping, incremental, concurrent, concurrent incremental, and V model.

Software Engineering Methodologies

Software engineering methodologies are designed to string or thread multiple software engineering notations together. This is done to achieve the goal of specifying, designing, and implementing software-based systems. They tend to be based on graphical or mathematical notations. These notations are used for capturing software requirements, software designs, and constructs for software implementation. Software engineering methodologies suffer from a dual personality. They focus only upon technical engineering activities. However, they fail to include fundamentally necessary principles in software project and quality management. The creators of software engineering methodologies do not value the activities of software project and quality management. Instead, they focus on software visualization. It would be better if they combined project and quality management with visualization. However, not all software engineering methodologies are bad. One or two have a unique blend of all key methods for SPI. Examples include structured analysis, structured design, information engineering, and object oriented analysis. Object-oriented design, Clean Room, and Rational Unified Process are popular examples. Extreme Programming, Agile Methods, Personal Software Process^{SM}, and Team Software Process^{SM} are even better examples.

Software Engineering Notations

Software engineering notations are the building blocks of software engineering methodologies. They are early attempts at formalizing methods for SPI. They are used to create visual representations of software constructs. This is done to facilitate rational and logical software development. Software engineering notations are meant to visually capture requirements and designs. They are designed to influence software engineers to do more than just computer programming. Individual software engineering notations are some of the earliest forms of in-depth software engineering guidance. Many software engineering notations have been haphazardly strung together to form software engineering methodologies. Similarly, software engineering notations offer no guidance for software project and quality management. These are the tenets of SPI, and software engineering for that matter. Examples include data flow diagrams, state transition diagrams, and entity relationship diagrams. Control specifications, structure charts, and program design languages are older examples. The Object Modeling Technique, Unified Modeling Language, and formal methods are newer examples.

Software Engineering Processes

Software engineering processes are designed to represent coarse-grained logical groupings of major software engineering activities. They tend to be some of the earliest forms of software engineering formalisms. Some software engineering processes formed the basis for entire software engineering standards. Software engineering standards are merely collections of software engineering activities. In any case, software engineering processes are thought of as major subactivities or subelements within the software life cycle. They are also considered subelements of a software project and software development process. Many at one time may have embodied the entire discipline of software engineering. Configuration management is an example of a process that once embodied the entire discipline of software engineering. While some software engineering processes add negligible value, others offer an overwhelming amount of benefits. These benefits often pay for the cost of all other software engineering processes combined. The Software Inspection Process is a good example of this. Use of one or two software engineering processes has led a few organizations to the peak of world-class operating performance. A few late 20th century software engineering methodologies have eclipsed the value of performing individual software processes. Software engineering processes are both a blessing and a curse.

Some software engineering processes are basically innocuous. However, they are so immensely popular as to cause some to ignore substantially important software engineering processes. Examples include software configuration management, software testing, and independent verification and validation. The Software Inspection Process, software defect classification, and software project management are very good examples. Popular examples also include software configuration management, software defect prevention, and software reuse. Commercial off-the-shelf integration, software architecture, and product line management are some of the latest examples.

Software Engineering Tools

Software engineering tools are designed to define and formalize software engineering processes. They are designed to automate tedious tasks that cannot be consistently performed by humans. At the same time, they add great value, increase software productivity, and increase work product output. More importantly, they perform many built-in verification and validation tasks. Large-scale investment in software engineering tools dates back to the 1970s. Key SPI methods that added the greatest value were not even present in public consciousness. Software engineering tools in the 1970s were extremely primitive and added only marginal value. They were often hosted on primitive but expensive computer systems. These computer systems were oftentimes counterproductive to use.

Software engineering tools, fueled by SPI methods and computer systems, will answer many SPI challenges in the 21st century. Examples include computer-aided software engineering tools, software project management tools, and software estimation tools. Code generation tools, graphical user interface management systems, and automated static analysis tools are good examples. Model checkers, automated software testing tools, and workflow automation tools are even better examples. Don't forget popular tools such as software process definition tools and software configuration management tools. Requirements management tools, office automation tools, Web-enabled tools, and operating systems are also good examples.

Software Engineering Measurement

Software engineering measurement is designed to institute quantitative analysis in the field of software engineering. Most other methods tend to have a qualitative element. Software engineering measurement is meant to elevate the field of computer programming to a true engineering discipline. This is accomplished by quantifying the essential properties of software. It is meant to be similar to what physics does for the classical engineering disciplines of mechanical and electrical engineering. Software engineering measurement is the shield of world-class software organizations. It is also the shield of organizations that have achieved peak operating efficiency. Yet, most organizations do not perform any software engineering measurement at all. One or two of the best software engineering methodologies have a blend of good software activities and software measurement. It is best to look at software measurement as an integrated discipline rather than a stand-alone process. Examples include software productivity metrics, software structure or design metrics, and software cost models. Software quality models, software reliability models, and customer satisfaction measurement are classical examples. Earned value management, the Taguchi method, House of Cards, and Quality Function Deployment are measurement examples.

Computer Programming Languages

Computer programming languages are natural language dialects, instructions, and commands which are used to control computers. People use computer programming languages to operate computers, task them to perform activities, and build applications. They are used to build operating systems, office automation suites, graphical processing tools, and useful productivity tools. Computer programming languages are the building blocks of software, applications, computers, and even the field of SPI. Many people believe that selection, use, and mastery of computer programming languages are the only significant SPI method. They embodied the fields of computer science and software engineering following the birth of the electronic computer. The first advances in computer science came with the invention of high-level, English-like computer programming languages. They were designed to consummate the marriage between humans and machines. A few popular examples of computer science breakthroughs are attributed to computer programming languages. These include the invention of COBOL for business applications, FORTRAN for math applications, and Ada for military use. Higher level, easier-to-understand, and English-like computer programming languages significantly improve productivity. The more computers can do, the easier it is to program, and the higher quality the code will be. Eventually, millions of armchair computer programmers created Web sites overnight using World Wide Web technologies. No SPI method has ever had the impact that Web-enabled technologies and related computer programming languages have. Examples include machine language, assembly, COBOL, FORTRAN, Algol, PL/1, Jovial, LISP, Ada, SQL, and BASIC. LOGOS, Pascal, C, C++, Ada95, Visual Basic, HTML, Java, Perl, and C# are some of the latest examples.

2.5 WHAT ARE KEY PRINCIPLES OF SPI?

A key principle of SPI consists of selecting a well-integrated software engineering methodology. It should have good software project management and software quality management activities. It should also have solid technical software activities and elements of quantitative software measurement.

Another key principle for SPI consists of using professional policy and procedure formats. This helps to define, communicate, and institutionalize good software engineering methodologies.

An organization can spend decades and millions of dollars allowing complete novices to use the various methods for SPI. SPI methods include general-purpose process improvement cycles and general-purpose process improvement criteria. Software process modeling notations, software engineering standards, and software engineering life cycles are SPI methods. Software engineering methodologies, software engineering notations, and software engineering processes are key methods. Software engineering tools, software engineering measurement, and computer programming languages are also SPI methods.

Alternatively, organizations can selectively apply professionally designed software engineering methodologies. Good software engineering methodologies are engineered based on decades of expert trial and error. An organization can hire an entry-level computer programmer to design the perfect process after decades of trial and error, or an organization can adopt proven software engineering methodologies on day one. This is a key principle for SPI.

2.6 WHAT ARE PITFALLS OF SPI?

Many approaches to SPI are draconian at best. They offer very little ROI at astronomical expense. Don't expect to find a silver bullet, especially among 20th century approaches to SPI. And don't put all of your eggs in one basket. Try a diversified approach. Research, analyze, and experiment with a variety of methods that offer a generous ROI of SPI at a nominal expense. Don't use a SPI method just because everyone else is doing it.

A new fad is born every year, often fueled by the unbridled enthusiasm of a new generation of computer programmers. Don't get swept up in youthful enthusiasm. Worse yet, don't be fooled by untested bureaucratic models from industry bodies and government research centers. Instead, responsibly steward your resources toward key SPI methods which offer a proven ROI.

2.7 WHO CARES ABOUT SPI?

Some of the people who care about SPI include software quality assurance personnel and SPI analysts, managers, and directors. Senior software engineering managers sometimes care about SPI. The field of software quality assurance is the predecessor or early prototype for the field of SPI. Software quality assurance analysts help select software engineering standards, life cycles, and methodologies. They help define software processes and ensure that software project management processes are properly executed. This makes software quality assurance analysts ideal champions of SPI. The fact that SPI professionals care about SPI does not have to be repeated. Senior software engineering managers care about SPI as well. They are concerned with operational excellence and satisfying customer standards. They are primarily responsible for ensuring that organizations achieve compliance with general-purpose process improvement criteria. Unfortunately, the list of people who care about SPI doesn't include the two most important parties. Software engineers and business unit managers, directors, and vice presidents rarely embrace the principles of SPI. Software engineers often view SPI as irrelevant, bothersome, and counterproductive. It is ironic that SPI is the exact opposite. SPI is highly relevant; it is designed to make life easier not harder, and to enhance productivity, not hinder it. Perhaps software engineers are merely reacting to poorly implemented SPI methods. Perhaps they just lack fundamental education. Maybe, in fact, SPI needs to be transparent to them. Business unit managers, directors, and vice presidents tend to be concerned with growing their businesses. This usually leads them to hire more people, shuffle political resources, and cut costs sharply. Business unit managers, directors, and vice presidents benefit the most from SPI.

3

METHODS FOR SOFTWARE PROCESS IMPROVEMENT

Methods for software process improvement (SPI) include de facto, emerging, and industry standards for improving quality, productivity, and performance. Methods for SPI are designed specifically to improve product quality and improve software project management performance. Several methods for SPI are designed to evaluate, certify, and qualify suppliers to serve government agencies. Some are designed to certify firms to adhere to regulations for international trade. Some methods for SPI are simple meetings to improve software quality. Some methods for SPI are technically challenging approaches to performing individual and group-based project management. Other methods for SPI are large sets of criteria designed for supplier selection and establishment of priorities for internal SPI. Methods for SPI share some common features regardless of their size, scope, and complexity. Methods for SPI are tedious, manually intensive, expensive, unpopular, and invoke fierce resistance. They invariably are seen as unnecessary bureaucracy among computer programmers and software engineers. Some of the methods for SPI are small and highly effective. Some have impressive results in spite of their expense. Some take years and millions of dollars to apply in spite of their popularity. The methods for SPI examined in this chapter all share common characteristics. They are well defined, repeatable, measurable, beneficial, and common in use. Another commonality is that they are difficult to apply and very expensive to use.

3.1 SOFTWARE INSPECTION PROCESS

The Software Inspection Process is a type of meeting that is held in order to identify defects in software work products. In reality, the Software Inspection Process is a highly structured and facilitated group review. It is held to objectively identify the maximum number of software defects. Its purpose is to improve software quality. The Software Inspection Process is a structured and neutrally facilitated meeting in which technical peers identify defects in software work products. The defects must be corrected, without suggesting solutions or interference from the originator of the work product. In short, the Software Inspection Process is for technical experts to identify defects that must be corrected. However, the technical experts cannot suggest design alternatives or subjective improvements to the product. Figure 1 illustrates the Software Inspection Process.

The Software Inspection Process may be held at the end of software life cycle phases. It may be held after software work products have been completed within individual phases. It may also be held when components of software work products have been completed. It is often held at critically important decision points within the software life cycle. The Software Inspection Process is a scheduled event in software project plans. It is not an ad hoc activity subject to preemption.

The Software Inspection Process consists of six major stages, phases, activities, subprocesses, components, or steps. The six major steps are planning, overview, preparation, meeting, rework, and follow-up. Each of the steps defines and differentiates the Software Inspection Process from any other type of meeting or review. They are designed to add value, structure, repeatability, and measurability. More importantly, the six major steps are designed to optimize the number of defects identified, thus ensuring optimal quality.

The Software Inspection Process is the most measured, analyzed, and used method in the history of software engineering. It is also the most ubiquitous, researched, and reported upon SPI method ever.

3.2 PERSONAL SOFTWARE PROCESS[SM]

The Personal Software Process[SM] is a training curriculum. It is designed to teach software engineers basic principles in software project and quality management. A goal of the Personal Software Process[SM] is to change the behavior of software engineers and teach them to measure their work. It also teaches them to analyze their measures and achieve performance goals. They often have a chance to see the benefits of software project and quality management. This is accomplished

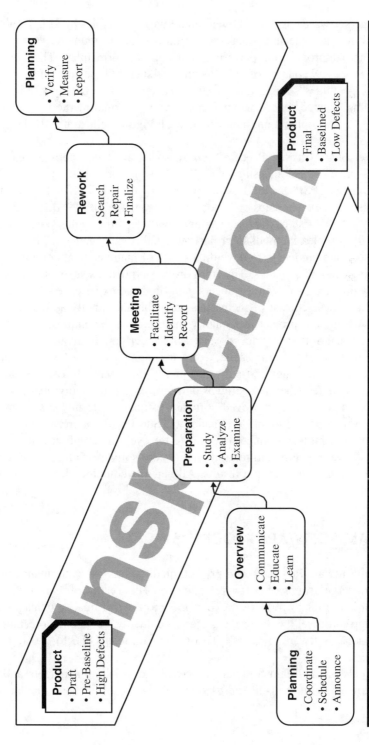

Figure 1   Software Inspection Process Stages

by teaching software engineers how to apply basic principles of SPI. They also learn how to make accurate plans and improve product quality, as well as measure and improve their performance using SPI principles. The Personal Software Process^{SM} consists of basic techniques such as time and defect recording. It also includes statistical size, cost, and quality estimating, testing, and earned value management. Checklists and reviews, formal methods, and cyclical life cycle development are included as well. Figure 2 illustrates the Personal Software Process^{SM}.

The Personal Software Process^{SM} consists of four major steps or plateaus. The steps are personal measurement (PSP^{SM}0), personal planning (PSP^{SM}1), personal quality (PSP^{SM}2), and cyclic process (PSP^{SM}3). The first three steps also contain incremental steps or minor variations, namely PSP^{SM}0.1, PSP^{SM}1.1, and PSP^{SM}2.1. The steps represent simple software life cycles consisting of increasingly complex methods in project and quality management. The training requires software engineers to develop a series of mathematical computer programs using each of the steps. The steps are also known as seven software life cycles. By doing so, software engineers gain firsthand experience with increasing benefits. These consist of increasing precision and quality associated with using basic software project and quality management techniques.

The Personal Software Process^{SM} has as its underlying foundation the notion that numerous benefits are possible. Software engineers are asked to combine earned value management and software quality management. They must find twice as many defects before testing as during testing using individual reviews.

The benefits include improved software estimation accuracy and greater software project precision and predictability. Shorter and more accurate software schedules, higher productivity, and faster cycle times often result. High levels of software quality and reliability, and zero software failures in fielding, use, and operation are common results. All benefits combined lead to substantially lower costs.

3.3 TEAM SOFTWARE PROCESS^{SM}

The Team Software Process^{SM} is a project, quality, and life cycle management method for large groups of software engineers. The Team Software Process^{SM} is a set of activities to form teams, perform project and quality management, and develop software. It extends the project and quality management techniques of the Personal Software Process^{SM}. This is done for teams of 3 to 150 software engineers.

The goals of the Team Software Process^{SM} are to show managers and engineers how to build self-directed teams. It also teaches them to plan and

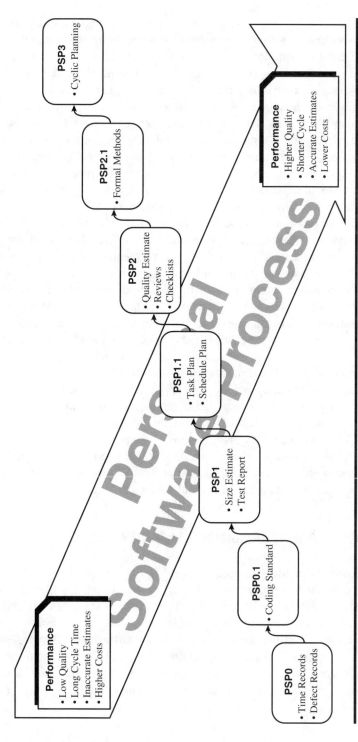

Figure 2 Personal Software Process[SM] Levels

manage their work, coach and motivate their teams, and sustain peak performance. Accelerated SPI and high-maturity behavior are the ultimate goals.

The Team Software Process[SM] consists of well-defined roles, a launch process, and statistical size, cost, and quality estimating. Earned value management, risk management, and integrated product teaming are included. There are also processes for development, maintenance, software inspections, and cyclical development. It is important to note that the Team Software Process[SM] is a rapidly evolving and constantly changing family of life cycles. It has many phases, processes, activities, scripts, forms, logs, and techniques. There were over 12 significant variations of the Team Software Process[SM] released in its first four years of existence. Figure 3 illustrates the Team Software Process[SM].

The Team Software Process[SM] consists of six major stages, phases, or scripts. The six major phase scripts are team launch, requirements, high-level design, implementation, release test, and postmortem. There are other significant scripts, processes, and activities as well that deserve mention. They include maintenance, unit test, inspection, and customer status meetings.

The team launch script is a distinctive element of the Team Software Process[SM]. It is a 10-step process that embodies team building, team integrating, and disciplined project management. The steps consist of establishing product and business goals, assigning roles, and defining team goals The next steps are produce a development strategy, build top-down and next-phase plans, and develop quality plans. Building bottom-up and balanced plans, conducting a risk assessment, and preparing management briefings and launch reports are next. The last steps are to hold management reviews and conduct a postmortem process to round out the team launch script.

The Team Software Process[SM] has many proven benefits. The benefits are improved size estimation, effort estimation, schedule estimation, defect density, and process yield. Further benefits of the Team Software Process[SM] are improved productivity, data accuracy, and process fidelity.

3.4 SOFTWARE CAPABILITY MATURITY MODEL®

The Software Capability Maturity Model® is a set of guidelines for selecting software suppliers and performing SPI. The Software Capability Maturity Model® is a set of fundamental criteria for software project management called key practices. The Software Capability Maturity Model® is a set of minimum screening criteria for discriminating among U.S. Department of Defense software suppliers. It is considered a set of criteria for analyzing the performance of software organizations. It helps them establish priorities for corrective action and guides them to the peak of operating efficiency.

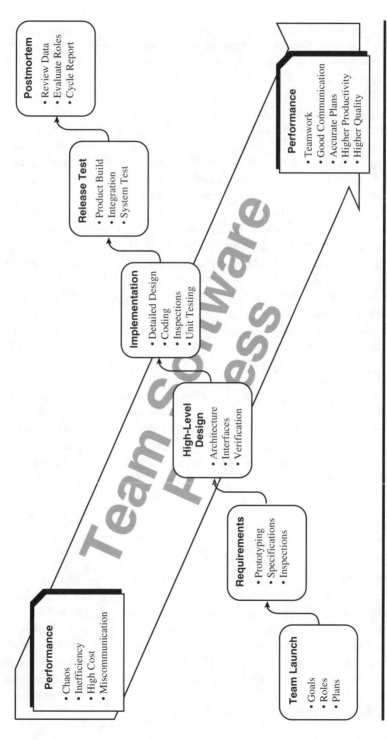

Figure 3 Team Software Process℠ Phases

There are two fundamental ways to apply the Software Capability Maturity Model®. The first is for a government agency or firm to use these criteria to judge how many of the key practices are met by suppliers. The second is for a software organization to use these criteria to judge how many of the key practices it meets.

The goal of the Software Capability Maturity Model® is to serve as a tool for government agencies. It is used to help them to discriminate among their suppliers based upon how good they are at software project management. A related goal is the improvement of software project management practices. Figure 4 illustrates the Software Capability Maturity Model®.

A total of 316 criteria or key practices comprise the Software Capability Maturity Model®. The 316 criteria or key practices of the Software Capability Maturity Model® are divided into five major plateaus called levels. The five levels are initial, repeatable, defined, managed, and optimizing. The five levels represent increasing compliance with the 316 criteria and use of basic principles in project management. The five levels are further subdivided into 18 key process areas. The key process areas represent logical groupings of the 316 criteria or key practices.

It is important to note that the 18 key process areas are even further divided into five common features. The first three common features are commitment to perform, ability to perform, and activities performed. The final two common features are measurement and analysis and verifying implementation. The 316 criteria are eventually divided among each of the common features within the key process areas. The common features are a distinctive characteristic of the Software Capability Maturity Model®. Adhering to the criteria within all of the common features is believed to enable successful SPI at the organizational level. A well-known firm exhibited 10-fold increases in cost efficiency, productivity, cycle time reduction, and quality using this model

3.5 ISO 9001

ISO 9001 is a set of requirements for quality management systems which must be met by firms within the European Union. ISO 9001 has quality management system requirements for firms to exhibit the ability to provide consistent products and services. ISO 9001 specifies the quality management system requirements for firms that want the ability to enhance customer satisfaction. ISO 9001 is a set of minimum requirements for firms to improve or professionally certify their quality management systems. ISO 9001 is for discriminating and selecting among suppliers whose quality management systems satisfy its requirements. ISO 9001 is for firms to design, implement, and improve their quality management systems to enhance customer satisfaction.

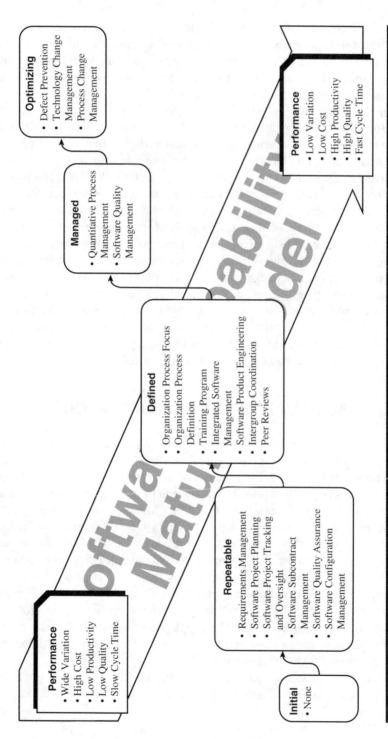

Figure 4 Software Capability Maturity Model® Levels

ISO 9001 consists of five broad categories of requirements for the design and certification of a firm's quality management system. The first three categories are quality management system, management responsibility, and resource management. Product realization and measurement, analysis, and improvement are the last two. Figure 5 illustrates ISO 9001.

ISO 9001 does share some similar characteristics with the common features of the Software Capability Maturity Model®. Management responsibility is the equivalent of the commitment to perform and verifying implementation common features. ISO 9001 has requirements for resource management which are the equivalent of the ability to perform common feature. ISO 9001 has requirements for product realization which are the equivalent of the activities performed common feature. Finally, measurement, analysis, and improvement is the equivalent of the measurement and analysis common feature.

ISO 9001 has two distinctive characteristics or elements. The first is its product realization clause which defines requirements for a basic product and service life cycle. Product realization consists of planning of product realization, customer-related processes, and design and development. Purchasing, product and service provision, and control and monitoring of measuring devices are also included. The second distinctive characteristic is its documentation requirements. It contains requirements for a quality policy, quality manual, quality procedures, planning documents, and quality records.

3.6 CAPABILITY MATURITY MODEL INTEGRATION®

Capability Maturity Model Integration® is a set of guidelines for selecting systems and software engineering suppliers. It is also used for performing process improvement. Capability Maturity Model Integration® is a set of criteria for process, project, and engineering management and support. Its criteria are called generic and specific practices. Capability Maturity Model Integration® is a robust set of criteria for discriminating among U.S. Department of Defense suppliers. Capability Maturity Model Integration® is a set of criteria for analyzing systems and software engineering performance. It helps them establish priorities for corrective action, and it guides them to the peak of operating efficiency. There are two ways to apply Capability Maturity Model Integration®. The first is for a U.S. Department of Defense agency or firm to judge how many of the practices are met by suppliers. The second is for an organization to use them for internal process improvement. Figure 6 illustrates Capability Maturity Model Integration®.

A total of 489 criteria or generic and specific practices comprise Capability Maturity Model Integration® staged representation. The 489 criteria are divided

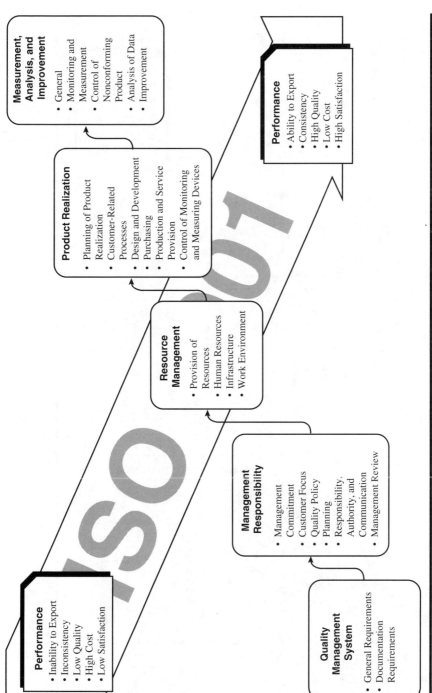

Figure 5   ISO 9001 Clauses

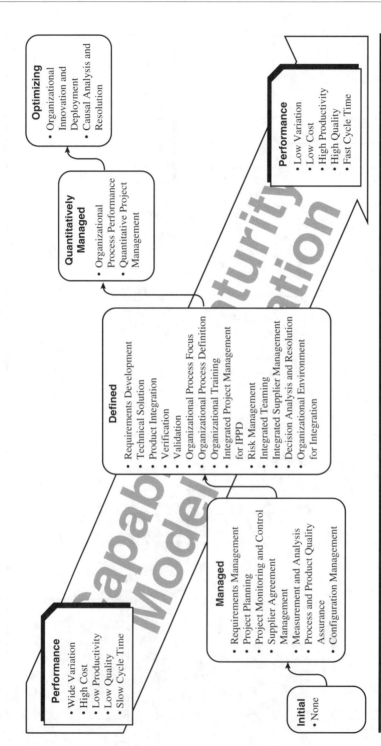

Figure 6 Capability Maturity Model Integration® Levels

into five major plateaus called levels in its staged representation. The five levels are initial, managed, defined, quantitatively managed, and optimizing. The five levels represent increasing compliance with the 489 criteria. They also represent increasing use of principles in basic project management. Process standardization, quantitative management, and continuous process improvement are included. The five levels are further subdivided into 25 process areas. The 25 process areas represent logical groupings of the 489 criteria. The 25 process areas have 12 generic practices which are further divided into four common features. The common features are commitment to perform, ability to perform, directing implementation, and verifying implementation. The common features are designed to enable process improvement at the organizational level.

A total of 614 criteria or practices comprise Capability Maturity Model Integration® continuous representation. The 614 criteria are divided into four broad categories in its continuous representation. It may be used instead of the five-level staged representation. The four categories are process management, project management, engineering, and support. The four categories are further divided into 25 process areas, which represent logical groupings of the 614 criteria. The 25 process areas have 17 generic practices which are further divided into six capability levels. The capability levels are incomplete, performed, managed, defined, quantitatively managed, and optimizing. The capability levels are designed to enable process improvement for any one of the 25 process areas. This results in peak operating efficiency for the chosen process area.

METHODS FOR RETURN ON INVESTMENT ANALYSIS

Methods for return on investment (ROI) include benefit, cost, benefit/cost ratio, ROI, net present value, and breakeven point. ROI methods in general are quite easy, indispensable, powerfully simplistic, and absolutely necessary in the field of software process improvement (SPI). It is ironic that ROI methods are not in common practice. The literature does not abound with ROI methods for SPI. The ROI literature that does exist is very hard to locate, appears infrequently, and is often confusing. There are dozens of very complex processes, methods, steps, formulas, terms, and concepts to absorb. In addition, ROI literature never fails to randomly select from dozens of formulas and present them in a haphazard manner. This only confounds the practice of ROI in the field of SPI. However, it is important to note that there are only a few significant formulas. They are small in number, and they are extremely simple to apply. They, of course, include benefit, cost, benefit/cost ratio, ROI, net present value, and breakeven point. In fact, these ROI formulas do not involve more than one or two significant terms or inputs. There are, however, some remaining challenges that must be addressed, and those happen to be the individual terms of these simplistic formulas, namely benefit and cost. Benefit is perhaps the most elusive input into the overly simplistic ROI formula. SPI literature does not abound with hard economic evidence of the benefits of SPI. Many believe there are no benefits, though they are convinced that SPI must plow forward. Most refuse to quantify the costs of SPI, because they are afraid of them. ROI formulas are simple, benefits do exist, and costs must be counted.

4.1 BENEFIT

Benefit is the amount of money which results from a SPI method. Benefit is the economic value resulting from a new and improved software process. What? Does this mean software processes have an economic value? Yes. Software processes have economic value.

Let's examine a common software process. How about software testing? Software testing is a process of evaluating a software product at the end of a software life cycle. It is done for the purpose of determining whether it satisfies its requirements. For example, let's say that the software is supposed to print a page. You look for the print function and invoke it (e.g., pull down the menu and release the mouse button on the print option). Your laser printer prints the page, and your software passes the test. That seems simple enough. What happens if the software does not print? Well, you have just found a problem, and the software does not pass the test. The requirement is not satisfied.

Does the process of software testing have economic value? Yes. Let's say that the printer problem takes 10 hours to find and fix. The economic value of your printer test is thus $1,000 at an hourly rate of $100. Now let's say that you can find and fix that defect before software testing in only one hour using the Software Inspection Process. The cost is $100. The benefit of the Software Inspection Process is thus $900! It costs $100 to find and fix the printer problem using the Software Inspection Process, whereas it costs $1,000 to find and fix the printer problem using the software testing process. Subtract the cost of the Software Inspection Process from the cost of software testing, and there you have it. While this example may seem overly simplistic, the benefits of the Software Inspection Process get even better. Figure 7 illustrates the formula for benefits.

Benefit is probably the most difficult concept to grasp in the field of SPI. Everything else is simple, including cost. With enough education, experience, and study, even astrophysics can be mastered. Grasp the concept of benefit and you have mastered the field of SPI.

$$Benefits = \sum_{i=1}^{n} Benefit_i$$

Figure 7 Formula for Benefits

4.2 COST

Cost is the amount of money that is spent on a SPI method. Cost is the economic consequence that is the result of creating a new and improved software process. Cost is the amount of money you must spend to get something back. SPI costs abound. Examples of SPI costs include the cost of training, the cost of travel, and the cost of buying that new SPI tool. Cost is an important factor.

Who wants to quantify the costs? Not very many! But everyone wants to quantify the benefits. Benefits are politically correct. Ask people for the benefits, and they will rattle off productivity, quality, and we'll feel better about ourselves. Cost is related to benefit. People are not very good at quantifying the economic value of benefits. That is, they don't know how much money they have made. In fact, they may even intuitively believe there are no benefits. They may believe the benefits are soft-side benefits and are therefore not economically quantifiable. The benefits are immeasurable, most believe. However, they just cannot be counted. And they should not be counted. Who would dare to question the benefits of the SPI method? Who would dare to count how much our SPI program is worth? Everyone knows that SPI is beneficial. Everyone knows that SPI adds value. It's just that the value is not quantifiable. Anyone who dares to quantify the economic value of an implicitly priceless SPI method is a troublemaker. Figure 8 illustrates the formula for costs.

If the benefits are priceless and immeasurable soft-side results, and there are no quantifiable economic benefits, then, by all means, let's not count the costs. If we place no benefit next to high cost, then we all look bad, SPI looks bad, and the SPI method is all for naught. So, let's not delve into the details of cost. In fact, let's not spend more than a few minutes counting the cost of the SPI method. Let's rattle off a nonsensical figure from the top of our heads. Let's see. The SPI method costs $1,000, the fee for the SPI trainer. And $1,000 is such a small price to pay for the hidden treasure that our SPI method represents.

Let's examine this so-called $1,000 SPI method. We had to train 100 people at $1,000 a person. That's $100,000. We had to fly 100 people coast to coast at a cost of $2,000 a person. That's $200,000. Each person stayed in a hotel for 10 nights at $100 per night. That's $100,000. It takes 100 hours to apply our SPI method at a rate of $100 per hour. That's $1 million. Let's see, so far the cost of our fancy SPI method is $1.4 million. It better yield more than $1.4

$$Cost = \sum_{i=1}^{n} Cost_i$$

Figure 8　Formula for Costs

million in benefits. If you insist that your immeasurable and unquantifiable treasure is worth the cost, you're probably out of your mind.

4.3 BENEFIT/COST RATIO

Benefit/cost ratio (B/CR) is simply the ratio of benefits to costs. B/CR is a measure of how much money is gained from using a SPI method. B/CR measures the economic magnitude of using a new and improved software process. For example, a B/CR of one to one or 1:1 means that for every dollar spent, one dollar is earned. That's a pretty good economic ratio. Many organizations would consider themselves fortunate, wise, and well prepared if they could achieve a B/CR of 1:1. What does this mean? Well, in simple terms, a B/CR of 1:1 means that for every dollar spent, one dollar in revenue is always earned. Translated into plain English, this would mean that everything is free. Pay a dollar for a meal, and get a dollar back in change. That's a free meal. Pay a dollar for your car's fuel, and get a dollar in return. That's a free ride. Figure 9 illustrates the formula for B/CR.

Let's look at one or two more examples. A B/CR of 2:1 means that for every dollar spent, two dollars is returned. Life is no longer free but instead is profitable if you can achieve a B/CR of 2:1. If you achieve a B/CR of 0.5:1, it means that for every dollar spent, 50 cents is returned. At first this seems unattractive. Perhaps even grounds for firing your accountant. However, upon closer examination, it doesn't seem so bad after all. What if it took 20 dollars to fill up your car, but you received 10 dollars in change? That would mean you are probably one lucky person. The point is to provide a simple explanation of B/CR and enlighten the reader with the range of possibilities.

Since many SPI methods are losing propositions, let's put this into context. If a SPI method has a B/CR of 0.5:1, 1:1, or 2:1, it means you will receive 50 cents, one dollar, or two dollars for every dollar spent. You will be instantly promoted to CEO if you can do this. You may stumble upon a SPI method that yields 10:1, 100:1, or even 1,000:1. That means for every dollar you spend, you get 10, 100, or 1,000 dollars in return. By gosh, you're a flaming genius. There are a few good SPI methods which have a B/CR in this range. Have your ears perked up yet?

$$B/CR = \frac{Benefit}{Cost}$$

Figure 9   Formula for Benefit/Cost Ratio

Well, they should, because there are several good SPI methods that exhibit a very good B/CR. The Software Inspection Process and Personal Software Process[SM] have good B/CR values.

4.4 RETURN ON INVESTMENT

ROI is the amount of money that is gained after spending an amount of money. ROI is the amount of money that is returned from an investment. That is, ROI refers to the amount of money that you earn above the principal you apply to the investment. For example, an ROI of 10% means that for every dollar you invest, 10 cents is returned. That is an impressive, unprecedented, and uncommon ROI. An ROI of 100% means that for every dollar invested, one dollar is earned. An ROI of 1,000% means that for every dollar invested, 10 dollars in profit is earned. ROI is a numerical measure of money or profit. ROI is often used out of context. Some people loosely refer to soft-side benefits as ROI. However, ROI is firmly grounded in terms of dollars and cents. Figure 10 illustrates the formula for ROI.

Before you decide to stop reading, throw this book in the garbage, and demand your money back, let's quickly put this into context. If a Wall Street investor calls you and offers an ROI of 1,000%, hang up the phone immediately! You would be doing very well if your retirement savings had only a slightly negative ROI, but product development is not like the stock market. It is not uncommon to expect an ROI of 100% or 1,000% in the field of high-technology design.

For example, if you manufacture semiconductors and your line puts out 9,999 defective memory chips for every 10,000 produced, you may want to spend a million dollars to improve it. If you can increase the yield to 100% and sell one million memory chips this year at a cost of two dollars per unit, it is worthwhile. What this means is that for a measly one million dollars, you have revenue of two million dollars, or an ROI of 100%. If instead of memory chips you make microprocessors that sell for 100 dollars, then your revenue is 100 million dollars. And it only cost you one million dollars. In other words, you just experienced a typical ROI of 9,900%.

$$ROI = \frac{Benefit - Cost}{Cost} \times 100\%$$

Figure 10 Formula for Return on Investment

The lesson here is not to confuse Wall Street and process improvement. A few SPI methods have similar economics and routinely yield an ROI of 10%, 100%, or even 1,000%. The Software Inspection Process, Personal Software Process[SM], and Team Software Process[SM] are just such SPI methods. They reduce defect populations by orders of magnitude at a nominal fee. These SPI methods increase product yields and can exhibit impressive ROI results. A few simple HTML instructions can yield a profitable Web site and one billion instant customers for a few minutes of investment. The ROI potential of using HTML is off the charts compared to C or C++.

ROI is very similar to B/CR and is a minor variation of it. B/CR gives you a ratio of benefits to costs. ROI gives you a similar ratio expressed as a percentage. With ROI, the costs are first subtracted from the benefits before dividing them by the costs. Subtracting the costs from the benefits isolates and quantifies the true benefits. Let's look at an example. If you spend one dollar on a SPI method that yields two dollars, your B/CR is 2:1. But is that a true measure of ROI? No! Is B/CR useful? Yes! However, ROI is even more useful than B/CR. Let's analyze the results of the same SPI method. You spend one dollar and receive two dollars back. The B/CR is 2:1, but the ROI is 100%. How does that work? First, you subtract the costs (two dollars back minus one dollar spent) and get a result of one dollar. Then you divide the *adjusted* benefits (which are one dollar) by the costs. That is, divide one dollar in modified benefits by one dollar in costs, which results in a value of one. Then multiply one by 100%. So, two dollars in benefits from one dollar in costs is a B/CR of 2:1 and an ROI of 100%. Both are useful measures of business value. B/CR is a rapid measure of business value, an easy concept to grasp, and conveys the value of the new SPI method. ROI is a more accurate measure of business value that gives us a better picture of what is happening with our SPI methods.

4.5 NET PRESENT VALUE

Net present value (NPV) is what money is worth in the future. NPV is the economic value of today's money in the future. NPV is the economic value of today's money in the future less inflation. For example, $10 today will be worth $9.52 a year from now, $7.84 5 years from now, and $6.14 10 years from now. This assumes a modest inflation rate of 5% per year. If that's your salary and your contract is locked into that rate for 10 years, you're in sad shape. Ten years from now you'll be making about $6.14 an hour. Figure 11 illustrates the formula for NPV.

NPV is a way of quantifying the economic value of money, so that you can properly determine its worth in the future. What does this have to do with SPI

$$NPV = \frac{Benefit}{(1 + Inflation\ Rate)^{Year}}$$

Figure 11   Formula for Net Present Value

methods? Well, SPI is all about the benefits. If you can quantify the economic value of the benefits, then you must discount their future value when calculating B/CR and ROI. For example, let's say that the benefits of the SPI method are $10 per year for the next 10 years. That is, our fancy new SPI method will yield $100 over the next 10 years. So, plugging $100 into the NPV formula indicates that the true benefit will be only $74.12 10 years from now. If our SPI method costs $10 and we did not use NPV, its B/CR is 10:1 and its ROI is 900%. Wow! However, using NPV, its B/CR is 7.4:1 and its ROI is 641%. That's still pretty impressive.

NPV can seem somewhat intimidating at first, but it is no more complex than B/CR and ROI. In fact, all three are perfectly valid measures for determining the economic value of the SPI method. Use all three. Some people would have you believe that NPV is the only formula that is meaningful to your economic analysis of SPI methods. Furthermore, they will attempt to confuse you with complex mathematics for NPV. They do this only to show off, intimidate you, and convince you to hire them to analyze the economics of your SPI methods. The intent in this book is to empower you with simple and easy-to-use methods for evaluating the economic value of your SPI methods.

4.6 BREAKEVEN POINT

The breakeven point is the numeric value at which the benefits overtake or exceed the costs. The breakeven point is when you begin to make a profit above some level of expenditure. It can be a unit of time or a number of work products. For instance, the breakeven point can be expressed as the number of hours a SPI method requires before a benefit is achieved, or it can be expressed as the number of lines of code that must be produced before a profit is achieved. Let's focus only on the breakeven point as the number of hours a new SPI method requires before benefits are achieved. Figure 12 illustrates the formula for breakeven point.

$$BEP = \frac{Cost}{1 - Old\ Productivity\ /\ New\ Productivity}$$

Figure 12   Formula for Breakeven Point

The breakeven point does not relate to B/CR, ROI, or NPV. However, it is an indispensable tool to determine when the benefits will be achieved. It is not enough to know that benefits will be achieved and what their value is at a given point in time. It becomes essential to know when to expect those benefits. The breakeven point is a classical method for economic forecasting that tells managers when the profits will begin flowing. Knowing this helps the decision-making process and optimizes the value of applying a new SPI method.

What does this formula tell us? Let's say the old SPI method requires 100,000 staff hours of effort to produce 10,000 lines of code. Let's also say the new SPI method requires 10,000 staff hours to produce 10,000 lines of code for the small price of 100 training hours. The breakeven point is a mere 111 hours. This means that 100 of those hours were our cost, and 11 hours were related to increased productivity. The new SPI method thus paid for itself after 111 hours, including the cost of instituting the new SPI method. But the new SPI method actually paid for itself after 11 hours of software project effort, which is roughly 1.5 staff days. Wow! You mean to say that SPI methods can pay for themselves in days? Indeed! In fact, the Software Inspection Process exhibits these properties when compared against software testing. In this example, the breakeven point tells the manager not to give up before the 111th hour, or the new SPI method was for naught. The breakeven point also tells the manager that every hour after the 111th hour yields a benefit. More importantly, it indicates that the costs of the new SPI method have been negated.

5

METHODS FOR BENEFIT ANALYSIS

Methods for benefit analysis are techniques to identify, measure, and quantify the benefits of software process improvement (SPI). Methods for benefit analysis are the cornerstone of SPI, SPI methods, and the return on investment (ROI) of SPI. Methods for benefit analysis are perhaps the most elusive, evasive, and least understood area in software engineering. Few know how to measure the benefits of software project management, software quality, and SPI. All other issues aside, methods for benefit analysis are the key enablers to understanding SPI and performing ROI of SPI. Methods for benefit analysis include measurement of productivity, defect density, quality, and defect removal efficiency. Measurements using the defect removal, software effort, and total life cycle cost models are also key methods for benefit analysis. This is by no means an exhaustive list of methods for benefit analysis. However, it is a virtual treasure trove of methods for benefit analysis that can fuel your SPI and ROI of SPI activities for years.

Productivity is a measure of how much and how fast software is produced. Defect density is a measure of the number of software defects. Quality is a measure of conformance to customer requirements. Defect removal efficiency is a measure of how effective your processes are at achieving software quality. The defect removal model is an estimate of how many defects escape your software process. It is also used to measure the effectiveness of your software processes. Software effort is a measure of how many hours it will take you to analyze, design, develop, and test your software. Total life cycle cost is an important method for estimating both software development and maintenance costs. The methods for benefit analysis build on one another and support the business case for SPI and ROI of SPI.

5.1 PRODUCTIVITY

Productivity is generally the amount of work that is performed. It is also the number of products and services created. Productivity is the rate, speed, or capacity of a software process. In this case, productivity is a measure of how fast and how many software products and services are rendered over a given period of time. The time period can be an hour, day, month, year, project length, or average for a software-producing enterprise. For example, a productivity of 25 lines of code per hour means that for every hour that is spent, 25 lines of code are produced.

Let's examine what a productivity of 25 lines of code per hour means. Does it mean that my programmers are pretty darn good? Does it mean that my programmers worked triple overtime for a few days, banging out code all night? Does it mean that productivity is a useless measure that tells me nothing about my process, operation, or firm? Does it mean that we should all begin looking for a few good super-programmers and fire anyone who can't keep up with them? The answer to these questions is a resounding "no." A productivity of 25 lines of code per hour is a simple ratio of total lines of code produced to the total number of project hours used. Figure 13 illustrates the formula for productivity.

In other words, the software analysts may have spent 100 hours developing requirements, the architects may have spent 100 hours on design, the programmers may have spent 100 hours on coding, and the testers may have spent 100 hours on integration, for a total of 400 hours. However, the programmers produced 10,000 lines of code. The lines of code were eventually divided by the 400 hours spent by the analysts, architects, programmers, and testers: 10,000 lines of code divided by 400 software project hours is 25 lines of code per hour. In fact, the programmers could not have produced their code without the requirements, design, and evaluation by the analysts, architects, and testers. Therefore, 25 lines of code per hour is the productivity of everyone, not just the computer programmers. This is a common point of confusion within software engineering.

$$Productivity = \frac{Lines\ of\ Code}{Hour}$$

Figure 13   Formula for Productivity

Productivity is just one of a few key measures which characterize the fields of software engineering, SPI, and ROI of SPI. Productivity cannot and should not be used in a vacuum, as a single-point, all-telling software measure. However, it should not be ignored. Productivity is a key measure for evaluating the benefits of SPI methods and thus the ROI of SPI. Productivity is a highly controversial measure for several reasons. First, many feel threatened by it, because they don't want to be hired, fired, or evaluated based on their individual productivity. It just sounds so cold and heartless to many people. Second, some people feel that there are better approaches to measuring software size, functionality, and complexity.

The bottom line on productivity is that it is a useful measure, it should be used responsibly, and it has many technical merits. However, you are free to choose your own measure of productivity other than the one presented here. Other highly relevant things to count include the number of software projects, number of releases, and number of documents. The number of requirements, number of design elements, and number of test cases may also be counted. The choices are limitless. Productivity is related to cost and cycle time. Increase productivity, and you reduce costs and cycle times. Reduce costs and cycle times, and you also reduce total life cycle costs. Productivity is more than just a measure of output. It is also related to cost efficiency, speed and cycle time, and total cost of ownership. Productivity is the source of vast benefits.

5.2 DEFECT DENSITY

Defect density is the number of errors or faults in software. Defect density is the estimated number of errors or faults remaining in the software after a software project is complete. Defect density is a ratio of residual defects to software size or lines of code. An example of defect density is 100, 10, or 1 defect(s) per thousand lines of code. What exactly do these figures mean or represent? A defect density of 100 defects per thousand lines of code means that for every thousand lines of code, 100 defects remain. Where do these defects remain? They are in the requirements, designs, code, and tests. If you have a software product with 10,000 lines of code, then this ratio indicates that you have 1,000 defects remaining. If your defect density is 10 defects per thousand lines of code, you have 100 defects remaining. If your defect density is 1 defect per thousand lines of code, you have 10 defects remaining. The smaller the ratio, the higher the quality of your software product. The larger the ratio, the lower the quality of your software product. Defect density is a classical measure of software quality. It is an excellent measure of benefits as they relate to SPI and ROI of SPI. Defect density enables us to perform a rich, wide, and

$$Defect\ Density = \frac{Defects}{Lines\ of\ Code}$$

Figure 14   Formula for Defect Density

almost infinite range and variety of benefit analyses. Figure 14 illustrates the formula for defect density.

Defect density is also a measure of customer satisfaction, as it pertains to customer needs, requirements, and expectations. Let's take a closer look at defect density. What does it really mean? What does it really tell us? What does it not mean or tell us? First, defect density measures the number of customer requirements that have not been satisfied by a software product. Second, defect density is a ratio of all requirements, design, code, and test defects to software size. Software size is merely a baseline against which to measure. If the defect density is 100 defects per thousand lines of code, there are 100 requirements, design, code, and test defects. This holds true if the software size is 1,000 defects. Defect density is not a measure of code quality. Defect density is not limited to just software source code. There can be a defect density for requirements, designs, code, and tests. However, defect density in general refers to the ratio of all defects to the amount of code that was produced.

There is a larger and more systemic issue associated with defect density. Defect density is used for managing software projects. What does that mean? If you had to choose three measures that indicate the success of a software project, defect density would be the first measure. It is a fundamental measure of product success. How is this so? A software project manager can establish a performance goal of one defect per thousand lines of code for a software project and then can periodically measure the defect density throughout the project. This would determine if the goal has been satisfied. Finally, a defect density of one defect per thousand lines of code means only one customer requirement went unsatisfied. In other words, if there were only a thousand lines of code, only one customer requirement went unsatisfied. Despite the antiquity of this classical measure, software project managers do not know how to manage using defect density. However, defect density is a key measure in high-maturity organizations, and it is a key measure for SPI and ROI of SPI.

5.3 QUALITY

Quality is conformance to customer requirements. It is the number of customer requirements that are met and satisfied or a measure of how many customer

$$Quality = 1 - \frac{Defects}{Lines\ of\ Code} \times 100\%$$

Figure 15   Formula for Quality

requirements a software product or service satisfies. Conversely, poor quality is nonconformance to customer requirements or the number of customer requirements that have not been met or satisfied. Poor quality is a measure of how many customer requirements a product or service satisfies. For example, if all customer requirements have been satisfied by a software product or service, then the quality is 100%. If half of the customer requirements are satisfied by the software product or service, then quality is 50%. Defect density is another way of expressing the same principles. In other words, defect density is a measure of conformance to customer requirements. That is, the number of defects per lines of code is a measure of quality. In fact, defect density is by far the most popular measure of quality in the field of software engineering. However, we will examine a variation of defect density that expresses conformance to customer requirements a little better. Figure 15 illustrates the formula for quality.

How did we translate conformance to customer requirements to the application of defect density? Well, first of all defects are another way of saying that a requirement has not been satisfied. Also, defects per lines of code is a simple ratio of defects to software size. Defects refer to all classes of defects, including requirements, design, code, and test defects. Like productivity, defects are normalized using software size as a standard way of expressing quality. For instance, three defects per lines of code may mean one requirement, design, and code defect was found.

Quality measurement, like productivity measurement, is highly controversial for several reasons. First, there are the conscientious objectors. They think that quality, like beauty, is in the eye of the beholder and cannot or should not be measured. Then there are those who say quality is a measure of cost. That is, they reason that higher quality products cost more and lower quality products cost less. Some say that quality is a measure of customer satisfaction, customer happiness, and quality of service. Of course, there are those who say quality is a measure of ease of use, expressed as usability, user friendliness, or the use of graphical user interfaces versus textual ones. Finally, some say quality is a product or service from a well-known blue-chip corporation or is a well-known brand. The industry success of an organization or firm is quality to some.

Certainly all of these popular and perhaps even pervasive or ubiquitous definitions of quality are correct, and they can certainly be quantified, measured, and used for ROI of SPI. However, the vast number of perceptions will be reduced here to a measure of conformance to customer requirements. This is not an arbitrary decision, as conformance to customer requirements is a standard measure of quality. Quality is sometimes even referred to as a long list of attributes including maintainability, reliability, usability, modularity, etc. However, let's assume that failure to address any one of dozens of minor attributes counts as one defect and that defects are a nonconformance to customer requirements.

5.4 DEFECT REMOVAL EFFICIENCY

Defect removal efficiency is the percentage of defects removed from software. It is the ratio of defects removed to defect escapes and defects injected. Defect removal efficiency is an indicator of how good or effective the software appraisal or review process has been. For example, defect removal efficiency is 70% if 70 out of every 100 defects are identified and removed. That is, they are removed by some form of appraisal activity. The Software Inspection Process and software testing are forms of appraisal activities.

Defect removal efficiency has a variety of useful purposes. It is an indicator of how effective quality management activities are on a phase-by-phase basis. Defect removal efficiency can indicate if there are problems in the quality management system that need correction. It can be used to manage quality throughout the software life cycle. Defect removal efficiency can be used as a measure to set process and product improvement goals. For instance, if the defect removal efficiency for testing is 30%, you may want to institute new people, processes, and tools to increase it to 40, 50, or even 80%. Defect removal efficiency is a method to analyze the effectiveness of individual processes, especially appraisal processes. It is one of the best methods to determine the effects of SPI. Figure 16 illustrates the formula for defect removal efficiency.

How does one interpret and apply the formula for defect removal efficiency? Let's start by defining each of its terms. Defects removed is the number of software defects identified by a software appraisal activity. Examples of popular software appraisal activities include individual reviews, the Software Inspection

$$DRE = \frac{Defects\ Removed}{Defects\ Escaped + Defects\ Injected} \times 100\%$$

Figure 16 Formula for Defect Removal Efficiency

Process, and testing. Automated static and dynamic analyses are even better forms of appraisal activities. Defects escaped is the number of defects that exist prior to the current time, that is, defects you inherit before you begin your work. If you are in the design phase, there may be preexisting analysis phase defects. If you are in the coding or testing phase, you may inherit preexisting analysis and design phase defects. Defects injected is the number of software defects committed in the current activity. For instance, if your task is to create the software architecture, then defects injected is the number of defects in your design. Let's say that you remove 90 defects in the design phase after inheriting 10 requirements defect escapes. Your defect removal efficiency is 90% if you inject 90 architecture defects in design.

We have kind of taken a time-independent point of view, which may be confusing. When is the best time to calculate defect removal efficiency? Defect removal efficiency is applied on a life-cycle-by-life-cycle basis, phase-by-phase basis, or appraisal-by-appraisal basis. Normally, defect removal efficiency is calculated on a phase-by-phase or activity-by-activity basis. This is done in order to evaluate the effectiveness of a phase or individual software process. Defect removal efficiency is a critical measure and key enabler for SPI and especially the ROI of SPI.

5.5 DEFECT REMOVAL MODEL

The defect removal model is a tool for managing software quality. It is a software project management method for software product quality. The defect removal model is a way for software project managers to plan, manage, and ensure the quality of their products. It is a tool that enables managers to plan, monitor, and optimize the application of appraisal activities. The Software Inspection Process, software testing, and automated static analysis are examples of appraisal activities. That is, on a phase-by-phase basis, software project managers will track the number of defects entering the phase. They will also track the number of defects injected during the phase and the number of defects exiting the phase. By doing this, they can establish software quality goals, design strategies to achieve the goals, and ultimately realize their goals. The defect removal model is a close cousin of defect removal efficiency, or, vice versa, defect removal efficiency is a close cousin of the defect removal model. The defect removal model yields the actual number of software defects that escape from a software life cycle phase or activity. Defect removal efficiency yields the percentage of defects removed by an activity. Figure 17 illustrates the formula for the defect removal model.

DRM = Defects Escaped + Defects Injected − Defects Removed

Figure 17   Formula for Defect Removal Model

Defects escaped is the number of software defects that exist prior to entering or performing a software activity or phase. Defects injected is the number of software defects committed during the phase or activity. Defects removed is the number of software defects identified and removed by a software appraisal activity. Let's say you enter the design phase and inherit 10 defects, create 90 architecture defects, and then remove 90 defects. The result of applying the defect removal model is 100 software defects less 90 software defects, or 10 software defects. The defect removal model is best applied on a phase-by-phase or activity-by-activity basis in order to optimize software quality. That is, use the defect removal model to track the number of defects that are being entered, injected, and removed. The defects are being removed from the requirements, design, code, and tests on a phase-by-phase basis.

The defect removal model is a tool for software project managers. The defect removal model is a way for software project managers to take charge of planning, managing, and optimizing quality. Gone are the days when software quality was a job for software test analysts and software quality assurance analysts. Software quality is the job of the software project manager. Software quality is just as important to managers as planning, managing, and optimizing cost and schedule performance. Software quality management using the defect removal model may be more important than cost and schedule performance. Why? Because cost and schedule performance are incontrovertibly linked to software quality performance. In other words, software project managers cannot achieve their cost and schedule targets without achieving their quality targets. If you don't achieve your software quality targets, both cost and schedule will be exceeded dramatically.

It is important to note that the defect removal model is only a tool. It does not have the precision and validity to be used for estimating software quality and reliability to any degree of accuracy, but it remains an important tool for enabling higher quality and reliability. Other forms of statistical quality and reliability models should be used for accurately estimating software quality and reliability. However, dollar for dollar, the defect removal model is by far one of the simplest, most useful, and easiest to understand tools. The defect removal model can be a persuasively effective method for optimizing software quality. Finally, the defect removal model is a critical source of key benefits for the fields of SPI and ROI of SPI.

5.6 SOFTWARE EFFORT

Software effort is the number of hours required for software development. It the number of hours needed for analysis, design, coding, and testing. Software effort is a unit of time, usually staff hours or staff months, which are an estimate of software development time. Software effort is the time required to analyze, design, develop, and test a software product. It does not usually include software maintenance effort, which must be estimated separately. For instance, the software effort based on Boehm's model is 39.55 staff months for 10,000 lines of code. Likewise, the software effort for the Walston/Felix, Bailey/Basili, and Doty models is 42.27, 15.81, and 58.82 staff months, respectively. The average effort of these models is 39.14 staff months or 6,783.85 staff hours to develop 10,000 lines of code. The effort includes analysis, design, code, and test hours. Once again, 6,783.85 hours does not include maintenance. These models are old and were probably designed or calibrated using software projects with millions of lines of code. Table 1 displays the formulas for software effort.

Software effort plays an important role in the analysis of costs and benefits and ultimately the ROI of SPI. Software effort models are used to estimate a portion of SPI costs, namely software development effort. There are other costs, such as training costs, maintenance costs, and the costs associated with using a new software process, and there are costs for special tools, special methods, and appraisal costs. What is important is that you use a software effort model that is right for your situation. It may be a commercial off-the-shelf software effort model, a bottom-up software effort estimate, or a parametric equation such as a linear or log-linear model designed especially for your data and environment. Let's assume that 25% of the software effort from these models is software testing. Deduct that in order to estimate software testing costs separately. Therefore, the average effort is 5,087.89 or 5,088 staff hours instead of 6,783.85. We will use this as a basis in future software effort estimates.

Table 1   Formulas for Software Effort

Source	Model*
Boehm	Months $= 3 \times \text{KSLOC}^{1.12}$
Walston/Felix	Months $= 5.2 \times \text{KSLOC}^{0.91}$
Bailey/Basili	Months $= 5.5 + 0.73 \times \text{KSLOC}^{1.15}$
Doty	Months $= 5.288 \times \text{KSLOC}^{1.047}$

* KSLOC = thousand source lines of code.

5.7 TOTAL LIFE CYCLE COST

Total life cycle cost represents software development and maintenance costs. Total life cycle cost is a method of determining both software development and maintenance costs. It quantifies analysis, design, development, test, and, more importantly, maintenance costs for software development. Very few people routinely estimate software development costs before a software project begins. The few who practice the science of software cost estimation only estimate development time. That is, they estimate the time it takes for analysis, design, coding, and testing. When estimating the benefits of a SPI method, they oftentimes only include analysis, design, coding, and testing benefits. However, software maintenance costs are almost never estimated, as a general rule of thumb. Likewise, the benefits of SPI for the software maintenance portion of the software life cycle are never estimated either. In fact, most people have never even heard of quantifying the costs and benefits to be obtained by analysis of postdelivery economics. Ironically, software maintenance costs have the potential to dwarf software development costs by over 20 times. That is, if you estimate your development time to be 1 month, the software maintenance time may be as high as 20 months. The software maintenance portion of the software life cycle is where the greatest benefits of SPI methods and ROI of SPI are found. Figure 18 illustrates the formula for total life cycle cost.

Total life cycle cost is a remarkably simple yet powerful concept. It is built upon the principles of defect density, quality, defect removal efficiency, and the defect removal model. Total life cycle cost is based on the economics of the Software Inspection Process, software testing, and software maintenance. A defect may be repaired in only 1 hour using the Software Inspection Process, whereas software testing requires 10 hours to fix a defect and software maintenance requires 100 hours to fix a defect. Don't be fooled by these basic ratios. This is a very conservative approach to analyzing the economics of software engineering. In fact, the Software Inspection Process can easily yield 10 defects per hour, whereas software testing can easily slip to 100 hours per defect and software maintenance typically hovers around 1,000 hours per defect. This is therefore a very conservative and kind model for software testing and software maintenance.

Let's examine what the total life cycle cost model is all about. Size refers to estimated software size in lines of code. The constant 10.51 is a simplification

$$TLC = Size \times 10.51 - Inspection\ Hours \times 99 - Test\ Hours \times 9$$

Figure 18   Formula for Total Life Cycle Cost

of software maintenance costs and defect injection rate. Inspection hours is the number of hours you plan to spend performing the Software Inspection Process. Test hours is the number of hours you plan to spend performing software testing. Let's cut to the chase. A 10,000-line-of-code system may cost up to 105,100 hours for software development and maintenance. For 100 hours of software testing, the total cost is reduced by an abysmal 1%. For 500 or 1,000 hours of software testing, the total life cycle cost drops by only 4 and 9%, respectively.

Before moving on, it is important to note that the typical amount of testing for a software release is 8 to 24 staff hours. If you spend 1,000 hours on testing, you would only reduce your total development and maintenance effort by less than 10% to 96,100 hours. Conversely, if you spend 100 hours on the Software Inspection Process, you will experience a drop in total life cycle cost of 10%. If you spend 500 hours on the Software Inspection Process, your total life cycle cost is reduced by almost 50%. If you spend 1,000 hours on the Software Inspection Process, the total life cycle effort is reduced by 94% to 6,100 hours. This is substantially less than a single staff year for a two-person project. The costs include analysis, design, coding, and testing phases, as well as the costs of the Software Inspection Process and software maintenance process.

The greatest benefits of SPI are found within the principles of defect density, quality, and defect removal efficiency. The defect removal model and especially total life cycle cost are sources of vast benefits, benefit data, and data for ROI of SPI. SPI methods that reduce or eliminate total life cycle costs have the greatest benefits and impact on the ROI of SPI.

6

METHODS FOR COST ANALYSIS

Methods for cost analysis are formulas, equations, and models to measure and quantify the effort, cost, and time of software process improvement (SPI) methods. Six cost models have been designed for the SPI methods we will examine here. Cost models are presented for the Software Inspection Process, Personal Software Process^SM, and Team Software Process^SM, as well as the Software Capability Maturity Model®, ISO 9001, and Capability Maturity Model Integration®. Cost analysis or quantifying the costs of a SPI method is an essential component of SPI and return on investment (ROI) of SPI. Not only is cost necessary for determining how much you need to spend for SPI or for input into an ROI equation, but knowing the cost of a SPI method is an integral part of the SPI method itself. Knowing costs is what it takes to successfully implement a SPI method and how to successfully manage a SPI initiative. In fact, knowing the cost of a SPI method indicates that you know the component parts of the SPI method. It also means you are familiar with the risks of implementing the SPI method and how to eliminate the obstacles. Knowing the cost of a SPI method certainly qualifies you as a professional in your field.

The major costs of a SPI method include education, process design, training, and implementation effort. Appraisal preparation, the appraisal itself, and any corrective action from appraisals are major cost items as well. The cost models presented here only address two major portions of the cost equation: implementation effort and process design. Why? An in-depth analysis of implementation effort is necessary to establish a foundation for cost analysis. In other words, you need to understand how costs relate to the SPI methods themselves. This chapter depicts how the cost models were designed and how they relate to the overall costs of each SPI method. The intention is to provide you with the skills to extend, adapt, and tailor these cost models for your organization. Furthermore, the intention is to show you how to design cost models for your own unique SPI method.

6.1 SOFTWARE INSPECTION PROCESS

The Software Inspection Process is a six-stage method for identifying defects. The six stages are planning, overview, preparation, meeting, rework, and follow-up. The planning stage is performed by a moderator in about 30 minutes for each pass through the Software Inspection Process. The overview stage is attended by the moderator, work product author, and all inspectors in about one hour for each pass. The preparation stage is performed by inspectors and takes about one hour. The meeting stage is attended by all participants and takes about two hours. The rework stage is performed by the work product author in about one hour. The follow-up stage is performed by the moderator in about 30 minutes. The total time required for a single pass through the Software Inspection Process is about 17 hours. Thus, the cost of the Software Inspection Process is the number of inspections times the sum of the effort for each role. The roles include the moderator, participants (team size), and inspectors (team size less one). The work product author also participates. Figure 19 illustrates the cost model for the Software Inspection Process.

The cost model for the Software Inspection Process consists of three variables or inputs. They are product size, review rate, and team size. The first two are combined to determine the number of times the Software Inspection Process must be used. Product size refers to the volume of the software product that must be inspected. For instance, the analysis phase may produce 10 requirements, and the design phase may produce 100 diagrams. The coding phase may produce 1,000 lines of code, and the testing phase may produce 10 test cases. The review rate refers to how fast the work products are inspected. For instance, suppose we inspect 1 requirement, 10 diagrams, 100 lines of code, and 1 test case per hour. The number of times the Software Inspection Process must be used is five for the requirements, five for the design, five for the code, and five for the tests. This is a total of 20 inspections. We have already determined

$$Hours = \frac{Product\ Size}{Review\ Rate \times 2} \times (Team\ Size \times 4 + 1)$$

Figure 19 Cost Model for Software Inspection Process

that each pass through the Software Inspection Process takes 17 hours, so the total effort for applying the Software Inspection Process to this project is 340 hours or 340 hours is 8.5 staff weeks.

That seems like an unreasonable amount of time. However, the Software Inspection Process yields a minimum of 1 major defect per inspection hour, so our 340 hours will yield 340 major software defects. It would require 3,400 hours of software testing to yield the same number of defects or 34,000 hours of software maintenance to fix them after product release, at a very minimum. The choice is yours — 340 hours for the Software Inspection Process or at least 34,000 hours for software maintenance. One last caution: reducing Software Inspection Process costs by increasing the review rates dramatically reduces its effectiveness. In other words, faster inspections reduce the number of software defects yielded to under one per hour. At the risk of sounding biased, it is important to note that individual reviews may be just as effective, and auto-mated static analysis could one day replace the Software Inspection Process and individual reviews altogether.

6.2 PERSONAL SOFTWARE PROCESS^{SM}

The Personal Software Process[SM] is a training curriculum. It teaches software engineers basic principles in software project and quality management. Beyond the classroom, the Personal Software Process[SM] consists of a basic software life cycle with five major stages. The five stages are planning, high-level design, high-level design review, development, and postmortem. Planning consists of developing program requirements, size estimates, and a cyclic development strategy and includes resource estimates, task and schedule plans, and defect estimates. High-level design consists of producing external specifications, module designs, prototypes, and a development strategy and includes documentation and issue tracking logs. High-level design review consists of verifying design coverage, state machines, logic, design consistency, and reuse and includes a development strategy as well as fixing defects. Development consists of pro-ducing module designs, reviewing designs, coding, and reviewing code and includes compiling, testing, and assessing the results. Postmortem consists of analyzing defects injected, defects removed, size, and time. Software engineers exhibit a productivity of 25 lines of code. This is for every hour spent in planning, high-level design, high-level design review, development, and post-mortem. It's a simple equation that simplifies to lines of code divided by 25. Figure 20 illustrates the cost model for the Personal Software Process[SM].

If it takes a software engineer 10 hours to go through all six stages, 250 lines of code result. If a software engineer produces 2,500 lines of code, it requires

$$Hours = \frac{Lines\ of\ Code}{25}$$

Figure 20 Cost Model for Personal Software Process^{SM}

100 hours to perform all six stages including coding. A 10,000 line of code system requires only 400 hours of planning, high-level design, high-level design review, development, and postmortem. The Personal Software Process^{SM} training curriculum consists of approximately 10 computer programming exercises. It is surprising to note that the productivity of individual software engineers does not seem to change across the 10 exercises, at least not the way productivity is measured in the classroom.

It is important to note that many consider the average productivity rate for the software industry to be one line of code per hour. Therefore, Personal Software Process^{SM} students are performing 25 times better than industry average. This includes the additional overhead of planning, design, development, reviews, and measurement. The Personal Software Process^{SM} shatters stereotypes associated with how long project and quality management require. That is, project and quality management can be performed 25 times faster than not using project and quality management at all.

As for the matter of how productivity is measured, productivity does improve with the Personal Software Process^{SM}. The Personal Software Process^{SM} results in near zero defects. That means total life cycle costs are reduced to the effort associated with development. Let's translate that into plain English. A 10,000-line-of-code system requires 105,100 hours to develop and maintain. This is true if the Software Inspection Process or software testing is not performed. That's a productivity of a single line of code every 9.5 hours. The Personal Software Process^{SM} yields a productivity of 25 lines of code per hour. That's a productivity increase of 263 times using the Personal Software Process^{SM}. However, it is questionable whether a productivity of 25 lines of code per hour is sustainable on large projects. Even though productivity using the Team Software Process^{SM} is four times lower than the Personal Software Process^{SM}, it is still very impressive.

6.3 TEAM SOFTWARE PROCESS^{SM}

The Team Software Process^{SM} is a method for teaching and operationalizing team building. It includes team working and project, quality, and life cycle management for groups of software engineers. The Team Software Process^{SM} builds upon the software project and quality management principles of the

Personal Software Process^{SM}. The Team Software Process^{SM} consists of six major phases. The six major phases are team launch, requirements, high-level design, implementation, release test, and postmortem. The Team Software Process^{SM} also has many lower level processes and scripts. However, it is not necessary to describe them here.

Team launch consists of establishing product and business goals and assigning roles and defining team goals. Team launch includes producing a development strategy, building top-down and next-phase plans, and developing quality plans. Building bottom-up and balanced plans, risk assessments, and preparing management briefings and launch reports are also included. Finally, team launch consists of holding management reviews and performing a launch postmortem.

Requirements consist of a requirements process overview, needs statement review, and needs statement clarification. It includes requirements tasks, task allocation, requirements documentation, system test plan, and requirements inspection. It also includes a system test plan inspection, requirements update, user requirements review, and requirements baseline.

High-level design consists of a design process review, high-level design, design standards, design tasks, and task allocation. It includes a design specification, integration testing plan, and design document inspection. It also includes a test plan inspection, design update, and update baseline.

Implementation consists of an implementation process overview, implementation planning, task allocation, and detailed design. It includes a unit test plan, test development, and detailed design inspection. It also includes coding, code inspection, unit test, component quality review, and component release.

Release test consists of a test process overview, test development, build, integration, system test, and documentation. It includes a postmortem process overview, process data review, and role performance evaluation. It also includes a cycle report preparation and role evaluation preparation.

Software engineers exhibit a productivity of 5.9347 lines of code for every hour spent using the Team Software Process^{SM}. This includes the team launch, requirements, high-level design, implementation, release test, and postmortem stages or phases. The equation can be simplified to lines of code divided by 5.9347. With over 20 major variations of the Team Software Process^{SM}, individual mileage may vary. Figure 21 illustrates the cost model for the Team Software Process^{SM}.

$$Hours = \frac{Lines\ of\ Code}{5.9347}$$

Figure 21 Cost Model for Team Software Process^{SM}

Software engineers require 168.5 hours to build a 1,000-line-of-code software product using the Team Software Process^{SM}. It takes that same team 1,685 hours to build a 10,000-line-of-code system using the Team Software Process^{SM}. This equation does not output programming time. It outputs the time spent in team launch, requirements, high-level design, implementation, release test, and postmortem. These figures indicate that a software project team can perform roughly six times faster than industry average. The team can do this while still performing state-of-the-art principles in software project, quality, and life cycle management — and produce zero defects to boot.

Let's examine the total life cycle costs of using the Team Software Process^{SM}. A 10,000-line-of-code system costs 1,685 hours using the Team Software Process^{SM}. A 10,000-line-of-code system costs 105,100 hours without using any of the principles of the Team Software Process^{SM}. This results in a productivity of 0.095 lines of code per hour. Therefore, using the Team Software Process^{SM} results in a productivity increase of more than 62 times. In other words, software project, quality, and life cycle management do not require any unnecessary overhead. Combined with team-building and team-working principles, it does not add any additional burden to the project cost. In fact, it repeals project costs.

It is not the intention in this book to ignore decades of research into log-linear models for software cost estimation. These models exhibit diseconomies of scale for complexity and size. It is important to note that early log-linear models were calibrated on systems with millions and tens of millions of lines of code and, conversely, were completely ineffective for accurately modeling small systems. Systems in the modern era of meta-programming languages tend to be smaller. They range in the hundreds and even thousands of lines of code. The simple linear models exhibited in this book are well suited for the programming-in-the-small era in which we reside. In other words, simple linear models may be ideally suited for estimating modern software projects.

6.4 SOFTWARE CAPABILITY MATURITY MODEL®

The Software Capability Maturity Model® is a minimum set of requirements for software project management. The Software Capability Maturity Model® is a set of criteria for the U.S. Department of Defense to use when selecting defense contractors. Many now use the Software Capability Maturity Model® as a standard for software process improvement. The Software Capability Maturity Model® consists of five levels: initial, repeatable, defined, managed, and optimizing. The initial level has no requirements. The repeatable level consists of requirements management, software project planning, and software project tracking and oversight. It includes software subcontract management, software qual-

$$Hours = 561 + 1,176 \times Number\ of\ Projects$$

Figure 22   Cost Model for Software Capability Maturity Model®

ity assurance, and software configuration management. The defined level consists of organizational process focus, organizational process definition, and training program. It includes integrated software management, software product engineering, intergroup coordination, and peer reviews. The managed level consists of quantitative process management and software quality management. The optimizing level consists of defect prevention, technology change management, and process change management.

The Software Capability Maturity Model® requires 561 hours to develop the policies and procedures necessary for Levels 2 and 3. It also requires 1,176 hours to develop the necessary documentation for each project. It is a simple equation expressed as the sum of 561 and the number of software projects multiplied by 1,176. Figure 22 illustrates the cost model for the Software Capability Maturity Model®.

Level 2 requires 6 policies and 24 procedures at 11 hours each. Level 3 requires 7 policies and 14 procedures at 11 hours each. That comes to 561 hours for 51 policies and procedures. Level 2 requires 532 hours for 8 documents, 19 work authorizations, 29 records, 34 reports, and 19 meeting minutes. Level 3 requires 644 hours for 20 documents, 11 work authorizations, 37 records, 21 reports, and 12 meeting minutes. That comes to 1,176 hours for 210 documents, work authorizations, records, reports, and meeting minutes. This is for a single software project.

The fixed part of the Software Capability Maturity Model® cost model is 561 hours. The variable portion is 1,176 hours, which is multiplied by the number of Software Capability Maturity Model®–compliant projects to be appraised. The only question, then, is to determine the number of projects to appraise. How many software projects need to spend a minimum of 1,176 hours? Usually only four to seven software projects are necessary. This applies to even the largest organization undergoing a Software Capability Maturity Model® appraisal. However, it is up to the discretion of the appraiser. You could take the opposite tack and require hundreds of software projects to be at Level 2 and 3. No appraiser would care to audit hundreds of projects. It is best not to incur the expense for such marginal gains. However, it is a common mistake of Software Capability Maturity Model® novices to require all projects to be Software Capability Maturity Model® compliant at enormous expense.

6.5 ISO 9001

ISO 9001 is a set of minimum requirements for quality management systems, as well as a set of criteria for certifying businesses within the European Union. It is also an international standard for quality and process improvement. ISO 9001 is composed of five broad categories of requirements for the design and certification of quality management systems. The five categories are quality management system, management responsibility, resource management, product realization, and measurement, analysis, and improvement. Quality management system consists of general requirements and documentation requirements. Management responsibility consists of management commitment, customer focus, quality policy, and planning. Responsibility, authority, communication, and management review round out management responsibility. Resource management consists of provision of resources, human resources, infrastructure, and work environment. Product realization consists of planning of product realization, customer-related processes, and design and development. Purchasing, production and services provision, and control of monitoring and measuring devices are also part of product realization. Measurement, analysis, and improvement consist of general requirements and monitoring and measurement. Control of nonconforming product, analysis of data, and improvement are also included. ISO 9001 requires about 546 hours to develop a quality policy, quality manual, and procedures for ISO 9001 registration. It also requires 560 hours to develop the necessary plans and records for each project. It is a simple equation expressed as the sum of 546 and the number of projects multiplied by 560. Figure 23 illustrates the cost model for ISO 9001.

The quality management system clause requires 21 policy statements at 3.4 hours and 21 quality manual paragraphs at 6.8 hours. This clause requires 5 procedures at 46.7 hours, 5 plans at 46.7 hours, and 21 records at 12.3 hours, for a total of 115.8 hours. The management responsibility clause requires 30 policy statements at 4.9 hours and 30 quality manual paragraphs at 9.7 hours. This clause requires 11 procedures at 102.7 hours, 11 plans at 102.7 hours, and 30 records at 17.5 hours, for a total of 237.4 hours.

The resource management clause requires 12 policy statements at 1.9 hours and 12 quality manual paragraphs at 3.9 hours. This clause requires 5 procedures at 46.7 hours, 5 plans at 46.7 hours, and 12 records at 7 hours, for a total of 106.2 hours. The product realization clause requires 54 policy statements at 8.8 hours and 54 quality manual paragraphs at 17.5 hours. This clause requires

$$Hours = 546 + 560 \times Number\ of\ Projects$$

Figure 23   Cost Model for ISO 9001

20 procedures at 186.7 hours, 20 plans at 186.7 hours, and 54 records at 31.5 hours, for a total of 431.1 hours.

Measurement and analysis and improvement requires 27 policy statements at 4.4 hours and 27 quality manual paragraphs at 8.8 hours. This clause requires 10 procedures at 93.3 hours, 10 plans at 93.3 hours, and 27 records at 15.8 hours, for a total of 215.5 hours.

ISO 9001 in its entirety requires 144 policy statements at 23.3 hours and 144 quality manual paragraphs at 46.7 hours. It requires 51 procedures at 476 hours, 51 plans at 476 hours, and 144 records at 84 hours, for a total of 1,106 hours. It is important to note that the 51 plans and 144 records which require 560 hours are only for one project.

The fixed part of the ISO 9001 cost model is 546 hours. The variable portion is 560 hours, which is multiplied by the number of ISO 9001–compliant projects to be audited. While Software Capability Maturity Model® appraisals and ISO 9001 audits are not similar in this regard, the design of the Software Capability Maturity Model® cost model was extended to the design of the ISO 9001 cost model for completeness and simplicity. The only question, then, is to determine the number of projects or project records to audit. How many projects need to spend a minimum of 560 hours to produce 51 plans and 144 records? Usually only four to seven projects are necessary for even the largest organization undergoing ISO 9001 registration. However, it is up to the discretion of the registrar. You could take the opposite tack and require hundreds of projects to be ISO 9001 compliant. No registrar would care to audit hundreds of projects. It is best not to undergo the expense for such marginal gains.

6.6 CAPABILITY MATURITY MODEL INTEGRATION®

Capability Maturity Model Integration® is a set of requirements for process and project management, engineering, and support, as well as a set of criteria for the U.S. Department of Defense to use when selecting defense contractors. Capability Maturity Model Integration® is the preferred method for process improvement within the U.S. Department of Defense community. The staged representation of Capability Maturity Model Integration® is composed of five levels. The five levels are initial, managed, defined, quantitatively managed, and optimizing.

The initial level consists of requirements management, project planning, and project monitoring and control. It includes supplier agreement management, measurement and analysis, and process and product quality assurance. It also includes configuration management. The defined level consists of requirements development, technical solution, product integration, verification, and valida-tion. It includes organizational process focus, organizational process definition,

$$Hours = 10,826 + 8,008 \times Number\ of\ Projects$$

Figure 24   Cost Model for Capability Maturity Model Integration®

and organizational training. It also includes integrated project management, risk management, integrated teaming, and integrated supplier management. Decision analysis and resolution and organizational environment for integration are also part of the defined level. The quantitatively managed level consists of organization process performance and quantitative project management. The optimizing level consists of organizational innovation and deployment and causal analysis and resolution.

Capability Maturity Model Integration® requires 10,826 hours to develop the policies and procedures for Levels 2 and 3. It also requires 8,008 hours to develop the necessary documentation for each project. It is a simple equation expressed as the sum of 10,826 and the number of projects multiplied by 8,008. Figure 24 illustrates the cost model for Capability Maturity Model Integration®.

Level 2 specific practices require 55 policies and procedures at 37.33 hours each. Level 3 specific practices require 109 policies and procedures at 37.33 hours each. That comes to 6,122 hours for 164 policies and procedures related to specific practices. Level 2 generic practices require 84 policies and procedures at 18.67 hours each. Level 3 generic practices require 168 policies and procedures at 18.67 hours each. That comes to 4,704 hours for 252 policies and procedures related to generic practices. Level 2 requires 138 work products at 18.67 hours each. Level 3 requires 291 work products at 18.67 hours each. That comes to 8,008 hours for 429 work products for a single software project.

The fixed part of the Capability Maturity Model Integration® cost model for reusable organizational software processes is 10,826 hours. The variable portion is 8,008 hours, which is multiplied by the number of Capability Maturity Model Integration®–compliant projects. The only question, then, is to determine the number of projects to appraise. How many projects need to spend a minimum of 8,008 hours? Usually only four to seven software projects are necessary for undergoing an appraisal using the staged representation. However, it is up to the discretion of the appraiser. You could take the opposite tack and require hundreds of projects to be at Levels 2 and 3 of the staged representation. No appraiser would care to audit hundreds of projects. It is best not to undergo this enormous expense. However, this is a common mistake of novices. That is, they make the error of forcing every project to be Capability Maturity Model Integration® compliant at great expense.

7

SOFTWARE INSPECTION PROCESS ROI METHODOLOGY

The return on investment (ROI) methodology for the Software Inspection Process is a procedure to measure, quantify, and analyze its economic value. The Software Inspection Process is a type of meeting which is held in order to identify defects in software work products. ROI is the amount of money gained, returned, or earned above the resources spent on the Software Inspection Process. Its ROI methodology is a six-part process that consists of estimating costs, benefits, benefit/cost ratio (B/CR), return on investment percent (ROI%), net present value (NPV), and breakeven point. The ROI methodology for the Software Inspection Process has unique elements for estimating costs, benefits, and B/CR. Its cost and benefit methodologies are complex, though its B/CR, ROI%, NPV, and breakeven point methodologies are simple. Key elements include the total life cycle cost model, which is used to estimate the benefits of using the Software Inspection Process. Figure 25 illustrates the ROI methodology for the Software Inspection Process.

7.1 INSPECTION COST METHODOLOGY

The cost methodology for the Software Inspection Process is a procedure to measure, quantify, and analyze the amount of money spent. The Software Inspection Process incurs cost to find defects, but results in lower overall software maintenance costs. Cost is the economic consequence of using the Soft-

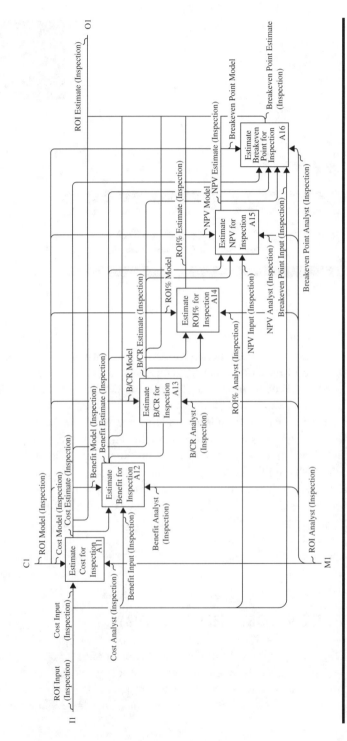

Figure 25 ROI Methodology for Software Inspection Process

ware Inspection Process to create a new and improved software process. Its cost methodology is a five-part process that consists of estimating training, software, meeting, test, and maintenance costs. The cost methodology for the Software Inspection Process has unique elements for estimating meeting and software maintenance costs. Its cost methodology consists of a complex composite of uniquely interrelated software cost and defect models. Key elements include the software, meeting, test, and maintenance cost models. These are used to approximate the complete costs of software development and maintenance, in conjunction with the Software Inspection Process. Figure 26 illustrates the cost methodology for the Software Inspection Process.

Estimate training cost for inspection: The objective of this activity is to estimate all of the training costs for the Software Inspection Process. This substep includes: multiply training rate, participant, and effort for inspection and add training time and training fee cost for inspection.

Estimate software cost (baseline) for inspection: The objective of this activity is to estimate the costs of software analysis, design, and implementation. This substep includes: estimate software cost (Boehm) for inspection, estimate software cost (Walston/Felix) for inspection, estimate software cost (Bailey/Basili) for inspection, estimate software cost (Doty) for inspection, and estimate software cost (average) for inspection.

In this case, the outputs of the software cost models by Boehm, Walston/Felix, Bailey/Basili, and Doty were averaged together. This was done as sort of a Delphi method to arrive at an average software cost. The reader is free to substitute contemporary cost models, such as COCOMO II, PRICE-S®, SLIM®, Knowledge Plan®, or any others, in order to accurately estimate software costs. The formulas for these models are illustrated in Chapter 5.

Estimate meeting cost for inspection: The objective of this activity is to estimate the cost for performing the Software Inspection Process. This substep includes: estimate meeting cost (BNR) for inspection, estimate meeting cost (Gilb) for inspection, estimate meeting cost (AT&T) for inspection, estimate meeting cost (HP) for inspection, estimate meeting cost (Rico) for inspection, and estimate meeting cost (average) for inspection.

The outputs of the BNR, Gilb, AT&T, HP, and Rico Software Inspection Process cost models were averaged together. Again, this was done as a Delphi method to arrive at an average Software Inspection Process cost. The formulas for these models are illustrated in the free Web Added Value™ materials available at www.jrosspub.com.

Estimate test cost for inspection: The objective of this activity is to estimate the cost of software testing based on defects escaping the Software Inspection Process. This substep includes: estimate starting defects for inspection, estimate meeting efficiency for inspection, estimate pre-test defects for inspection, es-

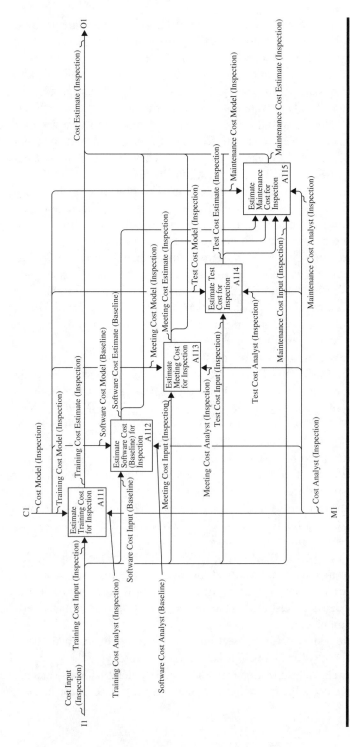

Figure 26 Cost Methodology for Software Inspection Process

timate test efficiency for inspection, estimate post-test defects for inspection, and estimate test cost (projected) for inspection.

Estimate maintenance cost for inspection: The objective of this activity is to estimate the cost of software maintenance based on defects escaping the Software Inspection Process and testing. This substep includes: estimate total life cycle cost for inspection and estimate maintenance cost (projected) for inspection.

7.2 INSPECTION BENEFIT METHODOLOGY

The benefit methodology for the Software Inspection Process is a procedure to measure, quantify, and analyze the amount of money returned. The Software Inspection Process eliminates defects early, when they are least expensive, resulting in lower maintenance costs. Benefit is the economic value of using the Software Inspection Process to create a new and improved software process. Its benefit methodology is a three-part process that consists of estimating test costs, total life cycle costs of testing, and benefits. Its benefit methodology consists of a variety of defect models used in combination. Key elements include the test cost model and the total life cycle cost model. These are used to compare the total life cycle costs of software testing to those of the Software Inspection Process. Figure 27 illustrates the benefit methodology for the Software Inspection Process.

Estimate test cost (baseline) for inspection: The objective of this activity is to estimate the cost of removing the maximum number of software defects using software testing. The substeps include: estimate post-test defects (baseline) for inspection; and estimate baseline test cost (projected) for inspection.

Estimate total life cycle cost (test) for inspection: The objective of this activity is to estimate software development and maintenance costs associated with using software testing. The substeps include: estimate total software cost (test) for inspection; estimate total test cost (test) for inspection; and subtract total test from software cost for inspection.

Estimate benefits (projected) for inspection: The objective of this activity is to compare software development and maintenance costs of testing and the Software Inspection Process. This substep includes: subtract total life cycle cost of inspection from test for inspection.

7.3 INSPECTION B/CR METHODOLOGY

The B/CR methodology for the Software Inspection Process is a procedure to measure, quantify, and analyze the ratio of benefits to costs. The ratio of benefits to costs for the Software Inspection Process is high because of reductions

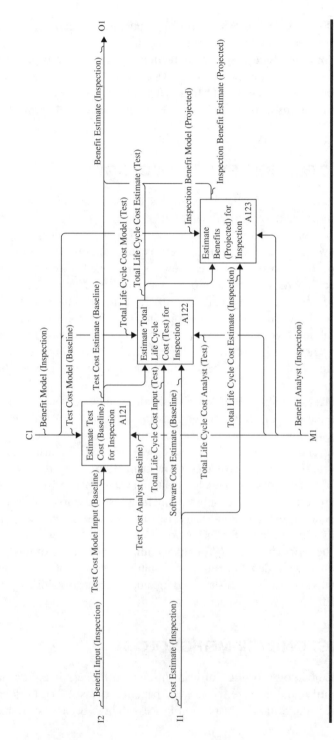

Figure 27 Benefit Methodology for Software Inspection Process

in software maintenance costs. B/CR is the economic magnitude of using the Software Inspection Process to create a new and improved software process. Its B/CR methodology is a two-part process that consists of estimating special costs and the benefit to cost ratio. Its benefit methodology consists of combining the benefits together with the special costs using a simple B/CR formula. Key elements include isolating the special, new, or additional costs and using the output of earlier total life cycle cost models. These are used to form an early picture of the economic value of the Software Inspection Process. Figure 28 illustrates the B/CR methodology for the Software Inspection Process.

Estimate special costs for inspection: The objective of this activity is to identify and separate the costs associated with the Software Inspection Process from common software development costs. This substep includes: add training and meeting costs for inspection.

Estimate benefit to cost ratio for inspection: The objective of this activity is to measure the magnitude of the benefits to the costs for implementing the Software Inspection Process. This substep includes: divide benefits by special costs for inspection.

7.4 INSPECTION ROI% METHODOLOGY

The ROI% methodology for the Software Inspection Process is a procedure to measure, quantify, and analyze the money returned. The ratio of net benefits to costs for the Software Inspection Process is high due to vast software maintenance cost savings. ROI% is the money earned from using the Software Inspection Process to create a new and improved software process. Its ROI% methodology is a two-part process that consists of estimating the benefit to cost ratio using net benefits versus gross benefits. Its benefit methodology consists of combining the net or adjusted benefits together with the special costs using the B/CR formula. Key elements include subtracting the special costs from the gross benefits to form net benefits. These are used to form a better picture of the magnitude of the benefits to the costs for the Software Inspection Process. (B/CR and ROI% are similar in that they are used to compare benefits to costs. However, B/CR uses gross benefits, while ROI% uses net benefits. Net benefits do not contain the implementation costs. Therefore, ROI% lowers the magnitude of benefits to costs versus using B/CR. The objective of using ROI% versus B/CR is to begin forming an accurate picture of the actual benefits of using a software process improvement method.) Figure 29 illustrates the ROI% methodology for the Software Inspection Process.

Estimate adjusted benefits for inspection: The objective of this activity is to validate the benefits of the Software Inspection Process by removing its costs. This substep includes: subtract special costs from benefits for inspection.

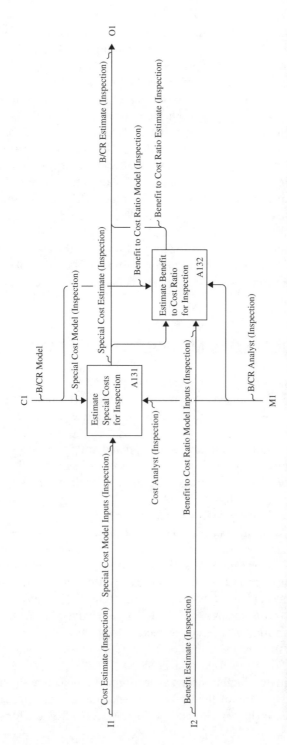

Figure 28 Benefit/Cost Ratio Methodology for Software Inspection Process

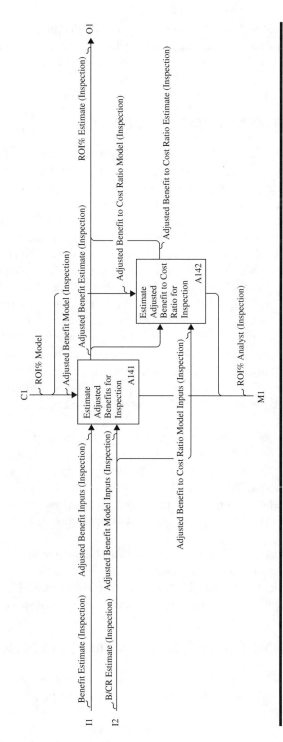

Figure 29 Return on Investment Percent Methodology for Software Inspection Process

Estimate adjusted benefit to cost ratio for inspection: The objective of this activity is to measure the magnitude of the net benefits to the costs for implementing the Software Inspection Process. This substep includes: divide adjusted benefits by special costs for inspection.

7.5 INSPECTION NPV METHODOLOGY

The NPV methodology for the Software Inspection Process is a procedure to measure, quantify, and analyze money returned less inflation. The ratio of discounted benefits to costs for the Software Inspection Process remains high due to reduced maintenance costs. NPV is the discounted money earned from using the Software Inspection Process to create a new and improved software process. Its NPV methodology is a three-part process that consists of estimating discounted benefits, special costs, and the benefit to cost ratio. Its benefit methodology consists of combining the discounted net benefits together with the special costs using the B/CR formula. Key elements include lowering the gross benefits to form the discounted benefits. These are used to form a realistic estimation of the magnitude of the benefits to the costs. (B/CR is a ratio of benefits to costs for objectively analyzing economic value. ROI% is used to avoid overstating the benefits. NPV is a skeptical and even cynical approach to ensure benefits are not overstated. All three of these methods should be used as exhibited by this NPV methodology. They are not mutually exclusive of one another.) Figure 30 illustrates the NPV methodology for the Software Inspection Process.

Estimate NPV of benefits for inspection: The objective of this activity is to discount the gross benefits of the Software Inspection Process based on inflation. This substep includes: divide benefits by devaluation rate for inspection.

Estimate adjusted NPV benefits for inspection: The objective of this activity is to validate the benefits of the Software Inspection Process by removing its costs. This substep includes: subtract special costs from NPV benefits for inspection.

Estimate adjusted NPV benefit to cost ratio for inspection: The objective of this activity is to measure the magnitude of the discounted net benefits to the costs for implementing the Software Inspection Process. This substep includes: divide adjusted NPV benefits by special costs for inspection.

7.6 INSPECTION BREAKEVEN POINT METHODOLOGY

The breakeven point methodology for the Software Inspection Process is a procedure to determine when benefits exceed costs. The benefits for the Soft-

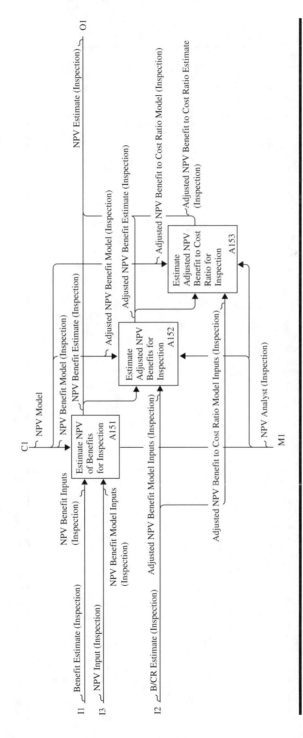

Figure 30 Net Present Value Methodology for Software Inspection Process

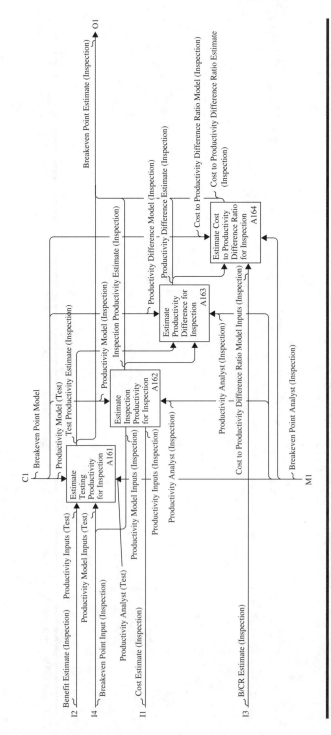

Figure 31 Breakeven Point Methodology for Software Inspection Process

ware Inspection Process rapidly exceed its cost due to reduced maintenance costs. Breakeven point is the value at which the benefits overtake the costs for using the Software Inspection Process. Its breakeven point methodology is a four-part process that consists of estimating productivity and the cost to productivity difference ratio. Its breakeven point methodology consists of combining costs with productivity difference using the breakeven point formula. Key elements include determining the ratio of productivity for the old and new software process improvement methods. These are used to determine the point when the benefits overtake the costs. Figure 31 illustrates the breakeven point methodology for the Software Inspection Process.

Estimate testing productivity for inspection: The objective of this activity is to determine the software productivity associated with using the software testing process. This substep includes: divide software size by total life cycle cost of testing for inspection.

Estimate inspection productivity for inspection: The objective of this activity is to determine the software productivity associated with using the Software Inspection Process. This substep includes: divide software size by total life cycle cost of inspection for inspection.

Estimate productivity difference for inspection: The objective of this activity is to compare the productivity of software testing to that of the Software Inspection Process. This substep includes: divide test productivity by inspection productivity for inspection.

Estimate cost to productivity difference ratio for inspection: The objective of this activity is to determine when the Software Inspection Process will begin paying for itself. This substep includes: divide special cost by one less productivity difference for inspection.

8

PERSONAL SOFTWARE PROCESS^{SM} ROI METHODOLOGY

The return on investment (ROI) methodology for the Personal Software Process^{SM} is a procedure to measure, quantify, and analyze its economic value. The Personal Software Process^{SM} is a training curriculum that is used to teach software project and quality management. ROI is the amount of money gained, returned, or earned above the resources spent on the Personal Software Process^{SM}. Its ROI methodology is a six-part process that consists of estimating costs, benefits, benefit/cost ratio (B/CR), ROI%, net present value (NPV), and breakeven point. The ROI methodology for the Personal Software Process^{SM} has unique elements for estimating costs, benefits, and B/CR. Its cost, benefit, B/CR, ROI%, NPV, and breakeven point methodologies are rather simple. Key elements include its software cost model and total life cycle cost model, which are used to estimate the costs and benefits of using the Personal Software Process^{SM}. Figure 32 illustrates the ROI methodology for the Personal Software Process^{SM}.

8.1 PSP^{SM} COST METHODOLOGY

The cost methodology for the Personal Software Process^{SM} is a procedure to measure, quantify, and analyze the amount of money spent. The Personal Software Process^{SM} incurs cost for training, but results in the lowest overall software maintenance costs. Cost is the economic consequence of using the Personal Software Process^{SM} to create a new and improved software process. Its cost

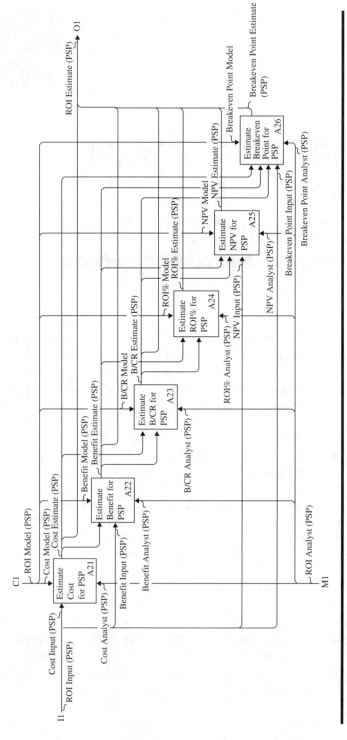

Figure 32 ROI Methodology for Personal Software Process[SM]

methodology is a two-part process that consists of estimating training and software costs. The cost methodology for the Personal Software Process^{SM} has unique elements for software development costs. Its cost methodology consists of a detailed accounting of training costs and the application of a rather simple software cost model. Key elements include the custom software effort model, which is based on historical productivity data. These are used to approximate the complete costs of software development, in conjunction with the Personal Software Process^{SM}. Figure 33 illustrates the cost methodology for the Personal Software Process^{SM}.

Estimate training cost for PSP^{SM}: The objective of this activity is to estimate all of the training costs for PSP^{SM}. This substep includes: estimate training time cost for PSP^{SM}, estimate nonclassroom time cost for PSP^{SM}, estimate travel cost for PSP^{SM}, and add training time, nonclassroom time, travel, and training fee cost for PSP^{SM}.

Estimate software cost for PSP^{SM}: The objective of this activity is to estimate the costs of software analysis, design, implementation, and test. This substep includes: divide software size by productivity for PSP^{SM}.

8.2 PSP^{SM} BENEFIT METHODOLOGY

The benefit methodology for the Personal Software Process^{SM} is a procedure to measure, quantify, and analyze the amount of money returned. The Personal Software Process^{SM} eliminates defects early and efficiently, when they are least expensive, resulting in no maintenance costs. Benefit is the economic value of using the Personal Software Process^{SM} to create a new and improved software process. Its benefit methodology is a four-part process that consists of estimating baseline software costs, test costs, total life cycle costs of testing, and benefits. Its benefit methodology consists of a variety of defect models used in combination. Key elements include the test cost model and the total life cycle cost model. These are used to compare the total life cycle costs of software testing to those of the Personal Software Process^{SM}. (Since the Personal Software Process^{SM} results in no estimated maintenance costs, the custom software cost model serves as a custom total life cycle cost model. The third substep is not necessary, but appears here to illustrate and highlight the process of estimating benefits.) Figure 34 illustrates the benefit methodology for the Personal Software Process^{SM}.

Estimate software cost (baseline) for PSP^{SM}: The objective of this activity is to estimate typical costs of software analysis, design, and implementation. This substep includes: estimate software cost (Boehm) for PSP^{SM}, estimate software cost (Walston/Felix) for PSP^{SM}, estimate software cost (Bailey/Basili) for PSP^{SM}, estimate software cost (Doty) for PSP^{SM}, and estimate software cost (average) for PSP^{SM}.

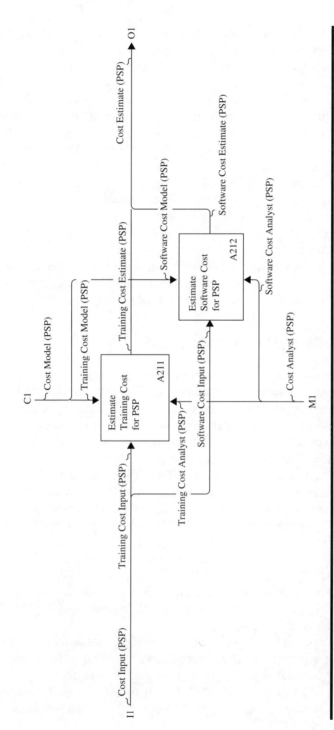

Figure 33 Cost Methodology for Personal Software Process[SM]

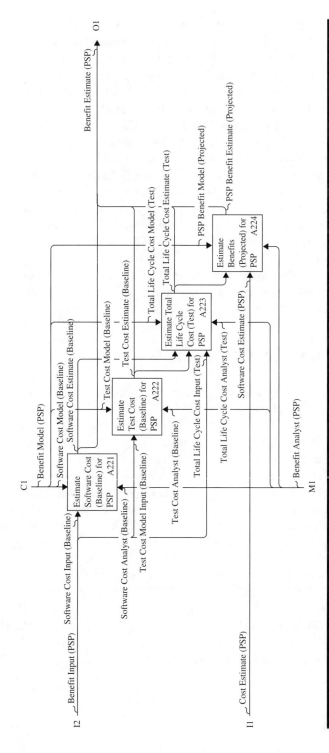

Figure 34 Benefit Methodology for Personal Software Process℠

In this case, the outputs of the software cost models by Boehm, Walston/ Felix, Bailey/Basili, and Doty were averaged together. This was done as sort of a Delphi method to arrive at an average software cost. The reader is free to substitute contemporary cost models, such as COCOMO II, PRICE-S®, SLIM®, Knowledge Plan®, or any others, in order to accurately estimate costs. The formulas for these models are illustrated in Chapter 5.

Estimate test cost (baseline) for PSP[SM]: The objective of this activity is to estimate the cost of removing the maximum number of software defects using software testing. This substep includes: estimate post-test defects (baseline) for PSP[SM] and estimate baseline test cost (projected) for PSP[SM].

Estimate total life cycle cost (test) for PSP[SM]: The objective of this activity is to estimate software development and maintenance costs associated with using software testing. This substep includes: estimate total software cost (test) for PSP[SM], estimate total test cost (test) for PSP[SM], and subtract total test from software cost for PSP[SM].

Estimate benefits (projected) for PSP[SM]: The objective of this activity is to compare development and maintenance costs of testing and PSP[SM]. This substep includes: subtract total life cycle cost of PSP[SM] from test for PSP[SM].

8.3 PSP[SM] B/CR METHODOLOGY

The B/CR methodology for the Personal Software Process[SM] is a procedure to measure, quantify, and analyze the ratio of benefits to costs. The ratio of benefits to costs for the Personal Software Process[SM] is high because maintenance costs are eliminated. B/CR is the economic magnitude of using the Personal Software Process[SM] to create a new and improved software process. Its B/CR methodology is a two-part process that consists of estimating special costs and the B/CR. Its benefit methodology consists of combining the benefits together with the special costs using a simple B/CR formula. Key elements include isolating the special, new, or additional costs and using the output of earlier total life cycle cost models. Figure 35 illustrates the B/CR methodology for the Personal Software Process[SM].

Estimate special costs for PSP[SM]: The objective of this activity is to identify and separate the costs associated with PSP[SM] from common software development costs. This substep includes: identify training cost for PSP[SM].

Estimate B/CR for PSP[SM]: The objective of this activity is to measure the magnitude of the benefits to the costs for implementing PSP[SM]. This substep includes: divide benefits by special costs for PSP[SM].

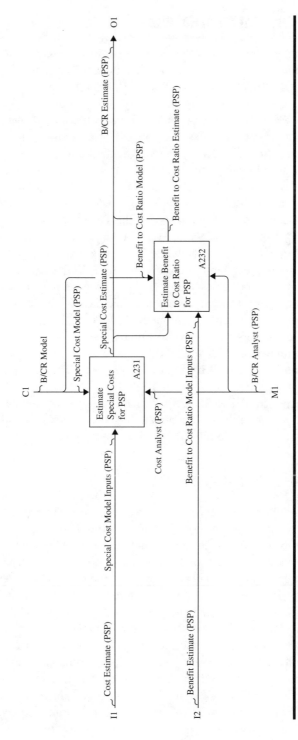

Figure 35 B/CR Methodology for Personal Software Process℠

8.4 PSP^SM ROI% METHODOLOGY

The ROI% methodology for the Personal Software Process^SM is a procedure to measure, quantify, and analyze the money returned. The ratio of net benefits to costs for the Personal Software Process^SM is high due to vast software maintenance cost savings. ROI% is the money earned from using the Personal Software Process^SM to create a new and improved software process. Its ROI% methodology is a two-part process that consists of estimating the B/CR using net benefits versus gross benefits. Its benefit methodology consists of combining the net or adjusted benefits together with the special costs using the B/CR formula. Key elements include subtracting the special costs from the gross benefits to form net benefits. These are used to form a better picture of the magnitude of the benefits to the costs for the Personal Software Process^SM. (B/CR and ROI% are similar in that they are used to compare benefits to costs. However, B/CR uses gross benefits, while ROI% uses net benefits. Net benefits do not contain the implementation costs. Therefore, ROI% lowers the magnitude of benefits to costs versus using B/CR. The objective of using ROI% versus B/CR is to begin forming an accurate picture of the actual benefits of using a software process improvement method.) Figure 36 illustrates the ROI% methodology for the Personal Software Process^SM.

Estimate adjusted benefits for PSP^SM: The objective of this activity is to validate the benefits of PSP^SM by removing its costs. This substep includes: subtract special costs from benefits for PSP^SM.

Estimate adjusted B/CR for PSP^SM: The objective of this activity is to measure the magnitude of the net benefits to the costs for implementing PSP^SM. This substep includes: divide adjusted benefits by special costs for PSP^SM.

8.5 PSP^SM NPV METHODOLOGY

The NPV methodology for the Personal Software Process^SM is a procedure to measure, quantify, and analyze money returned less inflation. The ratio of discounted benefits to costs for the Personal Software Process^SM remains high due to reduced maintenance costs. NPV is the discounted money earned from using the Personal Software Process^SM to create a new and improved software process. Its NPV methodology is a three-part process that consists of estimating discounted benefits, special costs, and the benefit to cost ratio. Its benefit methodology consists of combining the discounted net benefits together with the special costs using the B/CR formula. Key elements include lowering the gross benefits to form the discounted benefits. These are used to form a realistic estimation of the magnitude of the benefits to the costs. (B/CR is a ratio of benefits to costs for objectively analyzing economic value. ROI% is used to avoid overstating the benefits. NPV is a skeptical and even cynical approach to ensure benefits are not overstated. All

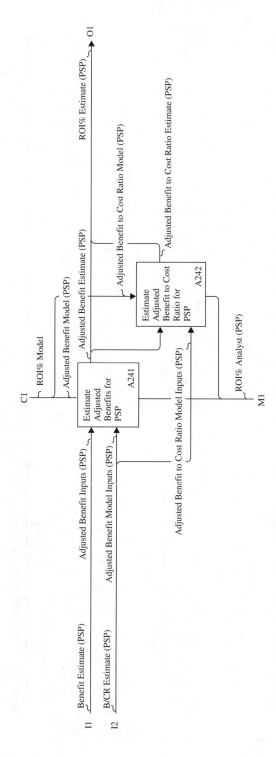

Figure 36 ROI% Methodology for Personal Software Process^{SM}

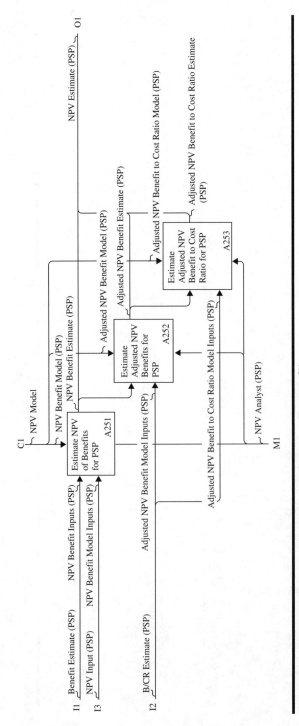

Figure 37 NPV Methodology for Personal Software Process[SM]

three of these methods should be used as exhibited by this NPV methodology. They are not mutually exclusive of one another.) Figure 37 illustrates the NPV methodology for the Personal Software Process^SM.

Estimate NPV of benefits for PSP^SM: The objective of this activity is to discount the gross benefits of PSP^SM based on inflation. This substep includes: divide benefits by devaluation rate for PSP^SM.

Estimate adjusted NPV benefits for PSP^SM: The objective of this activity is to validate the benefits of the PSP^SM by removing its costs. This substep includes: subtract special costs from NPV benefits for PSP^SM.

Estimate adjusted NPV B/CR for PSP^SM: The objective of this activity is to measure the magnitude of the discounted net benefits to the costs for implementing PSP^SM. This substep includes: divide adjusted NPV benefits by special costs for PSP^SM.

8.6 PSP^SM BREAKEVEN POINT METHODOLOGY

The breakeven point methodology for the Personal Software Process^SM is a procedure to determine when benefits exceed costs. The benefits for the Personal Software Process^SM rapidly exceed its cost due to reduced maintenance costs. Breakeven point is the value at which the benefits overtake the costs for using the Personal Software Process^SM. Its breakeven point methodology is a four-part process that consists of estimating productivity and the cost to productivity difference ratio. Its breakeven point methodology consists of combining costs with productivity difference using the breakeven point formula. Key elements include determining the ratio of productivity for the old and new software process improvement methods. These are used to determine the point when the benefits overtake the costs. Figure 38 illustrates the breakeven point methodology for the Personal Software Process^SM.

Estimate testing productivity for PSP^SM: The objective of this activity is to determine the software productivity associated with using the software testing process. This substep includes: divide software size by total life cycle cost of testing for PSP^SM.

Estimate PSP^SM productivity for PSP^SM: The objective of this activity is to determine the software productivity associated with using PSP^SM. This substep includes: divide software size by total life cycle cost of PSP^SM for PSP^SM.

Estimate productivity difference for PSP^SM: The objective of this activity is to compare the productivity of software testing to that of PSP^SM. This substep includes: divide test productivity by PSP^SM productivity for PSP^SM.

Estimate cost to productivity difference ratio for PSP^SM: The objective of this activity is to determine when PSP^SM will begin paying for itself. This substep includes: divide special cost by one less productivity difference for PSP^SM.

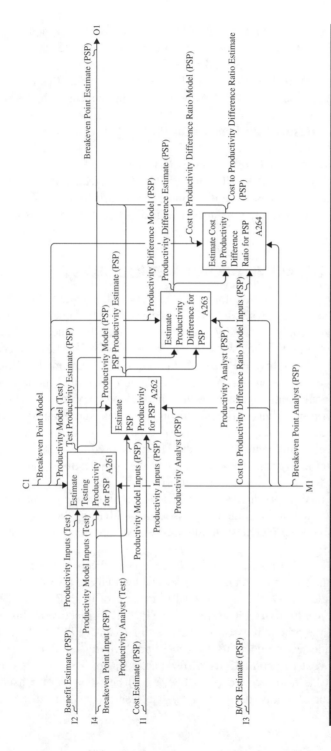

Figure 38 Breakeven Point Methodology for Personal Software Process℠

9

TEAM SOFTWARE PROCESS[SM] ROI METHODOLOGY

The return on investment (ROI) methodology for the Team Software Process[SM] is a procedure to measure, quantify, and analyze its economic value. The Team Software Process[SM] is a project, quality, and life cycle management method for large groups of software engineers. ROI is the amount of money gained, returned, or earned above the resources spent on the Team Software Process[SM]. Its ROI methodology is a six-part process that consists of estimating costs, benefits, benefit/cost ratio (B/CR), ROI%, net present value (NPV), and breakeven point. The ROI methodology for the Team Software Process[SM] has unique elements for estimating costs, benefits, and B/CR. Its cost, benefit, B/CR, ROI%, NPV, and breakeven point methodologies are rather simple. Key elements include its software cost model and total life cycle cost model, which are used to estimate the costs and benefits of using the Team Software Process[SM]. Figure 39 illustrates the ROI methodology for the Team Software Process[SM].

9.1 TSP[SM] COST METHODOLOGY

The cost methodology for the Team Software Process[SM] is a procedure to measure, quantify, and analyze the amount of money spent. The Team Software Process[SM] incurs cost for training, but results in one of the lowest overall software maintenance costs. Cost is the economic consequence of using the Team Software Process[SM] to create a new and improved software process. Its cost methodology is a two-part process that consists of estimating training and

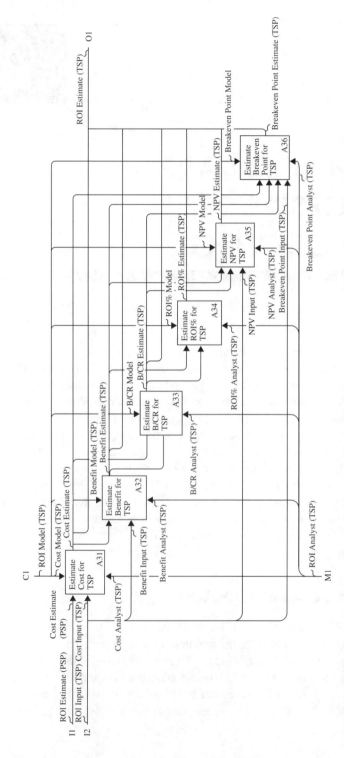

Figure 39 ROI Methodology for Team Software Process(SM)

software costs. The cost methodology for the Team Software Process℠ has unique elements for software development costs. Its cost methodology consists of a detailed accounting of training costs and the application of a rather simple software cost model. Key elements include the custom software effort model, which is based on historical productivity data. These are used to approximate the complete costs of software development, in conjunction with the Team Software Process℠. Figure 40 illustrates the cost methodology for the Team Software Process℠.

Estimate training cost for TSP℠: The objective of this activity is to estimate all of the training costs for TSP℠. This substep includes: estimate training time cost for TSP℠, estimate travel cost for TSP℠, and add training time, travel, and Personal Software Process℠ training cost for TSP℠.

Estimate software cost for TSP℠: The objective of this activity is to estimate the costs of software analysis, design, implementation, and test. This substep includes: divide software size by productivity for TSP℠.

9.2 TSP℠ BENEFIT METHODOLOGY

The benefit methodology for the Team Software Process℠ is a procedure to measure, quantify, and analyze the amount of money returned. The Team Software Process℠ eliminates defects early and efficiently, when they are least expensive, resulting in no maintenance costs. Benefit is the economic value of using the Team Software Process℠ to create a new and improved software process. Its benefit methodology is a four-part process that consists of estimating baseline software costs, test costs, total life cycle costs of testing, and benefits. Its benefit methodology consists of a variety of defect models used in combination. Key elements include the test cost model and the total life cycle cost model. These are used to compare the total life cycle costs of software testing to those of the Team Software Process℠. (Since the Team Software Process℠ results in no estimated maintenance costs, the custom software cost model serves as a custom total life cycle cost model. The third substep is not necessary, but appears here to illustrate and highlight the process of estimating benefits.) Figure 41 illustrates the benefit methodology for the Team Software Process℠.

Estimate software cost (baseline) for TSP℠: The objective of this activity is to estimate typical costs of software analysis, design, and implementation. This substep includes: estimate software cost (Boehm) for TSP℠, estimate software cost (Walston/Felix) for TSP℠, estimate software cost (Bailey/Basili) for TSP℠, estimate software cost (Doty) for TSP℠, and estimate software cost (average) for TSP℠.

In this case, the outputs of software cost models by Boehm, Walston/Felix, Bailey/Basili, and Doty were averaged together. This was done as sort of a

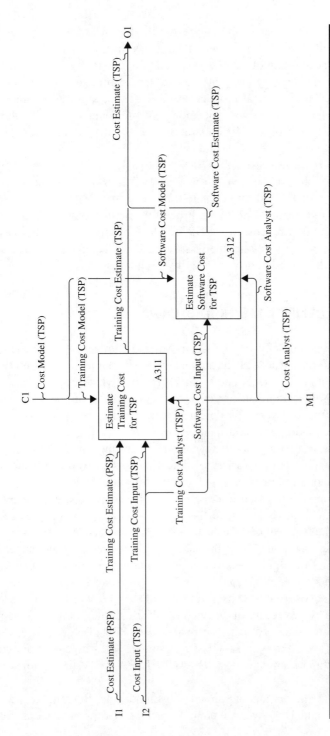

Figure 40 Cost Methodology for Team Software Process^{SM}

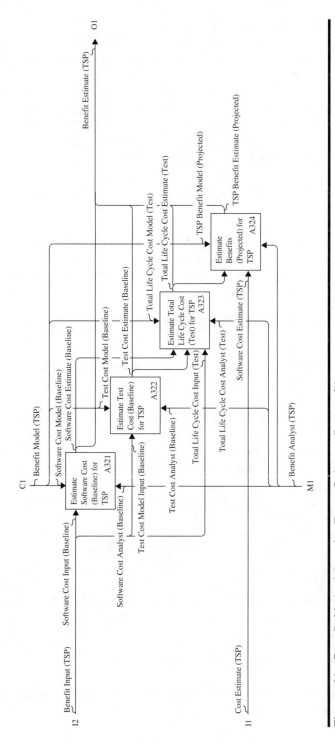

Figure 41 Benefit Methodology for Team Software Process℠

Delphi method to arrive at an average software cost. The reader is free to substitute contemporary cost models, such as COCOMO II, PRICE-S®, SLIM®, Knowledge Plan®, and others, in order to accurately estimate software costs. The formulas for these models are illustrated in Chapter 5.

Estimate test cost (baseline) for TSPSM: The objective of this activity is to estimate the cost of removing the maximum number of software defects using software testing. This substep includes: estimate post-test defects (baseline) for TSPSM and estimate baseline test cost (projected) for TSPSM.

Estimate total life cycle cost (test) for TSPSM: The objective of this activity is to estimate software development and maintenance costs associated with using software testing. This substep includes: estimate total software cost (test) for TSPSM, estimate total test cost (test) for TSPSM, and subtract total test from software cost for TSPSM.

Estimate benefits (projected) for TSPSM: The objective of this activity is to compare development and maintenance costs of testing and TSPSM. This substep includes: subtract total life cycle cost of TSPSM from test for TSPSM.

9.3 TSPSM B/CR METHODOLOGY

The B/CR methodology for the Team Software ProcessSM is a procedure to measure, quantify, and analyze the ratio of benefits to costs. The ratio of benefits to costs for the Team Software ProcessSM is high because maintenance costs are eliminated. B/CR is the economic magnitude of using the Team Software ProcessSM to create a new and improved software process. Its B/CR methodology is a two-part process that consists of estimating special costs and the B/CR. Its benefit methodology consists of combining the benefits together with the special costs using a simple B/CR formula. Key elements include isolating the special, new, or additional costs and using the output of earlier total life cycle cost models. Figure 42 illustrates the B/CR methodology for the Team Software ProcessSM.

Estimate special costs for TSPSM: The objective of this activity is to identify and separate the costs associated with TSPSM from common software development costs. This substep includes: identify training cost for TSPSM.

Estimate B/CR for TSPSM: The objective of this activity is to measure the magnitude of the benefits to the costs for implementing TSPSM. This substep includes: divide benefits by special costs for TSPSM.

9.4 TSPSM ROI% METHODOLOGY

The ROI% methodology for the Team Software ProcessSM is a procedure to measure, quantify, and analyze the money returned. The ratio of net benefits

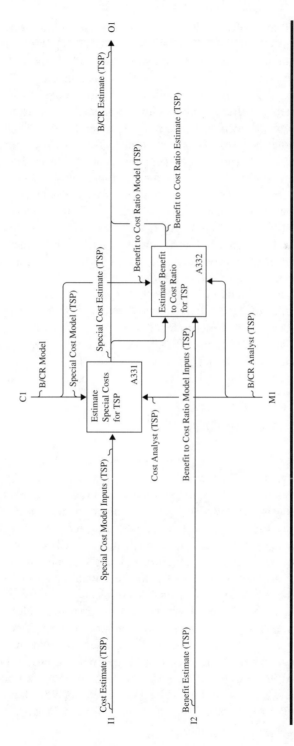

Figure 42 B/CR Methodology for Team Software Process℠

to costs for the Team Software Process^{SM} is high due to vast software maintenance cost savings. ROI% is the money earned from using the Team Software Process^{SM} to create a new and improved software process. Its ROI% methodology is a two part process that consists of estimating the B/CR using net benefits versus gross benefits. Its benefit methodology consists of combining the net or adjusted benefits together with the special costs using the B/CR formula. Key elements include subtracting the special costs from the gross benefits to form net benefits. These are used to form a better picture of the magnitude of the benefits to the costs for the Team Software Process^{SM}. (B/CR and ROI% are similar in that they are used to compare benefits to costs. However, B/CR uses gross benefits, while ROI% uses net benefits. Net benefits do not contain the implementation costs. Therefore, ROI% lowers the magnitude of benefits to costs versus using B/CR. The objective of using ROI% versus B/CR is to begin forming an accurate picture of the actual benefits of using a software process improvement method.) Figure 43 illustrates the ROI% methodology for the Team Software Process^{SM}.

Estimate adjusted benefits for TSP^{SM}: The objective of this activity is to validate the benefits of TSP^{SM} by removing its costs. This substep includes: subtract special costs from benefits for TSP^{SM}.

Estimate adjusted B/CR for TSP^{SM}: The objective of this activity is to measure the magnitude of the net benefits to the costs for implementing TSP^{SM}. This substep includes: divide adjusted benefits by special costs for TSP^{SM}.

9.5 TSP^{SM} NPV METHODOLOGY

The NPV methodology for the Team Software Process^{SM} is a procedure to measure, quantify, and analyze money returned less inflation. The ratio of discounted benefits to costs for the Team Software Process^{SM} remains high due to reduced maintenance costs. NPV is the discounted money earned from using the Team Software Process^{SM} to create a new and improved software process. Its NPV methodology is a three-part process that consists of estimating discounted benefits, special costs, and the B/CR. Its benefit methodology consists of combining the discounted net benefits together with the special costs using the B/CR formula. Key elements include lowering the gross benefits to form the discounted benefits. These are used to form a realistic estimation of the magnitude of the benefits to the costs. (B/CR is a ratio of benefits to costs for objectively analyzing economic value. ROI% is used to avoid overstating the benefits. NPV is a skeptical and even cynical approach to ensure benefits are not overstated. All three of these methods should be used as exhibited by this NPV methodology. They are not mutually exclusive of one another.) Figure 44 illustrates the NPV methodology for the Team Software Process^{SM}.

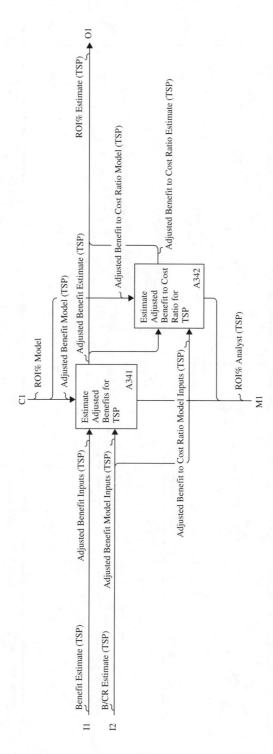

Figure 43 ROI% Methodology for Team Software Process℠

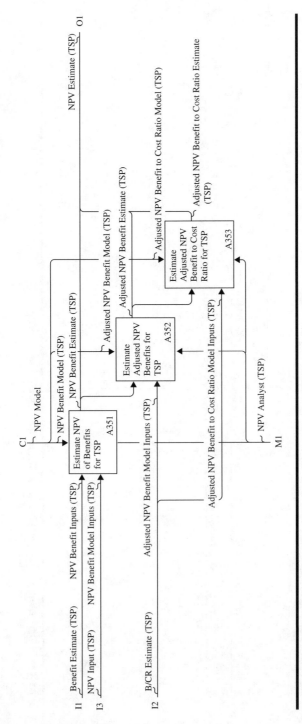

Figure 44 NPV Methodology for Team Software Process[SM]

Estimate NPV of benefits for TSP^{SM}: The objective of this activity is to discount the gross benefits of TSP^{SM} based on inflation. This substep includes: divide benefits by devaluation rate for TSP^{SM}.

Estimate adjusted NPV benefits for TSP^{SM}: The objective of this activity is to validate the benefits of TSP^{SM} by removing its costs. This substep includes: subtract special costs from NPV benefits for TSP^{SM}.

Estimate adjusted NPV B/CR for TSP^{SM}: The objective of this activity is to measure the magnitude of the discounted net benefits to the costs for implementing TSP^{SM}. This substep includes: divide adjusted NPV benefits by special costs for TSP^{SM}.

9.6 TSP^{SM} BREAKEVEN POINT METHODOLOGY

The breakeven point methodology for the Team Software Process^{SM} is a procedure to determine when benefits exceed costs. The benefits for the Team Software Process^{SM} rapidly exceed its cost due to reduced maintenance costs. Breakeven point is the value at which the benefits overtake the costs for using the Team Software Process^{SM}. Its breakeven point methodology is a four-part process that consists of estimating productivity and the cost to productivity difference ratio. Its breakeven point methodology consists of combining costs with productivity difference using the breakeven point formula. Key elements include determining the ratio of productivity for the old and new software process improvement methods. These are used to determine the point when the benefits overtake the costs. Figure 45 illustrates the breakeven point methodology for the Team Software Process^{SM}.

Estimate testing productivity for TSP^{SM}: The objective of this activity is to determine the software productivity associated with using the software testing process. This substep includes: divide software size by total life cycle cost of testing for TSP^{SM}.

Estimate TSP^{SM} productivity for TSP^{SM}: The objective of this activity is to determine the software productivity associated with using TSP^{SM}. This substep includes: divide software size by total life cycle cost of TSP^{SM} for TSP^{SM}.

Estimate productivity difference for TSP^{SM}: The objective of this activity is to compare the productivity of software testing to that of TSP^{SM}. This substep includes: divide test productivity by TSP^{SM} productivity for TSP^{SM}.

Estimate cost to productivity difference ratio for TSP^{SM}: The objective of this activity is to determine when TSP^{SM} will begin paying for itself. This substep includes: divide special cost by one less productivity difference for TSP^{SM}.

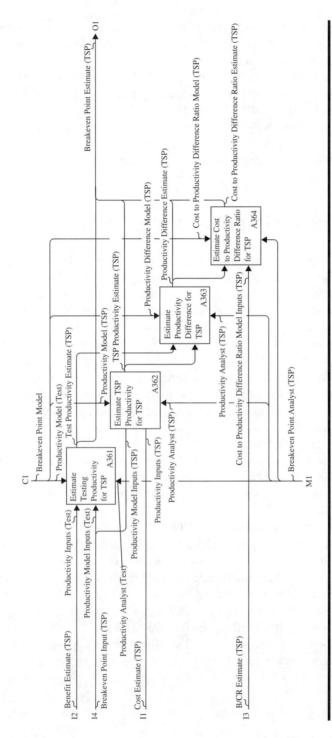

Figure 45 Breakeven Point Methodology for Team Software Process^{SM}

10

SOFTWARE CAPABILITY MATURITY MODEL® ROI METHODOLOGY

The return on investment (ROI) methodology for the Software Capability Maturity Model® is a procedure to measure, quantify, and analyze its economic value. The Software Capability Maturity Model® is a set of guidelines for selecting software suppliers and performing software process improvement. ROI is the amount of money gained, returned, or earned above the resources spent on the Software Capability Maturity Model®. Its ROI methodology is a six-part process that consists of estimating costs, benefits, benefit/cost ratio (B/CR), ROI%, net present value (NPV), and breakeven point. The ROI methodology for the Software Capability Maturity Model® has unique elements for estimating costs, benefits, and B/CR. Its cost and benefit methodologies are complex, although its B/CR, ROI%, NPV, and breakeven point methodologies are simple. Key elements include the process and total life cycle cost models, which are used to estimate its costs and benefits. Figure 46 illustrates the ROI methodology for the Software Capability Maturity Model®.

10.1 SW-CMM® COST METHODOLOGY

The cost methodology for the Software Capability Maturity Model® is a procedure to measure, quantify, and analyze the amount of money spent. The Software Capability Maturity Model® incurs cost to develop processes, result-

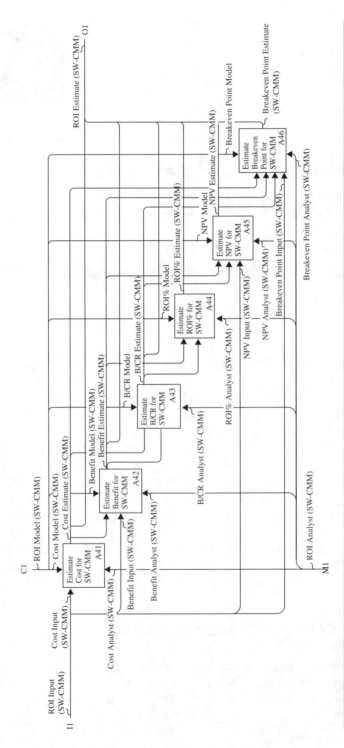

Figure 46 ROI Methodology for Software Capability Maturity Model®

ing in higher productivity and lower maintenance. Cost is the economic consequence of using the Software Capability Maturity Model® to create new and improved software processes. Its cost methodology is an eight-part process that consists of estimating process, product, preparation, assessment, software, meeting, test, and maintenance costs. The cost methodology for the Software Capability Maturity Model® has unique elements for estimating process costs. Key elements include the process, assessment, software development, meeting, test, and maintenance cost models. These are used to approximate the costs of software development and maintenance, in conjunction with the Software Capability Maturity Model®. Figure 47 illustrates the cost methodology for the Software Capability Maturity Model®.

Estimate process cost for SW-CMM®: The objective of this activity is to estimate the cost of developing policies and procedures for SW-CMM®. This substep includes: estimate Level 2 process cost for SW-CMM®, estimate Level 3 process cost for SW-CMM®, and estimate Level 2 and 3 process cost for SW-CMM®.

Estimate product cost for SW-CMM®: The objective of this activity is to estimate the cost of developing documents, work authorizations, records, reports, and meeting minutes for SW-CMM®. This substep includes: estimate Level 2 product cost for SW-CMM®, estimate Level 3 product cost for SW-CMM®, and estimate Level 2 and 3 product cost for SW-CMM®.

Estimate preparation cost for SW-CMM®: The objective of this activity is to estimate the cost of assessment indoctrination, assessment response conditioning, and mock assessments for SW-CMM®. This substep includes: estimate indoctrination cost for SW-CMM®, estimate response-conditioning cost for SW-CMM®, estimate mock assessment cost for SW-CMM®, and estimate indoctrination, response-conditioning, and mock assessment cost for SW-CMM®. (Assessment preparation is not necessarily a one-time activity. This activity may take place as many times as are necessary to prepare for the assessment. The goal is to pass the assessment the first time around, through iterative preparatory steps.)

Estimate assessment cost for SW-CMM®: The objective of this activity is to estimate the cost of assessment planning, assessment preparation, assessment meetings, and assessment follow-up for SW-CMM®. This substep includes: estimate assessment planning cost for SW-CMM®, estimate assessment preparation cost for SW-CMM®, estimate assessment meeting cost for SW-CMM®, estimate assessment follow-up cost for SW-CMM®, and estimate assessment planning, preparation, meeting, and follow-up cost for SW-CMM®.

Estimate software cost (baseline) for SW-CMM®: The objective of this activity is to estimate the costs of software analysis, design, and implementation. This substep includes: estimate software cost (Boehm) for SW-CMM®,

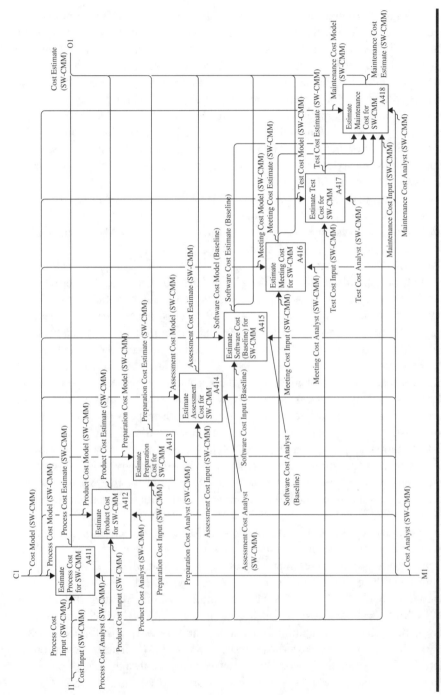

Figure 47 Cost Methodology for Software Capability Maturity Model®

estimate software cost (Walston/Felix) for SW-CMM®, estimate software cost (Bailey/Basili) for SW-CMM®, estimate software cost (Doty) for SW-CMM®, and estimate software cost (average) for SW-CMM®.

In this case, the outputs of the software cost models by Boehm, Walston/Felix, Bailey/Basili, and Doty were averaged together. This was done as sort of a Delphi method to arrive at an average software cost. The reader is free to substitute contemporary cost models, such as COCOMO II, PRICE-S®, SLIM®, Knowledge Plan®, or any others, in order to accurately estimate software costs. The formulas for these models are illustrated in Chapter 5.

Estimate meeting cost for SW-CMM®: The objective of this activity is to estimate the cost for performing the Software Inspection Process. This substep includes: estimate meeting cost (BNR) for SW-CMM®, estimate meeting cost (Gilb) for SW-CMM®, estimate meeting cost (AT&T) for SW-CMM®, estimate meeting cost (HP) for SW-CMM®, estimate meeting cost (Rico) for SW-CMM®, and estimate meeting cost (average) for SW-CMM®.

The outputs of the BNR, Gilb, AT&T, HP, and Rico Software Inspection Process cost models were averaged together. Again, this was done as a Delphi method to arrive at an average Software Inspection Process cost. The formulas for these models are illustrated in the free Web Added Value™ materials available at www.jrosspub.com.

Estimate test cost for SW-CMM®: The objective of this activity to estimate the cost of software testing based on defects escaping the Software Inspection Process. This substep includes: estimate starting defects for SW-CMM®, estimate meeting efficiency for SW-CMM®, estimate pre-test defects for SW-CMM®, estimate test efficiency for SW-CMM®, estimate post-test defects for SW-CMM®, and estimate test cost (projected) for SW-CMM®.

Estimate maintenance cost for SW-CMM®: The objective of this activity is to estimate the cost of software maintenance based on defects escaping the Software Inspection Process and testing. This substep includes: estimate total life cycle cost for SW-CMM® and estimate maintenance cost (projected) for SW-CMM®.

10.2 SW-CMM® BENEFIT METHODOLOGY

The benefit methodology for the Software Capability Maturity Model® is a procedure to measure, quantify, and analyze the amount of money returned. The Software Capability Maturity Model® results in higher productivity and quality, resulting in lower development and maintenance costs. The benefit is the economic value of using the Software Capability Maturity Model® to create a new and improved software process. Its benefit methodology is a three-part process that consists of estimating test costs, total life cycle costs of testing, and benefits. Its benefit methodology consists of a variety of defect models used in combination. Key elements include the test cost model and the total life cycle cost model. Some of the benefits are due to increased productivity, resulting in up to a 50% decrease in software development costs. Increased productivity is factored into the total life cycle cost model. These are used to compare the total life cycle costs of software testing to those of the Software Capability Maturity Model®. Figure 48 illustrates the benefit methodology for the Software Capability Maturity Model®.

Estimate test cost (baseline) for SW-CMM®: The objective of this activity is to estimate the cost of removing the maximum number of software defects using software testing. This substep includes: estimate post-test defects (baseline) for SW-CMM® and estimate baseline test cost (projected) for SW-CMM®.

Estimate total life cycle cost (test) for SW-CMM®: The objective of this activity is to estimate software development and maintenance costs associated with using software testing. This substep includes: estimate total software cost (test) for SW-CMM®, estimate total test cost (test) for SW-CMM®, and subtract total test from software cost for SW-CMM®.

Estimate benefits (projected) for SW-CMM®: The objective of this activity is to compare software development and maintenance costs of testing and SW-CMM®. This substep includes: subtract total life cycle cost of SW-CMM® from test for SW-CMM®.

10.3 SW-CMM® B/CR METHODOLOGY

The B/CR methodology for the Software Capability Maturity Model® is a procedure to measure, quantify, and analyze the ratio of benefits to costs. The ratio of benefits to costs for the Software Capability Maturity Model® is high because of productivity increases and reductions in software maintenance costs. In fact, the majority of the benefits are due to the institutionalization of peer reviews or the Software Inspection Process. Higher quality and lower maintenance costs result from using peer reviews. A small part of the benefits are derived from increased productivity. Adherence to U.S. Department of Defense policy for supplier selection results from using the Software Capability Maturity Model®. B/CR is the economic magnitude of using the Software Capability Maturity Model® to create a new and improved software process. Its B/CR methodology is a two-part process that consists of estimating special costs and the B/CR. Its benefit methodology consists of combining the benefits together with the special costs using a simple B/CR formula. Key elements include isolating the special, new, or additional costs and using the output of earlier total life cycle cost models. These are used to form an early picture of the

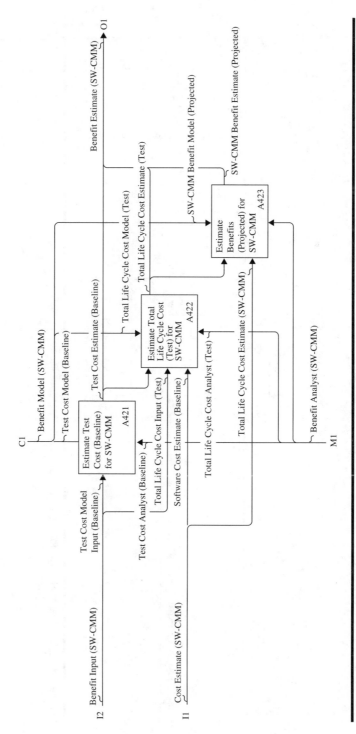

Figure 48   Benefit Methodology for Software Capability Maturity Model®

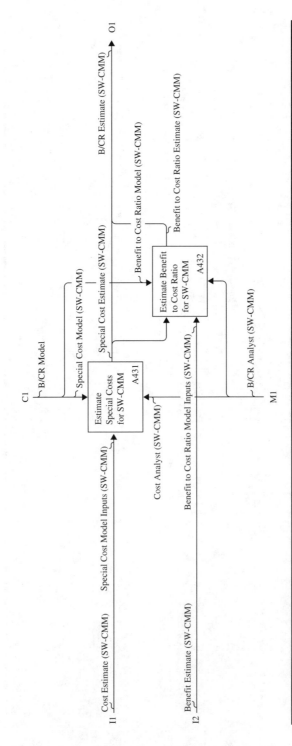

Figure 49 B/CR Methodology for Software Capability Maturity Model®

economic value of the Software Capability Maturity Model®. Figure 49 illustrates the B/CR methodology for the Software Capability Maturity Model®.

Estimate special costs for SW-CMM®: The objective of this activity is to identify and separate the costs associated with SW-CMM® from common software development costs. This substep includes: add process, product, preparation, assessment, and meeting costs for SW-CMM®.

Estimate B/CR for SW-CMM®: The objective of this activity is to measure the magnitude of the benefits to the costs for implementing SW-CMM®. This substep includes: divide benefits by special costs for SW-CMM®.

10.4 SW-CMM® ROI% METHODOLOGY

The ROI% methodology for the Software Capability Maturity Model® is a procedure to measure, quantify, and analyze the money returned. The ratio of net benefits to costs for the Software Capability Maturity Model® is high due to software maintenance cost savings. ROI% is the money earned from using the Software Capability Maturity Model® to create a new and improved software process. Its ROI% methodology is a two-part process that consists of estimating the B/CR using net benefits versus gross benefits. Its benefit methodology consists of combining the net or adjusted benefits together with the special costs using the B/CR formula. Key elements include subtracting the special costs from the gross benefits to form net benefits. These are used to form a better picture of the magnitude of the benefits to the costs for the Software Capability Maturity Model®. (B/CR and ROI% are similar in that they are used to compare benefits to costs. However, B/CR uses gross benefits, while ROI% uses net benefits. Net benefits do not contain the implementation costs. Therefore, ROI% lowers the magnitude of benefits to costs versus using B/CR.) Figure 50 illustrates the ROI% methodology for the Software Capability Maturity Model®.

Estimate adjusted benefits for SW-CMM®: The objective of this activity is to validate the benefits of SW-CMM® by removing its costs. This substep includes: subtract special costs from benefits for SW-CMM®.

Estimate adjusted B/CR for SW-CMM®: The objective of this activity is to measure the magnitude of the net benefits to the costs for implementing SW-CMM®. This substep includes: divide adjusted benefits by special costs for SW-CMM®.

10.5 SW-CMM® NPV METHODOLOGY

The NPV methodology for the Software Capability Maturity Model® is a procedure to measure, quantify, and analyze money returned less inflation. The

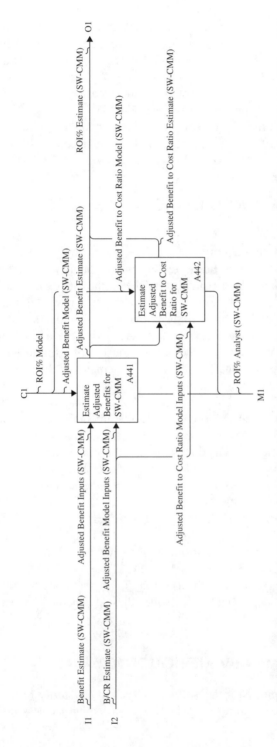

Figure 50 ROI% Methodology for Software Capability Maturity Model®

ratio of discounted benefits to costs for the Software Capability Maturity Model® remains high due to reduced maintenance costs. The reduced maintenance costs are largely due to the institutionalization or use of peer reviews or the Software Inspection Process. It is possible to have a smaller NPV if rigorous peer reviews are not utilized, and large residual software defect populations remain. Larger software defect populations result in larger software maintenance costs. NPV is the discounted money earned from using the Software Capability Maturity Model® to create a new and improved software process. Its NPV methodology is a three-part process that consists of estimating discounted benefits, special costs, and the B/CR. Its benefit methodology consists of combining the discounted net benefits together with the special costs using the B/CR formula. Key elements include lowering the gross benefits to form the discounted benefits. These are used to form a realistic estimation of the magnitude of the benefits to the costs. (B/CR is a ratio of benefits to costs for objectively analyzing economic value. ROI% is used to avoid overstating the benefits. NPV is a skeptical and even cynical approach to ensure benefits are not overstated. All three of these methods should be used as exhibited by this NPV methodology. They are not mutually exclusive of one another.) Figure 51 illustrates the NPV methodology for the Software Capability Maturity Model®.

Estimate NPV of benefits for SW-CMM®: The objective of this activity is to discount the gross benefits of SW-CMM® based on inflation. This substep includes: divide benefits by devaluation rate for SW-CMM®.

Estimate adjusted NPV benefits for SW-CMM®: The objective of this activity is to validate the benefits of SW-CMM® by removing its costs. This substep includes: subtract special costs from NPV benefits for SW-CMM®.

Estimate adjusted NPV B/CR for SW-CMM®: The objective of this activity is to measure the magnitude of the discounted net benefits to the costs for implementing SW-CMM®. This substep includes: divide adjusted NPV benefits by special costs for SW-CMM®.

10.6 SW-CMM® BREAKEVEN POINT METHODOLOGY

The breakeven point methodology for the Software Capability Maturity Model® is a procedure to determine when benefits exceed costs. The benefits of the Software Capability Maturity Model® rapidly exceed its cost due to reduced maintenance costs. Breakeven point is the value at which the benefits overtake the costs for using the Software Capability Maturity Model®. Its breakeven point methodology is a four-part process that consists of estimating productivity and the cost to productivity difference ratio. Its breakeven point methodology consists of combining costs with productivity difference using the breakeven point formula. Key elements include determining the ratio of productivity for

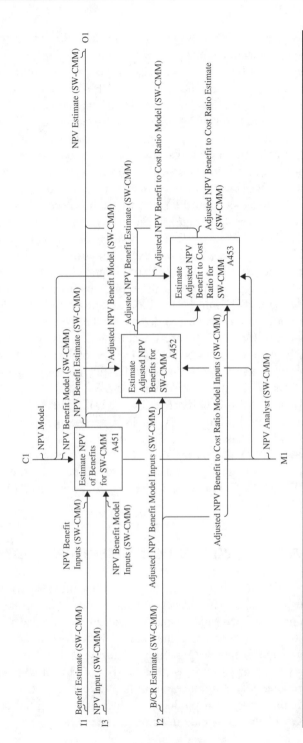

Figure 51 NPV Methodology for Software Capability Maturity Model®

the old and new software process improvement methods. These are used to determine the point when the benefits overtake the costs. (As indicated earlier, benefits, B/CR, ROI%, NPV, and breakeven point are directly impacted by the use of peer reviews. Rigorous peer reviews improve the economic outlook, while their absence hinders it.) Figure 52 illustrates the breakeven point methodology for the Software Capability Maturity Model®.

Estimate testing productivity for SW-CMM®: The objective of this activity is to determine the software productivity associated with using the software testing process. This substep includes: divide software size by total life cycle cost of testing for SW-CMM®.

Estimate SW-CMM® productivity for SW-CMM®: The objective of this activity is to determine the software productivity associated with using SW-CMM®. This substep includes: divide software size by total life cycle cost of SW-CMM® for SW-CMM®.

Estimate productivity difference for SW-CMM®: The objective of this activity is to compare the productivity of software testing to that of SW-CMM®. This substep includes: divide test productivity by SW-CMM® productivity for SW-CMM®.

Estimate cost to productivity difference ratio for SW-CMM®: The objective of this activity is to determine when SW-CMM® will begin paying for itself. This substep includes: divide special cost by one less productivity difference for SW-CMM®.

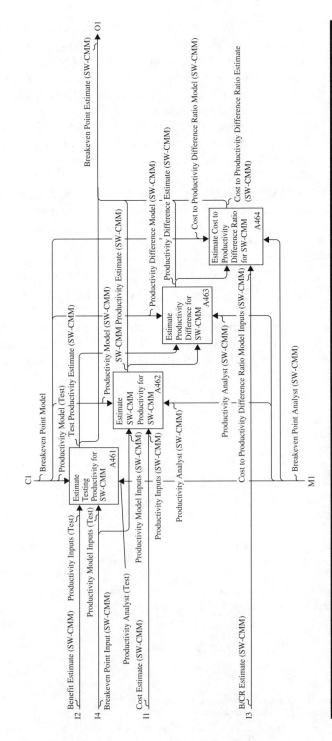

Figure 52 Breakeven Point Methodology for Software Capability Maturity Model®

11

ISO 9001 ROI METHODOLOGY

The return on investment (ROI) methodology for ISO 9001 is a procedure to measure, quantify, and analyze its economic value. ISO 9001 is a set of requirements for quality management systems which must be met by firms within the European Union. ROI is the amount of money gained, returned, or earned above the resources spent on ISO 9001. Its ROI methodology is a six-part process that consists of estimating costs, benefits, benefit/cost ratio (B/CR), ROI%, net present value (NPV), and breakeven point. The ROI methodology for ISO 9001 has unique elements for estimating costs, benefits, and B/CR. Its cost and benefit methodologies are complex, although its B/CR, ROI%, NPV, and breakeven point methodologies are simple. Key elements include the process and total life cycle cost models, which are used to estimate the costs and benefits of using ISO 9001. (Much of the data are in the form of opinion surveys, and data are difficult to find.) Figure 53 illustrates the ROI methodology for ISO 9001.

11.1 ISO 9001 COST METHODOLOGY

The cost methodology for ISO 9001 is a procedure to measure, quantify, and analyze the amount of money spent. ISO 9001 incurs cost to develop processes, resulting in higher productivity and lower maintenance. Cost is the economic consequence of using ISO 9001 to create a new and improved software process. Its cost methodology is a seven-part process that consists of estimating process, product, preparation, audit, software, test, and maintenance costs. The cost methodology for ISO 9001 has unique elements for estimating process costs. Key elements include the process, assessment, software development, test, and

115

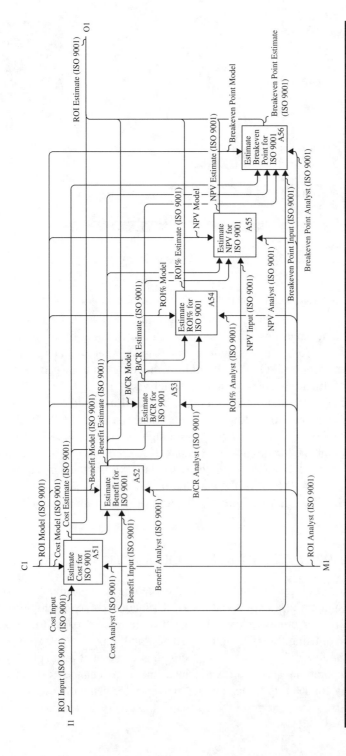

Figure 53 ROI Methodology for ISO 9001

maintenance cost models. These are used to approximate the costs of software development and maintenance, in conjunction with ISO 9001. The process and product cost model is based on a bottom-up approach to cost estimation. There are some top-down parametric cost models which are viewed as less accurate. Figure 54 illustrates the cost methodology for ISO 9001.

Estimate process cost for ISO 9001: The objective of this activity is to estimate the cost of developing policies, quality manuals, and procedures for ISO 9001. The substeps include: estimate policy cost for ISO 9001, estimate quality manual cost for ISO 9001, estimate procedure cost for ISO 9001, and estimate policy, quality manual, and procedure cost for ISO 9001.

Estimate product cost for ISO 9001: The objective of this activity is to estimate the cost of developing plans and records for ISO 9001. The substeps include: estimate plan cost for ISO 9001, estimate record cost for ISO 9001, and estimate plan and record cost for ISO 9001.

Estimate preparation cost for ISO 9001: The objective of this activity is to estimate the cost of indoctrination, response conditioning, and mock audits for ISO 9001. The substeps include: estimate indoctrination cost for ISO 9001, estimate response-conditioning cost for ISO 9001, estimate mock audit cost for ISO 9001, and estimate indoctrination, response-conditioning, and mock audit cost for ISO 9001.

Estimate audit cost for ISO 9001: The objective of this activity is to estimate the cost of audit planning, audit preparation, audit meetings, and audit follow-up for ISO 9001. The substeps include: estimate audit planning cost for ISO 9001, estimate audit preparation cost for ISO 9001, estimate audit meeting cost for ISO 9001, estimate audit follow-up cost for ISO 9001, and estimate audit planning, preparation, meeting, and follow-up cost for ISO 9001.

Estimate software cost (baseline) for ISO 9001: The objective of this activity is to estimate the costs of software analysis, design, and implementation. The substeps include: estimate software cost (Boehm) for ISO 9001, estimate software cost (Walston/Felix) for ISO 9001, estimate software cost (Bailey/Basili) for ISO 9001, estimate software cost (Doty) for ISO 9001, and estimate software cost (average) for ISO 9001.

In this case, the outputs of the software cost models by Boehm, Walston/Felix, Bailey/Basili, and Doty were averaged together. This was done as sort of a Delphi method to arrive at an average software cost. The reader is free to substitute contemporary cost models, such as COCOMO II, PRICE-S®, SLIM®, Knowledge Plan®, or any others, in order to accurately estimate software costs. The formulas for these models are illustrated in Chapter 5.

Estimate test cost for ISO 9001: The objective of this activity to estimate the cost of software testing based on estimated starting defect populations. The substeps include: estimate post-test defects for ISO 9001 and estimate test cost (projected) for ISO 9001.

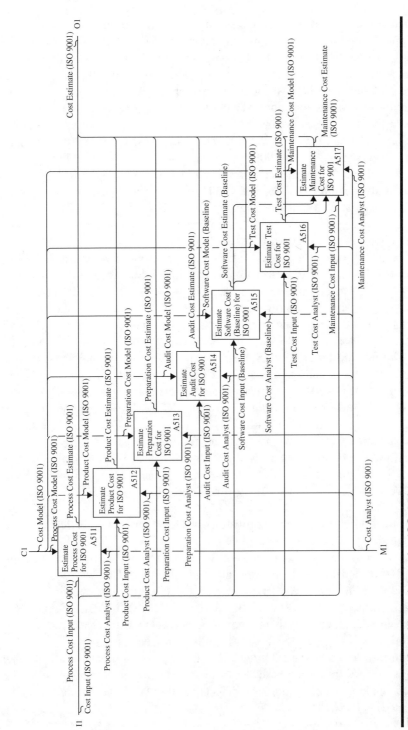

Figure 54 Cost Methodology for ISO 9001

Estimate maintenance cost for ISO 9001: The objective of this activity is to estimate the cost of software maintenance based on defects escaping the software testing process. The substeps include: estimate total life cycle cost for ISO 9001 and estimate maintenance cost (projected) for ISO 9001.

11.2 ISO 9001 BENEFIT METHODOLOGY

The benefit methodology for ISO 9001 is a procedure to measure, quantify, and analyze the amount of money returned. ISO 9001 results in higher productivity and quality, resulting in lower development and maintenance costs. Benefit is the economic value of using ISO 9001 to create a new and improved software process. Its benefit methodology is a three-part process that consists of estimating test costs, total life cycle costs of testing, and benefits. Its benefit methodology consists of a variety of defect models used in combination. Key elements include the test cost model and the total life cycle cost model. Some of the benefits are due to increased productivity, resulting in up to a 15% decrease in software development costs. Increased productivity is factored into the total life cycle cost model. The test and total life cycle cost models are used to compare the total life cycle costs of software testing to those of ISO 9001. Figure 55 illustrates the benefit methodology for ISO 9001.

Estimate test cost (baseline) for ISO 9001: The objective of this activity is to estimate the cost of removing the maximum number of software defects using software testing. The substeps include: estimate post-test defects (baseline) for ISO 9001 and estimate baseline test cost (projected) for ISO 9001.

Estimate total life cycle cost (test) for ISO 9001: The objective of this activity is to estimate software development and maintenance costs associated with using software testing. The substeps include: estimate total software cost (test) for ISO 9001, estimate total test cost (test) for ISO 9001, and subtract total test from software cost for ISO 9001.

Estimate benefits (projected) for ISO 9001: The objective of this activity is to compare software development and maintenance costs of testing and ISO 9001. This substep includes: subtract total life cycle cost of ISO 9001 from test for ISO 9001. It is assumed that rigorous testing was used prior to adaptation of ISO 9001. However, it is not assumed that peer reviews or the Software Inspection Process was used before, during, or after the deployment of ISO 9001.

11.3 ISO 9001 B/CR METHODOLOGY

The B/CR methodology for ISO 9001 is a procedure to measure, quantify, and analyze the ratio of benefits to costs. The ratio of benefits to costs for ISO 9001

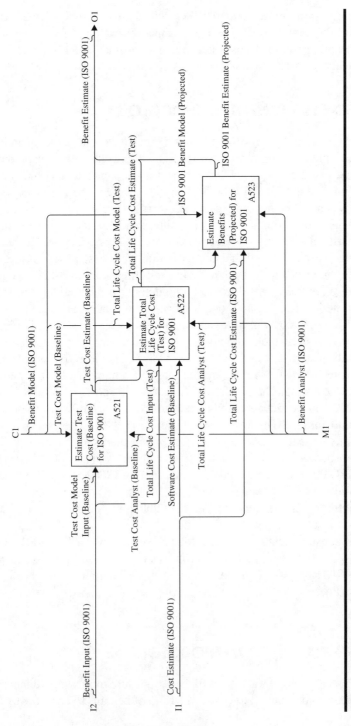

Figure 55 Benefit Methodology for ISO 9001

is moderate because of productivity increases and reductions in software maintenance costs. A large part of the benefits are due to reported productivity increases of 15% for ISO 9001. A moderate part of the benefits are derived from increased quality. The quality benefits of using ISO 9001 are reported to be as high as 13%. B/CR is the economic magnitude of using ISO 9001 to create a new and improved software process. Its B/CR methodology is a two-part process that consists of estimating special costs and the B/CR. Its benefit methodology consists of combining the benefits together with the special costs using a simple B/CR formula. Key elements include isolating the special, new, or additional costs and using the output of earlier total life cycle cost models. These are used to form an early picture of the economic value of ISO 9001. The objective is to establish a methodology for evaluating ROI. Personalized knowledge, study, or derivation of additional ISO 9001 benefits may increase B/CR, ROI%, NPV, and breakeven point. Figure 56 illustrates the B/CR methodology for ISO 9001.

Estimate special costs for ISO 9001: The objective of this activity is to identify and separate the costs associated with ISO 9001 from common software development costs. This substep includes: add process, product, preparation, and audit costs for ISO 9001.

Estimate B/CR for ISO 9001: The objective of this activity is to measure the magnitude of the benefits to the costs for implementing ISO 9001. This substep includes: divide benefits by special costs for ISO 9001.

11.4 ISO 9001 ROI% METHODOLOGY

The ROI% methodology for ISO 9001 is a procedure to measure, quantify, and analyze the money returned. The ratio of net benefits to costs for ISO 9001 is moderate due to software maintenance cost savings and minor productivity increases. ROI% is the money earned from using ISO 9001 to create a new and improved software process. Its ROI% methodology is a two-part process that consists of estimating the B/CR using net benefits versus gross benefits. Its benefit methodology consists of combining the net or adjusted benefits together with the special costs using the B/CR formula. Key elements include subtracting the special costs from the gross benefits to form net benefits. These are used to form a better picture of the magnitude of the benefits to the costs for ISO 9001. ROI% for ISO 9001 may be increased dramatically by the optimization of strategic clauses or process areas. (B/CR and ROI% are similar in that they are used to compare benefits to costs. However, B/CR uses gross benefits, while ROI% uses net benefits. Net benefits do not contain the implementation costs. Therefore, ROI% lowers the magnitude of benefits to costs versus using B/CR.) Figure 57 illustrates the ROI% methodology for ISO 9001.

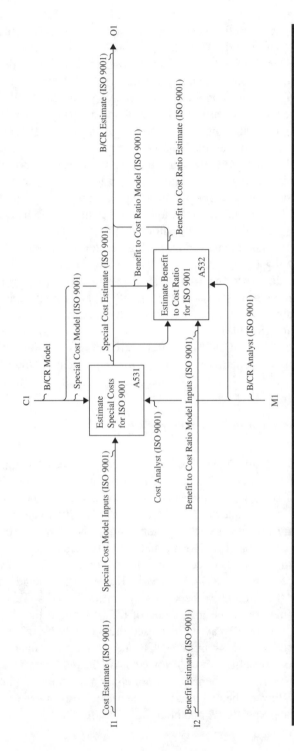

Figure 56 B/CR Methodology for ISO 9001

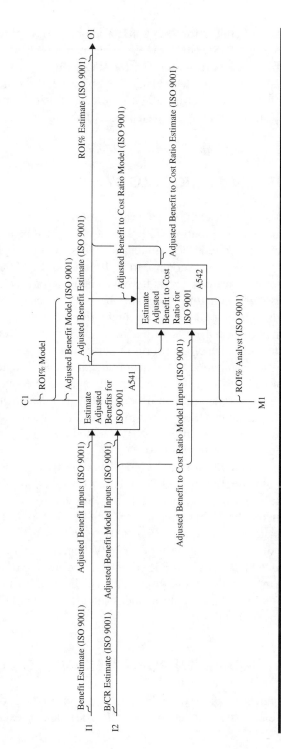

Figure 57   ROI% Methodology for ISO 9001

Estimate adjusted benefits for ISO 9001: The objective of this activity is to validate the benefits of ISO 9001 by removing its costs. This substep includes: subtract special costs from benefits for ISO 9001.

Estimate adjusted B/CR for ISO 9001: The objective of this activity is to measure the magnitude of the net benefits to the costs for implementing ISO 9001. This substep includes: divide adjusted benefits by special costs for ISO 9001.

11.5 ISO 9001 NPV METHODOLOGY

The NPV methodology for ISO 9001 is a procedure to measure, quantify, and analyze money returned less inflation. The ratio of discounted benefits to costs for ISO 9001 is good due to reduced maintenance costs and minor productivity increases. NPV is the discounted money earned from using ISO 9001 to create a new and improved software process. Its NPV methodology is a three-part process that consists of estimating discounted benefits, special costs, and the B/CR. Its benefit methodology consists of combining the discounted net benefits together with the special costs using the B/CR formula. Key elements include lowering the gross benefits to form the discounted benefits. These are used to form a realistic estimation of the magnitude of the benefits to the costs. (B/CR is a ratio of benefits to costs for objectively analyzing economic value. ROI% is used to avoid overstating the benefits. NPV is a skeptical and even cynical approach to ensure benefits are not overstated. All three of these methods should be used as exhibited by this NPV methodology.) Figure 58 illustrates the NPV methodology for ISO 9001.

Estimate NPV of benefits for ISO 9001: The objective of this activity is to discount the gross benefits of ISO 9001 based on inflation. This substep includes: divide benefits by devaluation rate for ISO 9001.

Estimate adjusted NPV benefits for ISO 9001: The objective of this activity is to validate the benefits of ISO 9001 by removing its costs. This substep includes: subtract special costs from NPV benefits for ISO 9001.

Estimate adjusted NPV B/CR for ISO 9001: The objective of this activity is to measure the magnitude of the discounted net benefits to the costs for implementing ISO 9001. This substep includes: divide adjusted NPV benefits by special costs for ISO 9001.

11.6 ISO 9001 BREAKEVEN POINT METHODOLOGY

The breakeven point methodology for ISO 9001 is a procedure to determine when benefits exceed costs. The benefits for ISO 9001 rapidly exceed its cost

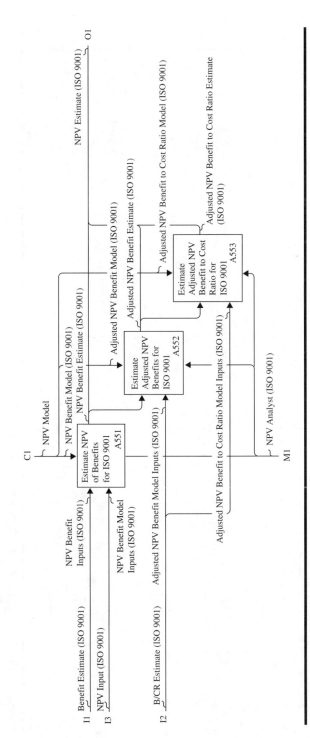

Figure 58 NPV Methodology for ISO 9001

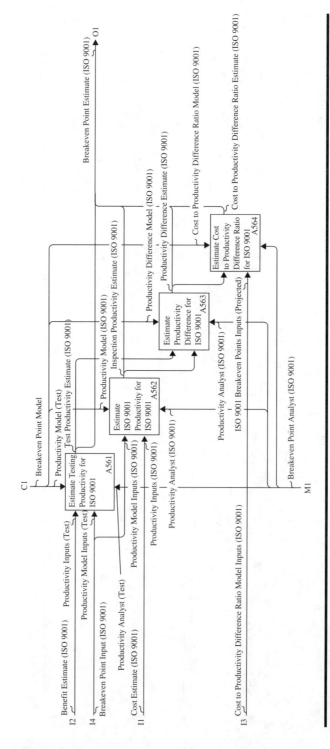

Figure 59 Breakeven Point Methodology for ISO 9001

due to reduced maintenance costs. Breakeven point is the value at which the benefits overtake the costs for using ISO 9001. Its breakeven point methodology is a four-part process that consists of estimating productivity and the cost to productivity difference ratio. Its breakeven point methodology consists of combining costs with productivity difference using the breakeven point formula. Key elements include determining the ratio of productivity for the old and new SPI methods. This is used to determine the point when the benefits overtake the costs. Figure 59 illustrates the breakeven point methodology for ISO 9001.

Estimate testing productivity for ISO 9001: The objective of this activity is to determine the software productivity associated with using the software testing process. This substep includes: divide software size by total life cycle cost of testing for ISO 9001.

Estimate ISO 9001 productivity for ISO 9001: The objective of this activity is to determine the software productivity associated with using ISO 9001. This substep includes: divide software size by total life cycle cost of ISO 9001 for ISO 9001.

Estimate productivity difference for ISO 9001: The objective of this activity is to compare the productivity of software testing to that of ISO 9001. This substep includes: divide test productivity by ISO 9001 productivity for ISO 9001.

Estimate cost to productivity difference ratio for ISO 9001: The objective of this activity is to determine when ISO 9001 will begin paying for itself. This substep includes: divide special cost by one less productivity difference for ISO 9001.

12

CAPABILITY MATURITY MODEL INTEGRATION® ROI METHODOLOGY

The return on investment (ROI) methodology for Capability Maturity Model Integration® is a procedure to measure, quantify, and analyze its economic value. Capability Maturity Model Integration® is a set of guidelines for selecting systems and software engineering suppliers and performing process improvement. ROI is the amount of money gained, returned, or earned above the resources spent on Capability Maturity Model Integration®. Its ROI methodology is a six-part process that consists of estimating costs, benefits, benefit/cost ratio (B/CR), ROI%, net present value (NPV), and breakeven point. The ROI methodology for Capability Maturity Model Integration® has unique elements for estimating costs, benefits, and B/CR. Its cost and benefit methodologies are complex, although its B/CR, ROI%, NPV, and breakeven point methodologies are simple. Key elements include the process and total life cycle cost models. Figure 60 illustrates the ROI methodology for Capability Maturity Model Integration®.

12.1 CMMI® COST METHODOLOGY

The cost methodology for Capability Maturity Model Integration® is a procedure to measure, quantify, and analyze the amount of money spent. Capability Maturity Model Integration® incurs cost to develop processes, resulting in higher

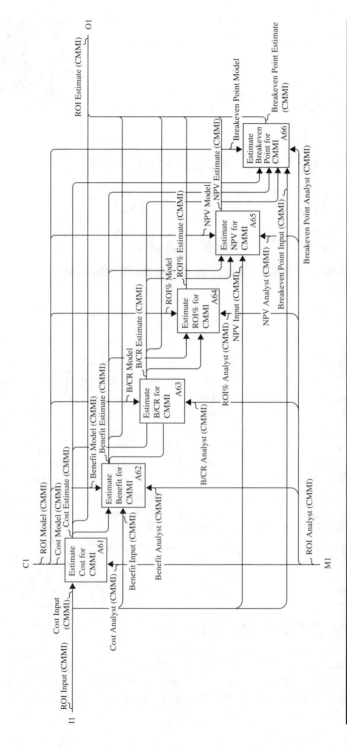

Figure 60 ROI Methodology for Capability Maturity Model Integration®

productivity and lower maintenance. Cost is the economic consequence of using Capability Maturity Model Integration® to create a new and improved software process. Its cost methodology is an eight-part process that consists of estimating process, product, preparation, assessment, software, meeting, test, and maintenance costs. The cost methodology for Capability Maturity Model Integration® has unique elements for estimating process costs. Key elements include the process, assessment, software development, meeting, test, and maintenance cost models. These are used to approximate the costs of software development and maintenance. Figure 61 illustrates the cost methodology for Capability Maturity Model Integration®.

Estimate process cost for CMMI®: The objective of this activity is to estimate the cost of developing policies and procedures for CMMI®. This substep includes: estimate Level 2 process cost for CMMI®, estimate Level 3 process cost for CMMI®, and estimate Level 2 and 3 process cost for CMMI®. (The process costs for CMMI® exceed those of the Software Capability Maturity Model®. CMMI® demands more rigor in process compliance and therefore more policies and procedures and more cost. SW-CMM® requires fewer policies and procedures and therefore lower process cost.)

Estimate product cost for CMMI®: The objective of this activity is to estimate the cost of developing plans, documents, records, and analyses for CMMI®. This substep includes: estimate Level 2 product cost for CMMI®, estimate Level 3 product cost for CMMI®, and estimate Level 2 and 3 product cost for CMMI®.

Estimate preparation cost for CMMI®: The objective of this activity is to estimate the cost of assessment indoctrination, assessment response conditioning, and mock assessments for CMMI®. This substep includes: estimate indoctrination cost for CMMI®, estimate response-conditioning cost for CMMI®, estimate mock assessment cost for CMMI®, and estimate indoctrination, response-conditioning, and mock assessment cost for CMMI®.

Estimate assessment cost for CMMI®: The objective of this activity is to estimate the cost of assessment planning, assessment preparation, assessment meetings, and assessment reporting for CMMI®. This substep includes: estimate plan and prepare for appraisal stage cost for CMMI®, estimate conduct appraisal stage cost for CMMI®, estimate report results cost for CMMI®, and estimate plan and prepare for appraisal, conduct appraisal stage, and report results stage cost for CMMI®.

Estimate software cost (baseline) for CMMI®: The objective of this activity is to estimate the costs of software analysis, design, and implementation. This substep includes: estimate software cost (Boehm) for CMMI®, estimate software cost (Walston/Felix) for CMMI®, estimate software cost (Bailey/Basili) for CMMI®, estimate software cost (Doty) for CMMI®, and estimate software cost (average) for CMMI®.

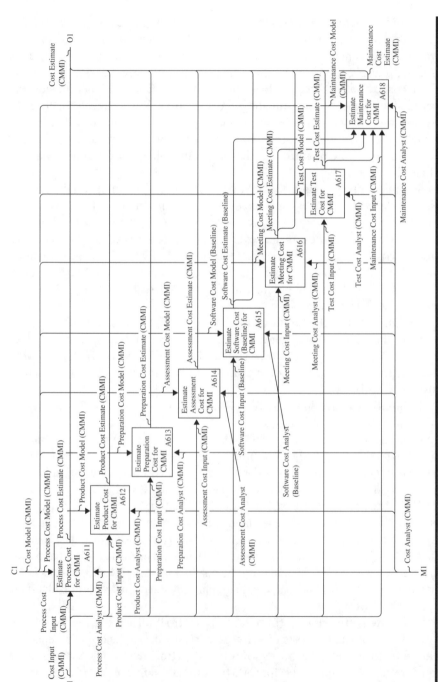

Figure 61 Cost Methodology for Capability Maturity Model Integration®

In this case, the outputs of the software cost models by Boehm, Walston/Felix, Bailey/Basili, and Doty were averaged together. This was done as sort of a Delphi method to arrive at an average software cost. The reader is free to substitute contemporary cost models, such as COCOMO II, PRICE-S®, SLIM®, Knowledge Plan®, or any others, in order to accurately estimate software costs. The formulas for these models are illustrated in Chapter 5.

Estimate meeting cost for CMMI®: The objective of this activity is to estimate the cost for performing the Software Inspection Process. This substep includes: estimate meeting cost (BNR) for CMMI®, estimate meeting cost (Gilb) for CMMI®, estimate meeting cost (AT&T) for CMMI®, estimate meeting cost (HP) for CMMI®, estimate meeting cost (Rico) for CMMI®, and estimate meeting cost (average) for CMMI®.

The outputs of the BNR, Gilb, HP, AT&T, and Rico Software Inspection Process cost models were averaged together. Again, this was done as a Delphi method to arrive at an average Software Inspection Process cost. The formulas for these models are illustrated in the free Web Added Value™ materials available at www.jrosspub.com.

Estimate test cost for CMMI®: The objective of this activity is to estimate the cost of software testing based on defects escaping the Software Inspection Process. This substep includes: estimate starting defects for CMMI®, estimate meeting efficiency for CMMI®, estimate pre-test defects for CMMI®, estimate test efficiency for CMMI®, estimate post-test defects for CMMI®, and estimate test cost (projected) for CMMI®.

Estimate maintenance cost for CMMI®: The objective of this activity is to estimate the cost of software maintenance based on defects escaping the Software Inspection Process and testing. This substep includes: estimate total life cycle cost for CMMI® and estimate maintenance cost (projected) for CMMI®.

12.2 CMMI® BENEFIT METHODOLOGY

The benefit methodology for Capability Maturity Model Integration® is a procedure to measure, quantify, and analyze the amount of money returned. Capability Maturity Model Integration® results in higher productivity and quality, resulting in lower development and maintenance costs. Benefit is the economic value of using Capability Maturity Model Integration® to create a new and improved software process. Its benefit methodology is a three-part process that consists of estimating test costs, total life cycle costs of testing, and benefits. Its benefit methodology consists of a variety of defect models used in combination. Key elements include the test cost model and the total life cycle cost model. Some of the benefits are due to increased productivity, resulting in up

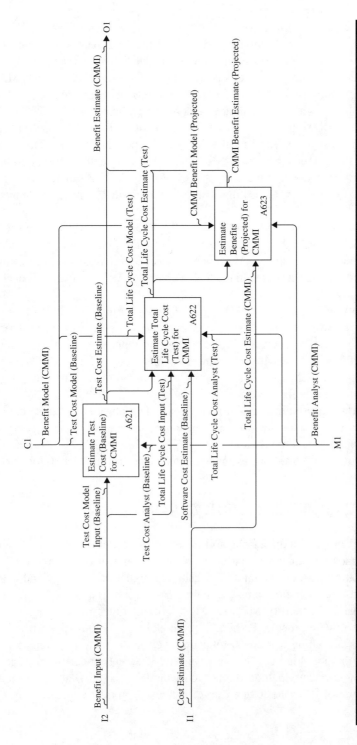

Figure 62 Benefit Methodology for Capability Maturity Model Integration®

to a 50% decrease in software development costs. Increased productivity is factored into the total life cycle cost model. The test and total life cycle cost models are used to compare the total life cycle costs of software testing to those of the Capability Maturity Model Integration®. Figure 62 illustrates the benefit methodology for Capability Maturity Model Integration®.

Estimate test cost (baseline) for CMMI®: The objective of this activity is to estimate the cost of removing the maximum number of software defects using software testing. This substep includes: estimate post-test defects (baseline) for CMMI® and estimate baseline test cost (projected) for CMMI®.

Estimate total life cycle cost (test) for CMMI®: The objective of this activity is to estimate software development and maintenance costs associated with using software testing. This substep includes: estimate total software cost (test) for CMMI®, estimate total test cost (test) for CMMI®, and subtract total test from software cost for CMMI®.

Estimate benefits (projected) for CMMI®: The objective of this activity is to compare software development and maintenance costs of testing and CMMI®. This substep includes: subtract total life cycle cost of CMMI® from test for CMMI®.

12.3 CMMI® B/CR METHODOLOGY

The B/CR methodology for Capability Maturity Model Integration® is a procedure to measure, quantify, and analyze the ratio of benefits to costs. The ratio of benefits to costs for Capability Maturity Model Integration® is high because of productivity increases and reductions in software maintenance costs. In fact, the majority of the benefits are due to the institutionalization of peer reviews or the Software Inspection Process. Higher quality and lower maintenance costs result from using peer reviews. A small part of the benefits are derived from increased productivity. Adherence to U.S. Department of Defense policy for supplier selection results from using Capability Maturity Model Integration®. B/CR is the economic magnitude of using Capability Maturity Model Integration® to create a new and improved software process. Its B/CR methodology is a two-part process that consists of estimating special costs and the B/CR. Its benefit methodology consists of combining the benefits together with the special costs using a simple B/CR formula. Key elements include isolating the special, new, or additional costs and using the output of earlier total life cycle cost models. These are used to form an early picture of the economic value of Capability Maturity Model Integration®. Figure 63 illustrates the B/CR methodology for Capability Maturity Model Integration®.

Estimate special costs for CMMI®: The objective of this activity is to identify and separate the costs associated with CMMI® from common software

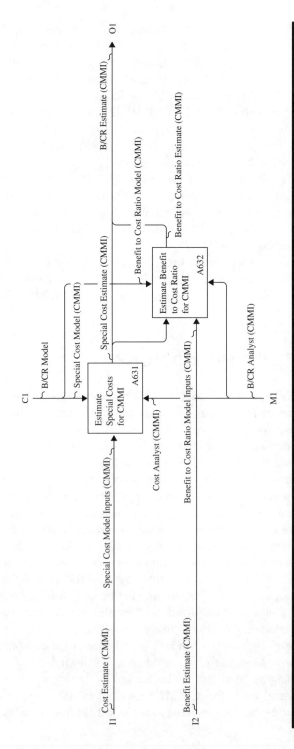

Figure 63 B/CR Methodology for Capability Maturity Model Integration®

development costs. This substep includes: add process, product, preparation, assessment, and meeting costs for CMMI®.

Estimate B/CR for CMMI®: The objective of this activity is to measure the magnitude of the benefits to the costs for implementing the Capability Maturity Model Integration®. This substep includes: divide benefits by special costs for CMMI®.

12.4   CMMI® ROI% METHODOLOGY

The ROI% methodology for Capability Maturity Model Integration® is a procedure to measure, quantify, and analyze the money returned. The ratio of net benefits to costs for Capability Maturity Model Integration® is high due to software maintenance cost savings. ROI% is the money earned from using Capability Maturity Model Integration® to create a new and improved software process. Its ROI% methodology is a two-part process that consists of estimating the B/CR using net benefits versus gross benefits. Its benefit methodology consists of combining the net or adjusted benefits together with the special costs using the B/CR formula. Key elements include subtracting the special costs from the gross benefits to form net benefits. These are used to form a better picture of the magnitude of the benefits to the costs for Capability Maturity Model Integration®. (B/CR and ROI% are similar in that they are used to compare benefits to costs. However, B/CR uses gross benefits, while ROI% uses net benefits. Net benefits do not contain the implementation costs. Therefore, ROI% lowers the magnitude of benefits to costs versus using B/CR.) Figure 64 illustrates the ROI% methodology for Capability Maturity Model Integration®.

Estimate adjusted benefits for CMMI®: The objective of this activity is to validate the benefits of CMMI® by removing its costs. This substep includes: subtract special costs from benefits for CMMI®.

Estimate adjusted B/CR for CMMI®: The objective of this activity is to measure the magnitude of the net benefits to the costs for implementing CMMI®. This substep includes: divide adjusted benefits by special costs for CMMI®.

12.5   CMMI® NPV METHODOLOGY

The NPV methodology for Capability Maturity Model Integration® is a procedure to measure, quantify, and analyze money returned less inflation. The ratio of discounted benefits to costs for Capability Maturity Model Integration® remains high due to reduced maintenance costs. The reduced maintenance costs are largely due to the institutionalization or use of peer reviews or the Software

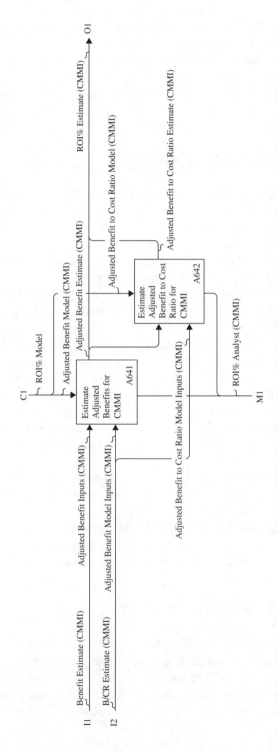

Figure 64 ROI% Methodology for Capability Maturity Model Integration®

Inspection Process. It is possible to have a smaller NPV if rigorous peer reviews are not utilized and large residual software defect populations remain. Larger software defect populations result in larger software maintenance costs. NPV is the discounted money earned from using Capability Maturity Model Integration® to create a new and improved software process. Its NPV methodology is a three-part process that consists of estimating discounted benefits, special costs, and the B/CR. Its benefit methodology consists of combining the discounted net benefits together with the special costs using the B/CR formula. Key elements include lowering the gross benefits to form the discounted benefits. These are used to form a realistic estimation of the magnitude of the benefits to the costs. (B/CR is a ratio of benefits to costs for objectively analyzing economic value. ROI% is used to avoid overstating the benefits. NPV is a skeptical and even cynical approach to ensure benefits are not overstated. All three of these methods should be used as exhibited by this NPV methodology.) Figure 65 illustrates the NPV methodology for Capability Maturity Model Integration®.

Estimate NPV of benefits for CMMI®: The objective of this activity is to discount the gross benefits of CMMI® based on inflation. This substep includes: divide benefits by devaluation rate for CMMI®.

Estimate adjusted NPV benefits for CMMI®: The objective of this activity is to validate the benefits of CMMI® by removing its costs. This substep includes: subtract special costs from NPV benefits for CMMI®.

Estimate adjusted NPV B/CR for CMMI®: The objective of this activity is to measure the magnitude of the discounted net benefits to the costs for implementing CMMI®. This substep includes: divide adjusted NPV benefits by special costs for CMMI®.

12.6 CMMI® BREAKEVEN POINT METHODOLOGY

The breakeven point methodology for Capability Maturity Model Integration® is a procedure to determine when benefits exceed costs. The benefits for Capability Maturity Model Integration® rapidly exceed its cost due to reduced maintenance costs. Breakeven point is the value at which the benefits overtake the costs for using Capability Maturity Model Integration®. Its breakeven point methodology is a four-part process that consists of estimating productivity and the cost to productivity difference ratio. Its breakeven point methodology consists of combining costs with productivity difference using the breakeven point formula. Key elements include determining the ratio of productivity for the old and new software process improvement methods. These are used to determine the point when the benefits overtake the costs. (As indicated earlier, benefits,

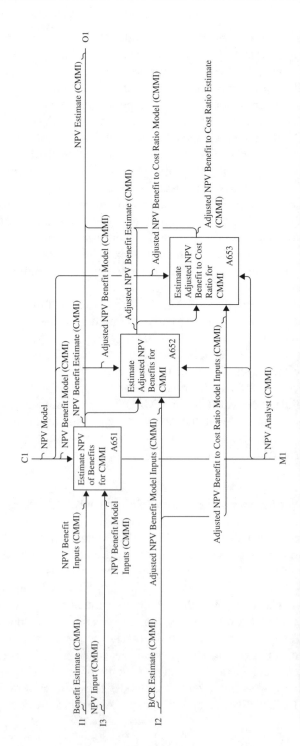

Figure 65 NPV Methodology for Capability Maturity Model Integration®

B/CR, ROI%, NPV, and breakeven point are directly impacted by the use of peer reviews. Rigorous peer reviews improve the economic outlook, while their absence hinders it.) Figure 66 illustrates the breakeven point methodology for Capability Maturity Model Integration®.

Estimate testing productivity for CMMI®: The objective of this activity is to determine the software productivity associated with using the software testing process. This substep includes: divide software size by total life cycle cost of testing for CMMI®.

Estimate CMMI® productivity for CMMI®: The objective of this activity is to determine the software productivity associated with using CMMI®. This substep includes: divide software size by total life cycle cost of CMMI® for CMMI®.

Estimate productivity difference for CMMI®: The objective of this activity is to compare the productivity of software testing to that of CMMI®. This substep includes: divide test productivity by CMMI® productivity for CMMI®.

Estimate cost to productivity difference ratio for CMMI®: The objective of this activity is to determine when CMMI® will begin paying for itself. This substep includes: divide special cost by one less productivity difference for CMMI®.

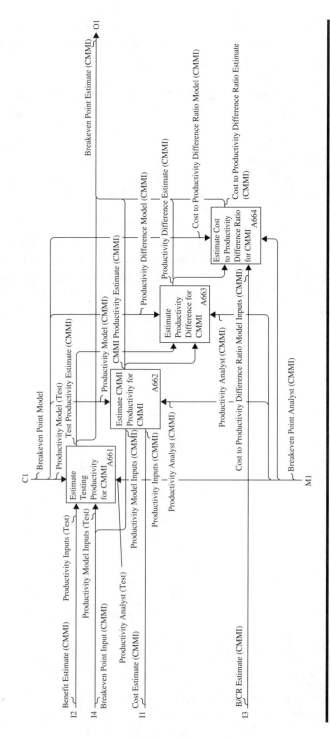

Figure 66 Breakeven Point Methodology for Capability Maturity Model Integration®

13

COSTS

Costs are the amount of money that is necessary to implement one or more software process improvement (SPI) methods. Costs are the expenses associated with applying, using, and exploiting SPI methods. Costs are the resources that are necessary to deploy and institutionalize SPI methods in a software organization or firm. Costs or cost factors consist of training, process development, and product development. Appraisal preparation, appraisals, product development, inspections, tests, and maintenance are major costs. Training refers to SPI methods that rely on formal classroom training as the principal delivery mechanism for the SPI method. Process development refers to SPI methods that require organizations to design and develop policies and procedures. Product development refers to SPI methods that require the development of special work products or project artifacts for projects. Appraisal preparation refers to SPI methods that necessitate advanced preparation by software project members. Appraisal refers to SPI methods that require a formal assessment or audit of activities and artifacts to verify their use. Product development refers to the costs of analyzing, designing, and coding software products using software effort models. The inspection cost factor consists of SPI methods that use the Software Inspection Process. The test cost factor consists of the costs of testing software products for all SPI methods. Finally, the maintenance cost factor consists of the total life cycle costs of all SPI methods. Some costs entirely consist of training. Some costs are associated with expensive appraisals and audits. However, most SPI methods have common costs such as software effort.

13.1 SOFTWARE INSPECTION PROCESS

Let's begin by modeling the training costs for implementing the Software Inspection Process on a four-person project. The average market price for

Software Inspection Process training is about $410 per person. The average length of time for Software Inspection Process training is 3 days or 24 business hours. At a minimum cost of $100 per hour, training time comes to $2,400. Add $410 and $2,400 and the total is $2,810 per person for Software Inspection Process training. Multiply $2,810 by four people and that comes to $11,240 to train four people to perform the Software Inspection Process.

Let's also assume our software effort is 5,088 hours to analyze, design, and code 10,000 lines of code. Multiply 5,088 by $100 per hour. Our software cost is now $508,800 to analyze, design, and code 10,000 lines of code.

Now let's examine the cost of implementing the Software Inspection Process by our four trained inspectors. Let's assume the project will develop 10,000 software source lines of code (SLOC), which is common for a modern Web project. (Inspections of requirements, designs, and tests drive the costs even higher, but are omitted for the sake of simplicity.) At a Software Inspection Process rate of 240 SLOC per meeting, that comes to approximately 41.67 meetings. (The optimal inspection rate is 120 SLOC per meeting, so we are lowering the cost and efficiency of inspections a little.) Software Inspection Process runs require 17 hours for planning, overviews, preparation, meetings, rework, and follow-up. We then multiply 41.67 by 17 for a total of 708.33 hours. Once again at $100 per hour, that comes to $70,833 for our four trained inspectors to perform the Software Inspection Process on 10,000 SLOC.

Now let's estimate the cost of software testing. Remember that the Software Inspection Process finds about one defect for every hour spent doing inspections, so we have probably nabbed 708 software defects by now. If we estimate that we started with 1,000 software defects, we have 292 software defects remaining after our nearly 42 Software Inspection Process runs. Let's further assume that our software testing process nabs two-thirds of the remaining 292 defects or 195 software defects. Let's also assume it takes 10 hours to find each of the 195 software defects. That comes to 1,950 software testing hours and at a rate of $100 per hour is $195,000 for software testing.

But we are not done yet. Now let's use our total life cycle cost model. The formula is software size multiplied by 10.51, less the inspection hours times 99, and less the test hours times 9. Our total life cycle cost for using the Software Inspection Process is 17,425.33 hours. If we subtract the 5,088 hours of software effort, 708 hours of inspection effort, and 1,950 hours of software testing effort, that leaves us with 9,679 hours in residual software maintenance costs, or $967,900. Table 2 illustrates the costs of the Software Inspection Process.

Now we are ready to estimate the complete costs of using the Software Inspection Process to produce 10,000 lines of code. Add $11,240 for training, $508,800 in software development costs, and $70,833 in Software Inspection

Table 2   Estimated Cost of Software Inspection Process

Factor	Cost
Training	$11,240
Development	$508,800
Inspections	$70,833
Testing	$195,000
Maintenance	$967,900
Total	**$1,753,773**

Process costs. Also add $195,000 in software testing costs and $967,900 in software maintenance costs. The complete cost to use the Software Inspection Process to help produce 10,000 lines of code is $1,753,773.

13.2 PERSONAL SOFTWARE PROCESS^SM

Let's begin by modeling the training costs for implementing the Personal Software Process^SM on a four-person project. The Software Engineering Institute's price for Personal Software Process^SM training is $5,000 per person. The costs for airfare, hotels, meals, and parking are about $5,400 for two weeks. The length of time for Personal Software Process^SM training is 10 days or 80 business hours. Each hour of classroom time requires approximately one hour of nonclassroom time for a total of 80 more hours. At a minimum cost of $100 per hour, training time comes to $16,000. Add $5,000, $5,400, and $16,000 and the total is $26,400 per person for Personal Software Process^SM training. Multiply $26,400 by four people and that comes to $105,600 to train four people to perform the Personal Software Process^SM.

Now let's examine the cost of implementing Personal Software Process^SM by our four trained engineers. Let's assume the project will develop 10,000 lines of code, which once again is not unlikely for a Web project in modern times. At an average productivity rate of 25 lines of code per hour, that comes to approximately 400 hours. At $100 per hour, that is $40,000 for our engineers to produce 10,000 lines of code using the Personal Software Process^SM.

As an aside, the costs of individual reviews instead of inspections and testing are already included in the $40,000. The Personal Software Process^SM results in zero defects upon release. Therefore, there are no additional software maintenance costs using our approach to estimating maintenance effort. Software maintenance is determined by estimating the costs of repairing software defects that have been released to customers. Table 3 illustrates the costs of the Personal Software Process^SM.

Table 3   Estimated Cost of Personal Software Process^{SM}

Factor	Cost
Training	$105,600
Development	$40,000
Total	**$145,600**

Now we are ready to estimate the complete costs of using the Personal Software Process^{SM} to help produce 10,000 lines of code. Add $105,600 for training and $40,000 in software development costs. The complete cost to use the Personal Software Process^{SM} to help produce 10,000 lines of code is $145,600.

13.3   TEAM SOFTWARE PROCESS^{SM}

Let's begin by modeling the training costs for implementing the Team Software Process^{SM} on a four-person project. The Software Engineering Institute's price for Team Software Process^{SM} training is $4,000 per person. The costs for airfare, hotels, meals, and parking are about $2,700 for one week. The length of time for Team Software Process^{SM} training is five days or 40 business hours. At a minimum cost of $100 per hour, training time comes to $4,000. Add $4,000, $2,700, and $4,000 and the total is $10,700 per person for Team Software Process^{SM}–specific training. Add the $26,400 for Personal Software Process^{SM} training to the $10,700 for Team Software Process^{SM} training. The total overall costs come to $37,100 per person. Multiply $37,100 by four people and that comes to $148,400 to train four people to perform the Team Software Process^{SM}.

Now let's examine the cost of implementing the Team Software Process^{SM} by our four trained engineers. Let's assume the project will develop 10,000 lines of code, which once again is not unlikely for a Web project. At an average productivity rate of 5.9347 lines of code per hour, that comes to approximately 1,685 hours. At $100 per hour, that comes to $168,501 for our engineers to produce 10,000 lines of code.

As an aside, the costs of team reviews instead of inspections and testing are already included in the $168,501 implementation cost. The Team Software Process^{SM} results in zero defects upon release. Therefore, there are no additional software maintenance costs using our approach to estimating software maintenance effort. Software maintenance is determined by estimating the costs of repairing software defects that have been released to customers. Table 4 illustrates the costs of the Team Software Process^{SM}.

Now we are ready to estimate the complete costs of using the Team Software Process^{SM} to help produce 10,000 lines of code. Add $148,400 for training

Table 4   Estimated Cost of Team Software Process^SM

Factor	Cost
Training	$148,400
Development	$168,501
Total	**$316,901**

and $168,501 in software development costs. The complete cost to use the Team Software Process^SM to help produce 10,000 lines of code is $316,901.

Remember that use of the Team Software Process^SM requires training in the Personal Software Process^SM first. Therefore, the training costs also include the Personal Software Process^SM training costs as well.

13.4 SOFTWARE CAPABILITY MATURITY MODEL®

Let's begin by modeling the costs for developing the policies and procedures for Software Capability Maturity Model® Levels 2 and 3. Software Capability Maturity Model® Levels 2 and 3 require 13 policies and 38 procedures at 11 hours each. That comes to 561 hours for 51 Software Capability Maturity Model® Level 2 and 3 policies and procedures. Multiply 561 by $100, and the cost of developing Level 2 and 3 policies and procedures is $56,100.

Now let's examine the cost of putting Software Capability Maturity Model® Levels 2 and 3 into practice for a single software project. Levels 2 and 3 require 28 documents, 30 work authorizations, 66 records, 55 reports, and 30 meeting minutes at 5.63 hours each. That comes to 1,176 hours for 209 Level 2 and 3 documents, work authorizations, records, reports, and meeting minutes. This is for a single software project. Multiply 1,176 by $100, and the cost of Level 2 and 3 documents, work authorizations, records, reports, and meeting minutes is $117,600. This too is for a single software project.

Let's estimate one software project with four people in 13 indoctrination courses at 2 hours each, which totals 104 hours. Let's similarly estimate one software project with four people in 13 response-conditioning courses at 2 hours, which totals another 104 hours. Finally, let's estimate one software project with four people in one 40-hour mock assessment or two 20-hour mock assessments, which totals 160 hours. Now let's add 104 indoctrination hours, 104 response-conditioning hours, and 160 mock assessment hours. That totals 368 assessment preparation hours. Finally, let's multiply 368 by $100 for a total of $36,800 in assessment preparation costs.

Let's not forget the assessment itself. An assessment requires up to 642 hours of internal labor (not including the assessor's effort). However, for our one project of four people let's estimate 13 hours for planning and 47 hours for preparation. Additionally, let's estimate 129 hours for the appraisal itself and 12 hours of follow-up, which totals 201 hours for the assessment. Now multiply 201 by $100 for a total labor cost of $20,100 plus $10,000 in assessment fees for a total cost of $30,100.

Let's also assume our software effort is 5,088 hours to analyze, design, and code 10,000 lines of code. Multiply 5,088 by $100 per hour, and our cost is now $508,800 to analyze, design, and code 10,000 lines of code. However, software productivity can double at Level 3, so let's adjust our software cost to $254,400.

Let's also assume our Level 2 and 3–compliant software project will use the Software Inspection Process. At a Software Inspection Process rate of 240 SLOC per meeting, that comes to approximately 41.67 meetings. (The optimal inspection rate is 120 SLOC per meeting, so we are lowering the cost and efficiency of inspections a little.) Software Inspection Process runs require 17 hours for planning, overviews, preparation, meetings, rework, and follow-up. We then multiply 41.67 by 17 for a total of 708.33 hours. Once again at $100 per hour, that comes to $70,833 for our four trained inspectors to perform the Software Inspection Process on 10,000 SLOC.

Now let's estimate the cost of software testing. Remember that the Software Inspection Process finds about one defect for every hour spent doing inspections, so we have probably nabbed 708 software defects by now. If we estimate that we started with 1,000 software defects, we have 292 software defects remaining after our nearly 42 Software Inspection Process runs. Let's further assume that our software testing process nabs two-thirds of the remaining 292 defects or 195 software defects. Let's also assume it takes 10 hours to find each of the 195 software defects. That comes to 1,950 software testing hours and at a rate of $100 per hour is $195,000 for software testing.

But we are not done yet. Now let's use our total life cycle cost model. The formula is software size multiplied by 10.2544, less the inspection hours times 99, and less the test hours times 9. (0.2544 is 50% of 0.5088, which is due to a 100% productivity increase associated with Level 3 compliance.) Our total life cycle cost for using the Software Capability Maturity Model® is 14,869.33 hours. Subtract the 2,544 hours of software effort, 708 hours of inspection effort, and 1,950 hours of software testing effort and that leaves us with 9,667 hours in residual software maintenance costs, or $966,700. Table 5 illustrates the costs of the Software Capability Maturity Model®.

Now we are ready to estimate the complete costs of using Levels 2 and 3 to help produce 10,000 lines of code. Add $56,100 for processes, $117,600 for products, $36,800 for preparation, $30,100 for assessment, and $254,400 for development. Also add $70,833 for inspections, $195,000 for software testing,

Table 5   Estimated Cost of Software Capability Maturity Model®

Factor	Cost
Processes	$56,100
Products	$117,600
Preparation	$36,800
Assessment	$30,100
Development	$254,400
Inspection	$70,833
Test	$195,000
Maintenance	$966,700
Total	**$1,727,533**

and $966,700 for software maintenance. The complete cost to use Levels 2 and 3 to help produce 10,000 lines of code is $1,727,533.

13.5 ISO 9001

Let's begin by modeling the costs for developing the policies and procedures for ISO 9001. ISO 9001 requires 144 policy statements, 144 quality manual paragraphs, and 51 procedures at 1.61 hours each. That comes to 546 hours for 339 ISO 9001 policy statements, quality manual paragraphs, and procedures. Multiply 546 by $100, and the cost of developing ISO 9001 policies and procedures is $54,600.

Now let's examine the cost of putting ISO 9001 into practice for a single software project. ISO 9001 requires 51 plans and 144 records at about 2.87 hours each. That comes to 560 hours for 195 ISO 9001 plans and records for a single software project. Multiply 560 by $100, and the cost of ISO 9001 plans and records is $56,000 for a single software project.

Let's estimate one software project with four people in 23 indoctrination courses at 1 hour each, which totals 92 hours. Let's similarly estimate one project with four people in 23 response-conditioning courses at 1 hour each, which also totals 92 hours. Finally, let's estimate one software project with four people in one 20 hour mock quality system audit, for a total of 80 hours. Now let's add 92 indoctrination hours, 92 response-conditioning hours, and 80 mock quality system audit hours. That totals 264 quality system audit preparation hours. Finally, let's multiply 264 by $100 for a total of $26,400 in quality system audit preparation costs.

Let's not forget the quality system audit itself. An ISO 9001 quality system audit may cost around $48,000. However, let's isolate this cost to $12,000 per software project. Typically, internal labor associated with quality system audits is about twice the cost of the audit itself. Therefore, let's assume $24,000 in internal costs to support the actual quality system audit. Adding $12,000 in external costs and $24,000 in internal costs, we arrive at $36,000 per quality system audit per project.

Let's also assume our software effort is 5,088 hours to analyze, design, and code 10,000 lines of code. Multiply 5,088 by $100 per hour, and our software cost is now $508,800 to analyze, design, and code 10,000 lines of code. However, software productivity can increase by about 13% with ISO 9001, so let's adjust our software cost to $442,656.

Now let's estimate the cost of software testing. Let's assume that we started with 1,000 software defects. Let's further assume that our software testing process nabs two-thirds of our 1,000 defects or 667 software defects. Let's also assume it takes 10 hours to find each of the 667 software defects. That comes to 6,670 software testing hours and at a rate of $100 per hour is $667,000 for software testing.

But we are not done yet. Now let's use our total life cycle cost model. The formula is software size multiplied by 10.442656, less the test hours times nine. (0.442656 is 87% of 0.5088, which is due to a 13% productivity increase associated with using ISO 9001.) Our total life cycle cost for using ISO 9001 is 44,396.56 hours. Let's subtract the 4,427 hours of software effort and 6,670 hours of software testing effort. That leaves us with 33,300 hours in residual software maintenance costs. However, there is also a 15% increase in software quality due to using ISO 9001. This lowers our software maintenance hours to 28,305 and at a rate of $100 per hour is $2,830,500. Table 6 illustrates the costs of ISO 9001.

Now we are ready to estimate the complete costs of using the ISO 9001 to help produce 10,000 lines of code. Add $54,600 for processes, $56,000 for products, $26,400 for preparation, $36,000 for audit, and $442,656 for development. Also add $667,000 for software testing and $2,830,500 for software

Table 6   Estimated Cost of Software ISO 9001

Factor	Cost
Processes	$54,600
Products	$56,000
Preparation	$26,400
Audit	$36,000
Development	$442,656
Test	$667,000
Maintenance	$2,830,500
Total	**$4,113,156**

maintenance. The complete cost to use the ISO 9001 to help produce 10,000 lines of code is $4,113,156.

13.6 CAPABILITY MATURITY MODEL INTEGRATION®

Let's begin by modeling the costs for developing the policies and procedures for Capability Maturity Model Integration® Levels 2 and 3. Capability Maturity Model Integration® Levels 2 and 3 require 416 policies and procedures at approximately 26.02 hours each. That comes to 10,826 hours for 416 Capability Maturity Model Integration® Level 2 and 3 policies and procedures. Multiply 10,826 by $100. The cost of developing Capability Maturity Model Integration® Level 2 and 3 policies and procedures is $1,082,600. However, let's assume only half of this cost is for software engineering and adjust it accordingly to $541,300.

Now let's examine the cost of putting Capability Maturity Model Integration® Levels 2 and 3 into practice for a single project. Capability Maturity Model Integration® Levels 2 and 3 require 429 work products at about 18.67 hours each. That comes to 8,008 hours for 429 Capability Maturity Model Integration® Level 2 and 3 work products for a single project. Multiply 8,008 by $100, and the cost of Capability Maturity Model Integration® Level 2 and 3 work products is $800,800 for a single project. However, let's assume only half of this cost is for software engineering and adjust it accordingly to $400,400.

Let's estimate one project with eight people in 20 indoctrination courses at 2 hours each, which totals 320 hours. Let's similarly estimate one project with eight people in 20 response-conditioning courses at 2 hours each, which also totals 320 hours. Finally, let's estimate one project with eight people in one 40-hour mock assessment or two 20-hour mock assessments, which totals 320 hours. Now let's add 320 indoctrination hours, 320 response-conditioning hours, and 320 mock assessment hours. That totals 960 hours. Finally, let's multiply 960 by $100 for a total of $96,000 in assessment preparation costs. Half of this is software engineering, which amounts to $48,000.

Let's not forget the assessment itself. For our one software project with four people, let's estimate 127 hours for the plan and prepare for appraisal stage, 204 hours for the conduct appraisal stage, and 21 hours for the report results stage. That totals 352 hours. Multiply 352 by $100 for an internal labor estimate of $35,200. Add an assessment fee of $12,500 for a total assessment cost of $47,700.

Let's also assume our software effort is 5,088 hours to analyze, design, and code 10,000 lines of code. Multiply 5,088 by $100 per hour, and our software cost is now $508,800 to analyze, design, and code 10,000 lines of code. However, software productivity can double at Level 3, so let's adjust our software cost to $254,400.

Let's also assume our Capability Maturity Model Integration® Level 2 and 3–compliant software project will use the Software Inspection Process. At a Software Inspection Process rate of 240 SLOC per meeting, that comes to approximately 41.67 meetings. (The optimal inspection rate is 120 SLOC per meeting, so we are lowering the cost and efficiency of inspections a little.) Software Inspection Process runs require 17 hours for planning, overviews, preparation, meetings, rework, and follow-up. We then multiply 41.67 by 17 for a total of 708.33 hours. Once again at $100 per hour, that comes to $70,833 for our four trained inspectors to perform the Software Inspection Process on 10,000 SLOC.

Now let's estimate the cost of software testing. Remember that the Software Inspection Process finds about one defect for every hour spent doing inspections, so we have probably nabbed 708 software defects by now. If we estimate that we started with 1,000 software defects, we have 292 software defects remaining after our nearly 42 Software Inspection Process runs. Let's further assume that our software testing process nabs two-thirds of our remaining 292 defects or 195 software defects. Let's also assume it takes 10 hours to find each of the 195 software defects. That comes to 1,950 software testing hours and at a rate of $100 per hour is $195,000 for software testing.

But we are not done yet. Now let's use our total life cycle cost model. The formula is software size multiplied by 10.2544, less the inspection hours times 99, and less the test hours times 9. (0.2544 is 50% of 0.5088, which is due to a 100% productivity increase associated with Level 3 compliance.) Our total life cycle cost for using the Capability Maturity Model Integration® is 14,869.33 hours. Let's subtract the 2,544 hours of software effort, 708 hours of inspection effort, and 1,950 hours of software testing effort. That leaves us with 9,667

Table 7   Estimated Cost of Capability Maturity Model Integration®

Factor	Cost
Processes	$541,300
Products	$400,400
Preparation	$48,000
Assessment	$47,700
Development	$254,400
Inspection	$70,833
Test	$195,000
Maintenance	$966,700
Total	**$2,524,333**

hours in residual software maintenance costs, or $966,700. Table 7 illustrates the costs of Capability Maturity Model Integration®.

Now we are ready to estimate the complete costs of using Levels 2 and 3 to help produce 10,000 lines of code. Add $541,300 for processes, $400,400 for products, $48,000 for preparation, $47,700 for assessment, and $254,400 for development. Also add $70,833 for the Software Inspection Process, $195,000 for software testing, and $966,700 for software maintenance. The complete cost to use Levels 2 and 3 to help produce 10,000 lines of code is $2,524,333.

14

BENEFITS

The benefits of software process improvement (SPI) methods come from increased quality and thus decreased software maintenance and total life cycle costs. That is, most popular SPI methods are specifically designed to increase the quality of the software product. Many popular SPI methods are software quality management systems, because they are designed to improve quality. What strategy will we use for determining the benefits of any one SPI method? We will determine what the software maintenance and total life cycle costs are before and after introduction of the SPI method. That is, first we will determine what the software maintenance and total life cycle costs are before introduction of the SPI method. Then we will determine what the software maintenance and total life cycle costs are after introduction of the SPI method.

The only issue is to determine whether the new and old software maintenance and total life cycle costs include testing costs. That is, does the software organization have a rigorous software testing process? We will assume the software organization does not have a rigorous software testing process, which is most likely the case. Without testing, the software maintenance and total life cycle costs are much higher. Likewise, we can assume the software organization does have a rigorous software testing process, which is probably not the case. With rigorous testing, the software maintenance and total life cycle costs are much lower. Thus, if good software testing is already in place, then the benefits are much lower. If good software testing is not in place, then the benefits are much higher. We will assume a good software testing process is in place, in order to be conservative.

14.1 SOFTWARE INSPECTION PROCESS

Let's begin by modeling the costs for analyzing, designing, and developing 10,000 lines of code. Let's further assume our software effort is 5,088 hours to analyze, design, and code 10,000 lines of code.

Let's also begin by estimating the cost of software testing, and assume that good software testing is in place so as to be conservative. Let's assume that we started with 1,000 software defects. Let's further assume that our software testing process nabs two-thirds of our 1,000 defects or 667 software defects. Let's also assume it takes 10 hours to find each of the 667 software defects. That comes to 6,670 software testing hours.

Let's use our total life cycle cost model to determine the cost of developing 10,000 lines of code using software testing. The formula is software size multiplied by 10.51, less the test hours times nine. Our total life cycle cost for using software testing alone is 45,099.97 hours. Multiply 45,099.97 by $100, and the total life cycle cost of using software testing is $4,509,997 to develop 10,000 lines of code.

Now let's use our total life cycle cost model to determine the cost of developing 10,000 lines of code using inspections. The formula is software size multiplied by 10.51, less the inspection hours times 99, and less the test hours times 9. Our total life cycle cost for using the Software Inspection Process is 17,425.33 hours. Multiply 17,425.33 by $100. The total life cycle cost of using the Software Inspection Process is $1,742,533 to develop 10,000 lines of code. Table 8 illustrates the benefits of the Software Inspection Process.

Now we are ready to estimate the benefits of using the Software Inspection Process to help produce 10,000 lines of code. Subtract $1,742,533 from $4,509,997, which represents total life cycle costs. The benefits of using the Software Inspection Process to help produce 10,000 lines of code are $2,767,464.

14.2 PERSONAL SOFTWARE PROCESS[SM]

Let's begin by modeling the costs for analyzing, designing, and developing 10,000 lines of code. Let's further assume our software effort is 5,088 hours to analyze, design, and code 10,000 lines of code.

Table 8   Estimated Benefits of Software Inspection Process

State	Total Life Cycle Cost
Before Inspections	$4,509,997
After Inspections	$1,742,533
Benefits	**$2,767,464**

Table 9   Estimated Benefits of Personal Software Process[SM]

State	Total Life Cycle Cost
Before PSP[SM]	$4,509,997
After PSP[SM]	$40,000
Benefits	**$4,469,997**

Let's also begin by estimating the cost of software testing and assume that good software testing is in place so as to be conservative. Let's assume that we started with 1,000 software defects. Let's further assume that our software testing process nabs two-thirds of our 1,000 defects or 667 software defects. Let's also assume it takes 10 hours to find each of the 667 software defects. That comes to 6,670 software testing hours.

Let's use our total life cycle cost model to determine the cost of developing 10,000 lines of code using software testing. The formula is software size multiplied by 10.51, less the test hours times nine. Our total life cycle cost for using software testing alone is 45,099.97 hours. Multiply 45,099.97 by $100, and the total life cycle cost of using software testing is $4,509,997 to develop 10,000 lines of code.

Now let's determine the total life cycle cost of developing 10,000 lines of code using the Personal Software Process[SM]. The formula is software size divided by 25. Our total life cycle cost for using the Personal Software Process[SM] is 400 hours. Multiply 400 by $100. The total life cycle cost of using the Personal Software Process[SM] is $40,000 to develop 10,000 lines of code. Table 9 illustrates the benefits of the Personal Software Process[SM].

Now we are ready to estimate the benefits of using the Personal Software Process[SM] to help produce 10,000 lines of code. Subtract $40,000 from $4,509,997, which represents total life cycle costs. The benefits of using the Personal Software Process[SM] to help produce 10,000 lines of code are $4,469,997.

14.3 TEAM SOFTWARE PROCESS[SM]

Let's begin by modeling the costs for analyzing, designing, and developing 10,000 lines of code. Let's further assume our software effort is 5,088 hours to analyze, design, and code 10,000 lines of code.

Let's also begin by estimating the cost of software testing and assume that good software testing is in place so as to be conservative. Let's assume that we started with 1,000 software defects. Let's further assume that our software testing process nabs two-thirds of our 1,000 defects or 667 software defects. Let's also assume it takes 10 hours to find each of the 667 software defects. That comes to 6,670 software testing hours.

Table 10 Estimated Benefits of Team Software Process^{SM}

State	Total Life Cycle Cost
Before TSP^{SM}	$4,509,997
After TSP^{SM}	$168,501
Benefits	**$4,341,496**

Let's use our total life cycle cost model to determine the cost of developing 10,000 lines of code using software testing. The formula is software size multiplied by 10.51, less the test hours times nine. Our total life cycle cost for using software testing alone is 45,099.97 hours. Multiply 45,099.97 by $100, and the total life cycle cost of using software testing is $4,509,997 to develop 10,000 lines of code.

Now let's determine the total life cycle cost of developing 10,000 lines of code using the Team Software Process^{SM}. The formula is software size divided by 5.9347. Our total life cycle cost for using the Team Software Process^{SM} is 1,685 hours. Multiply 1,685 by $100. The total life cycle cost of using the Team Software Process^{SM} is $168,501 to develop 10,000 lines of code. Table 10 illustrates the benefits of the Team Software Process^{SM}.

Now we are ready to estimate the benefits of using the Team Software Process^{SM} to help produce 10,000 lines of code. Subtract $168,501 from $4,509,997, which represents total life cycle costs. The benefits of using the Team Software Process^{SM} to help produce 10,000 lines of code are $4,341,496.

14.4 SOFTWARE CAPABILITY MATURITY MODEL®

Let's begin by modeling the costs for analyzing, designing, and developing 10,000 lines of code. Let's further assume our software effort is 5,088 hours to analyze, design, and code 10,000 lines of code.

Let's also begin by estimating the cost of software testing and assume that good software testing is in place so as to be conservative. Let's assume that we started with 1,000 software defects. Let's further assume that our software testing process nabs two-thirds of our 1,000 defects or 667 software defects. Let's also assume it takes 10 hours to find each of the 667 software defects. That comes to 6,670 software testing hours.

Let's use our total life cycle cost model to determine the cost of developing 10,000 lines of code using software testing. The formula is software size multiplied by 10.51, less the test hours times nine. Our total life cycle cost for using software testing alone is 45,099.97 hours. Multiply 45,099.97 by $100,

Table 11 Estimated Benefits of Software Capability Maturity Model®

State	Total Life Cycle Cost
Before SW-CMM®	$4,509,997
After SW-CMM®	$1,486,933
Benefits	**$3,023,064**

and the total life cycle cost of using software testing is $4,509,997 to develop 10,000 lines of code.

Now let's use our total life cycle cost model to determine the cost of developing 10,000 lines of code using the Software Capability Maturity Model®. The formula is software size multiplied by 10.2544, less the inspection hours times 99, and less the test hours times 9. (0.2544 is 50% of 0.5088, which is due to a 100% productivity increase associated with Level 3 compliance.) Our total life cycle cost of using the Software Capability Maturity Model® is 14,869.33 hours. Multiply 14,869.33 by $100. The total life cycle cost of using the Software Capability Maturity Model® is $1,486,933 to develop 10,000 lines of code. Table 11 illustrates the benefits of the Software Capability Maturity Model®.

Now we are ready to estimate the benefits of using the Software Capability Maturity Model® to help produce 10,000 lines of code. Subtract $1,486,933 from $4,509,997, which represents total life cycle costs. The benefits of using the Software Capability Maturity Model® to help produce 10,000 lines of code are $3,023,064.

14.5 ISO 9001

Let's begin by modeling the costs for analyzing, designing, and developing 10,000 lines of code. Let's further assume our software effort is 5,088 hours to analyze, design, and code 10,000 lines of code.

Let's also begin by estimating the cost of software testing and assume that good software testing is in place so as to be conservative. Let's assume that we started with 1,000 software defects. Let's further assume that our software testing process nabs two-thirds of our 1,000 defects or 667 software defects. Let's also assume it takes 10 hours to find each of the 667 software defects. That comes to 6,670 software testing hours.

Let's use our total life cycle cost model to determine the cost of developing 10,000 lines of code using software testing. The formula is software size multiplied by 10.51, less the test hours times nine. Our total life cycle cost for using software testing alone is 45,099.97 hours. Multiply 45,099.97 by $100,

Table 12   Estimated Benefits of ISO 9001

State	Total Life Cycle Cost
Before ISO 9001	$4,509,997
After ISO 9001	$3,940,156
Benefits	**$569,841**

and the total life cycle cost of using software testing is $4,509,997 to develop 10,000 lines of code.

Now let's use our total life cycle cost model to determine the cost of developing 10,000 lines of code using ISO 9001. The formula is software size multiplied by 10.442656, less the test hours times nine. (0.442656 is 87% of 0.5088, which is due to a 13% productivity increase associated with using ISO 9001.) Our total life cycle cost for using ISO 9001 is 44,396.56 hours. There is also a 15% increase in software quality due to using ISO 9001, which lowers our software maintenance hours by 4,995. Therefore, our adjusted total life cycle cost for using ISO 9001 is 39,401.56 hours. Multiply 39,401.56 by $100. The adjusted total life cycle cost of using ISO 9001 is $3,940,156 to develop 10,000 lines of code. Table 12 illustrates the benefits of ISO 9001.

Now we are ready to estimate the benefits of using ISO 9001 to help produce 10,000 lines of code. Subtract $3,940,156 from $4,509,997, which represents total life cycle costs. The benefits of using ISO 9001 to produce 10,000 lines of code are $569,841.

Some studies indicate that the benefits of ISO 9001 are higher than we have assumed here. For instance, some studies indicate that the quality increase associated with using ISO 9001 is 30%, 40%, or even 50%. Use the quality margins associated with your enterprise instead of the assumptions we have used here.

14.6 CAPABILITY MATURITY MODEL INTEGRATION®

Let's begin by modeling the costs for analyzing, designing, and developing 10,000 lines of code. Let's further assume our software effort is 5,088 hours to analyze, design, and code 10,000 lines of code.

Let's also begin by estimating the cost of software testing and assume that good software testing is in place so as to be conservative. Let's assume that we started with 1,000 software defects. Let's further assume that our software testing process nabs two-thirds of our 1,000 defects or 667 software defects. Let's also assume it takes 10 hours to find each of the 667 software defects. That comes to 6,670 software testing hours.

Table 13 Estimated Benefits of Capability Maturity Model Integration®

State	Total Life Cycle Cost
Before CMMI®	$4,509,997
After CMMI®	$1,486,933
Benefits	**$3,023,064**

Let's use our total life cycle cost model to determine the cost of developing 10,000 lines of code using software testing. The formula is software size multiplied by 10.51, less the test hours times nine. Our total life cycle cost for using software testing alone is 45,099.97 hours. Multiply 45,099.97 by $100, and the total life cycle cost of using software testing is $4,509,997 to develop 10,000 lines of code.

Now let's use our total life cycle cost model to determine the cost of developing 10,000 lines of code using Capability Maturity Model Integration®. The formula is software size multiplied by 10.2544, less the inspection hours times 99, and less the test hours times 9. (0.2544 is 50% of 0.5088, which is due to a 100% productivity increase associated with Level 3 compliance.) Our total life cycle cost for using the Capability Maturity Model Integration® is 14,869.33 hours. Multiply 14,869.33 by $100. The total life cycle cost of using the Capability Maturity Model Integration® is $1,486,933 to develop 10,000 lines of code. Table 13 illustrates the benefits of Capability Maturity Model Integration®.

Now we are ready to estimate the benefits of using Capability Maturity Model Integration® to help produce 10,000 lines of code. Subtract $1,486,933 from $4,509,997, which represents total life cycle costs. The benefits of using Capability Maturity Model Integration® to help produce 10,000 lines of code are $3,023,064.

15

BENEFIT/COST RATIO

The benefit/cost ratio (B/CR) of software process improvement (SPI) methods is a ratio of benefits to costs. B/CR is how much money is gained from a SPI method. It is the economic magnitude of a new and improved software process. B/CR is an instant measure of how much additional money we have gained, saved, or received from using a SPI method. In other words, B/CR tells us whether the SPI method was worth all of the time, trouble, expense, and investment. There are only two parts, terms, or components to this very simple equation: benefits and costs. All we have left to do is identify the benefits of our chosen SPI method and the costs of our chosen SPI method. Therein lies the challenge — to determine which benefits to use, and which costs to use in the B/CR model.

The benefits are the difference between the software maintenance and total life cycle costs. The costs are estimated before and after the introduction of the SPI method. That is, we subtract the new software maintenance and total life cycle costs after introducing the SPI method from the old costs. This assumes that the software maintenance and total life cycle costs of the new SPI method are lower, resulting in cost savings. We have already shown this to be the case for the SPI methods examined here.

The costs, on the other hand, require some selective analysis. What costs constitute the cost term of the B/CR equation? Should we use total costs? Should we use total life cycle costs? Should we use software development and maintenance costs? The answer is not so obvious. The costs that we will use for the B/CR model consist of training, process, product, preparation, assessment, and inspection costs. We will exclude development costs, test costs, and maintenance costs. Why? The costs that we will include consist of all of the special, new, or additional costs that are necessary to introduce the SPI method. Software development, test, and software maintenance costs are the assumed baseline. They must be performed in spite of the new SPI method. They are the platform from which we are departing with the introduction of the new SPI method.

15.1 SOFTWARE INSPECTION PROCESS

The benefits of using the Software Inspection Process to help produce 10,000 lines of code are $2,767,464. This was obtained by subtracting $1,742,533 in new total life cycle costs from $4,509,997 in old total life cycle costs.

The special, new, or additional costs that are required to introduce inspections consist of the training and inspection costs. The training costs to prepare four people to use inspections to help produce 10,000 lines of code are $11,240. The inspection cost for our four trained inspectors to evaluate 10,000 lines of code is $70,833. This amounts to nearly 42 Software Inspection Process runs. That totals $82,073 to introduce the Software Inspection Process as a SPI method.

The development cost of $508,000, testing cost of $195,000, and maintenance cost of $967,900 were not included. The development, testing, and maintenance costs either stayed the same or decreased. Had the development, testing, or maintenance costs increased, the differences or the increases would have been included. Table 14 illustrates the B/CR of the Software Inspection Process.

Now we are ready to determine the B/CR of the Software Inspection Process to help produce 10,000 lines of code. Divide the benefits of $2,767,464 by the costs of $82,073 for the Software Inspection Process. The B/CR of using the Software Inspection Process to help produce 10,000 lines of code is 34:1.

15.2 PERSONAL SOFTWARE PROCESS^{SM}

The benefits of using the Personal Software Process^{SM} to help produce 10,000 lines of code are $4,469,997. This was obtained by subtracting $40,000 in new total life cycle costs from $4,509,997 in old total life cycle costs.

Table 14 B/CR of Software Inspection Process

SPI Method	Benefits/Costs
Inspection Benefits	$2,767,464
Inspection Costs	$82,073
B/CR	**34:1**

Table 15   B/CR of Personal Software Process[SM]

SPI Method	Benefits/Costs
PSP[SM] Benefits	$4,469,997
PSP[SM] Costs	$105,600
B/CR	**42:1**

The special, new, or additional costs that are required to introduce the Personal Software Process[SM] consist of only the training cost. The training cost to use the Personal Software Process[SM] to help produce 10,000 lines of code is $105,600. This is a conservative estimate of Personal Software Process[SM] training costs. There are many more courses that must be taken.

The development cost of $40,000 was not included as a Personal Software Process[SM] cost. The development cost actually decreased. Had the development cost of the Personal Software Process[SM] increased, the difference or increase would have been included. Table 15 illustrates the B/CR of the Personal Software Process[SM].

Now we are ready to determine the B/CR of the Personal Software Process[SM] to help produce 10,000 lines of code. Divide the benefits of $4,469,997 by the costs of $105,600 for the Personal Software Process[SM]. The B/CR of using the Personal Software Process[SM] to help produce 10,000 lines of code is 42:1.

15.3 TEAM SOFTWARE PROCESS[SM]

The benefits of using the Team Software Process[SM] to help produce 10,000 lines of code are $4,341,496. This was obtained by subtracting $168,501 in new total life cycle costs from $4,509,997 in old total life cycle costs.

The special, new, or additional costs that are required to introduce the Team Software Process[SM] consist of only the training cost. The training cost to use the Team Software Process[SM] to help produce 10,000 lines of code is $148,400.

This is a conservative estimate of Team Software Process[SM] training costs. There are many more courses that must be taken.

The development cost of $168,501 was not included as a Team Software Process[SM] cost. The development cost actually decreased. Had the development cost of using the Team Software Process[SM] increased, the difference or increase would have been included. Table 16 illustrates the B/CR of the Team Software Process[SM].

Now we are ready to determine the B/CR of the Team Software Process[SM] to help produce 10,000 lines of code. Divide the benefits of $4,341,496 by the

Table 16   B/CR of Team Software Process^{SM}

SPI Method	Benefits/Costs
TSP^{SM} Benefits	$4,341,496
TSP^{SM} Costs	$148,400
B/CR	**29:1**

costs of $148,400 for the Team Software Process^{SM}. The B/CR of using the Team Software Process^{SM} to help produce 10,000 lines of code is 29:1.

15.4 SOFTWARE CAPABILITY MATURITY MODEL®

The benefits of using the Software Capability Maturity Model® to help produce 10,000 lines of code are $3,023,064. This was obtained by subtracting $1,486,933 in new total life cycle costs from $4,509,997 in old total life cycle costs.

The special, new, or additional costs that are required consist of process, product, preparation, assessment, and inspection costs. The special costs that are necessary to help produce 10,000 lines of code are $56,100, $117,600, $36,800, $30,100, and $70,833, respectively. This totals $311,433 to introduce the Software Capability Maturity Model® as a SPI method.

The development cost of $254,400, testing cost of $195,000, and maintenance cost of $966,700 were not included as special costs. The development, testing, and maintenance costs either stayed the same or decreased. Had the development, testing, or maintenance costs increased, the differences or the increases would have been included. Table 17 illustrates the B/CR of the Software Capability Maturity Model®.

Now we are ready to determine the B/CR of the Software Capability Maturity Model® to help produce 10,000 lines of code. Divide the benefits of $3,023,064 by the costs of $311,433 for the Software Capability Maturity Model®. The B/CR of using the Software Capability Maturity Model® to help produce 10,000 lines of code is 10:1.

Table 17   B/CR of Software Capability Maturity Model®

SPI Method	Benefits/Costs
SW-CMM® Benefits	$3,023,064
SW-CMM® Costs	$311,433
B/CR	**10:1**

Table 18   B/CR of ISO 9001

SPI Method	Benefits/Costs
ISO 9001 Benefits	$569,841
ISO 9001 Costs	$173,000
B/CR	**3:1**

15.5 ISO 9001

The benefits of using ISO 9001 to help produce 10,000 lines of code are $569,841. This was obtained by subtracting $3,940,156 in new total life cycle costs from $4,509,997 in old total life cycle costs.

The special, new, or additional costs that are required to use ISO 9001 consist of process, product, preparation, and audit costs. The specials costs that are necessary to produce 10,000 lines of code are $54,600, $56,000, $26,400, and $36,000, respectively. This totals $173,000 to introduce ISO 9001 as a SPI method.

The development cost of $442,656, testing cost of $667,000, and maintenance cost of $2,830,500 were not included as ISO 9001 costs. The development, testing, and maintenance costs either stayed the same or decreased. Had the development, testing, or maintenance costs increased, the differences or the increases would have been included. Table 18 illustrates the B/CR of ISO 9001.

Now we are ready to determine the B/CR of ISO 9001 to help produce 10,000 lines of code. Divide the benefits of $569,841 by the costs of $173,000 for ISO 9001. The B/CR of using ISO 9001 to help produce 10,000 lines of code is 3:1.

15.6 CAPABILITY MATURITY MODEL INTEGRATION®

The benefits of using Capability Maturity Model Integration® to help produce 10,000 lines of code are $3,023,064. This was obtained by subtracting $1,486,933 in new total life cycle costs from $4,509,997 in old total life cycle costs.

The special, new, or additional costs that are required consist of process, product, preparation, assessment, and inspection costs. The special costs to use Capability Maturity Model Integration® are $541,300, $400,400, $48,000, $47,700, and $70,833, respectively. This totals $1,108,233 to introduce Capability Maturity Model Integration® as a SPI method.

The development cost of $254,400, testing cost of $195,000, and maintenance cost of $966,700 were not included as special costs. The development,

Table 19 B/CR of Capability Maturity Model Integration®

SPI Method	Benefits/Costs
CMMI® Benefits	$3,023,064
CMMI® Costs	$1,108,233
B/CR	**3:1**

testing, and maintenance costs either stayed the same or decreased. Had the development, testing, or maintenance costs increased, the differences or the increases would have been included. Table 19 illustrates the B/CR of Capability Maturity Model Integration®.

Now we are ready to determine the B/CR of Capability Maturity Model Integration® to help produce 10,000 lines of code. Divide the benefits of $3,023,064 by the costs of $1,108,233 for Capability Maturity Model Integration®. The B/CR of using Capability Maturity Model Integration® to help produce 10,000 lines of code is 3:1.

16

RETURN ON INVESTMENT

The return on investment (ROI) of software process improvement (SPI) methods is the amount of money gained, returned, or earned above the resources that are spent. ROI is a solid measure of how much additional money we have gained, saved, or received from using a SPI method. ROI begins to clear the landscape. It helps us determine whether the SPI method was worth all of the time, trouble, expense, and investment in a new SPI method. Once again, there are only two parts, terms, or components to the simple ROI equation: benefits and costs. We have already identified the benefits of our chosen SPI method and the costs up to this point. Essentially, ROI consists of dividing the benefits by the costs.

However, the ROI model requires an additional manipulation of the benefits and costs. Before dividing the benefits by the costs, the costs must first be subtracted from the benefits. What? The ROI model assumes that the benefits are not truly benefits until the costs have first been eliminated, paid for, or covered. That is, benefits usually represent the gross windfall, savings, or revenue of using a SPI method. However, in order to achieve the benefits, some measure of investment is required. Therefore, the benefits came at a cost that must be accounted for, isolated, and eliminated. That is what the ROI model does. First, we will identify our benefits. Then we will subtract from the gross benefits the costs that were necessary to achieve the benefits. Then we will divide the adjusted benefits by the costs, in order to determine what is known as ROI. Whereas benefit/cost ratio (B/CR) is used to evaluate gross benefits, ROI is used to evaluate net benefits, or gross benefits less the costs of SPI.

16.1 SOFTWARE INSPECTION PROCESS

The benefits of using the Software Inspection Process to help produce 10,000 lines of code are $2,767,464. This was obtained by subtracting $1,742,533 in new total life cycle costs from $4,509,997 in old total life cycle costs.

The special, new, or additional costs that are required to introduce inspections consist of the training and inspection cost itself. The training costs to prepare four people to use inspections to help produce 10,000 lines of code are $11,240. The inspection cost for our four trained inspectors to evaluate 10,000 lines of code is $70,833. This amounts to nearly 42 Software Inspection Process runs. That totals $82,073 to introduce the Software Inspection Process as a SPI method.

The development cost of $508,000, testing cost of $195,000, and maintenance cost of $967,900 were not included. The development, testing, and maintenance costs either stayed the same or decreased. Had the development, testing, or maintenance costs increased, the differences or the increases would have been included.

Let's determine the B/CR of the Software Inspection Process to help produce 10,000 lines of code. Divide the benefits of $2,767,464 by the costs of $82,073 for the Software Inspection Process. The B/CR of using the Software Inspection Process to help produce 10,000 lines of code is 34:1.

However, the benefits of the Software Inspection Process must be adjusted, by first removing the costs. That is, the costs of inserting the Software Inspection Process as a SPI method must first be removed from the gross benefits. We will call these the adjusted benefits of the Software Inspection Process. Subtract $82,073 in Software Inspection Process costs from $2,767,464 in gross Software Inspection Process benefits. The result is $2,685,391 in adjusted benefits. Table 20 illustrates the ROI of the Software Inspection Process.

Now we are ready to determine the ROI of the Software Inspection Process to help produce 10,000 lines of code. Divide the adjusted benefits of $2,685,391 by the costs of $82,073 for the Software Inspection Process. Multiply the result

Table 20   ROI of Software Inspection Process

SPI Method	Benefits/Costs
Inspection Benefits (Gross)	$2,767,464
Inspection Costs	$82,073
Inspection B/CR	34:1
Inspection Benefits (Adjusted)	$2,685,391
ROI	**3,272%**

by 100%. The ROI of using the Software Inspection Process to help produce 10,000 lines of code is 3,272%.

16.2 PERSONAL SOFTWARE PROCESS^{SM}

The benefits of using the Personal Software Process^{SM} to help produce 10,000 lines of code are $4,469,997. This was obtained by subtracting $40,000 in new total life cycle costs from $4,509,997 in old total life cycle costs.

The special, new, or additional costs that are required to introduce the Personal Software Process^{SM} consist of only the training cost. The training cost to use the Personal Software Process^{SM} to help produce 10,000 lines of code is $105,600.

The development cost of $40,000 was not included as a Personal Software Process^{SM} cost. The development cost actually decreased. Had the development cost of the Personal Software Process^{SM} increased, the difference or increase would have been included.

Let's determine the B/CR of the Personal Software Process^{SM} to help produce 10,000 lines of code. Divide the benefits of $4,469,997 by the costs of $105,600 for the Personal Software Process^{SM}. The B/CR of using the Personal Software Process^{SM} to help produce 10,000 lines of code is 42:1.

However, the benefits of the Personal Software Process^{SM} must be adjusted, by first removing the costs. That is, the costs of inserting the Personal Software Process^{SM} as a SPI method must first be removed from the gross benefits. We will call these the adjusted benefits of the Personal Software Process^{SM}. Subtract $105,600 in Personal Software Process^{SM} costs from $4,469,997 in gross Personal Software Process^{SM} benefits. The result is $4,364,397 in adjusted benefits. Table 21 illustrates the ROI of the Personal Software Process^{SM}.

Now we are ready to determine the ROI of the Personal Software Process^{SM} to help produce 10,000 lines of code. Divide the adjusted benefits of $4,364,397 by the costs of $105,600 for the Personal Software Process^{SM}. Multiply the

Table 21   ROI of Personal Software Process^{SM}

SPI Method	Benefits/Costs
PSP^{SM} Benefits (Gross)	$4,469,997
PSP^{SM} Costs	$105,600
PSP^{SM} B/CR	42:1
PSP^{SM} Benefits (Adjusted)	$4,364,397
ROI	**4,133%**

result by 100%. The ROI of using the Personal Software Process[SM] to help produce 10,000 lines of code is 4,133%.

16.3 TEAM SOFTWARE PROCESS[SM]

The benefits of using the Team Software Process[SM] to help produce 10,000 lines of code are $4,341,496. This was obtained by subtracting $168,501 in new total life cycle costs from $4,509,997 in old total life cycle costs.

The special, new, or additional costs that are required to introduce the Team Software Process[SM] consist of only the training cost. The training cost to use the Team Software Process[SM] to help produce 10,000 lines of code is $148,400.

The development cost of $168,501 was not included as a Team Software Process[SM] cost. The development cost actually decreased. Had the development cost of using the Team Software Process[SM] increased, the difference or increase would have been included.

Let's determine the B/CR of the Team Software Process[SM] to help produce 10,000 lines of code. Divide the benefits of $4,341,496 by the costs of $148,400 for the Team Software Process[SM]. The B/CR of using the Team Software Process[SM] to help produce 10,000 lines of code is 29:1.

However, the benefits of the Team Software Process[SM] must be adjusted, by first removing the costs. That is, the costs of inserting the Team Software Process[SM] as a SPI method must first be removed from the gross benefits. We'll call these the adjusted benefits of the Team Software Process[SM]. Subtract $148,400 in Team Software Process[SM] costs from $4,341,496 in gross Team Software Process[SM] benefits. The result is $4,193,096 in adjusted benefits. Table 22 illustrates the ROI of the Team Software Process[SM].

Now we are ready to determine the ROI of the Team Software Process[SM] to help produce 10,000 lines of code. Divide the adjusted benefits of $4,193,096 by the costs of $148,400 for the Team Software Process[SM]. Multiply the result by 100%. The ROI of using the Team Software Process[SM] to help produce 10,000 lines of code is 2,826%.

Table 22   ROI of Team Software Process[SM]

SPI Method	Benefits/Costs
TSP[SM] Benefits (Gross)	$4,341,496
TSP[SM] Costs	$148,400
TSP[SM] B/CR	29:1
TSP[SM] Benefits (Adjusted)	$4,193,096
ROI	**2,826%**

16.4 SOFTWARE CAPABILITY MATURITY MODEL®

The benefits of using the Software Capability Maturity Model® to help produce 10,000 lines of code are $3,023,064. This was obtained by subtracting $1,486,933 in new total life cycle costs from $4,509,997 in old total life cycle costs.

The special, new, or additional costs that are required consist of process, product, preparation, assessment, and inspection costs. The special costs that are necessary to help produce 10,000 lines of code are $56,100, $117,600, $36,800, $30,100, and $70,833, respectively. This totals $311,433 to introduce the Software Capability Maturity Model® as a SPI method.

The development cost of $254,400, testing cost of $195,000, and maintenance cost of $966,700 were not included as special costs. The development, testing, and maintenance costs either stayed the same or decreased. Had the development, testing, or maintenance costs increased, the differences or the increases would have been included.

Let's determine the B/CR of the Software Capability Maturity Model® to help produce 10,000 lines of code. Divide the benefits of $3,023,064 by the costs of $311,433 for the Software Capability Maturity Model®. The B/CR of using the Software Capability Maturity Model® to help produce 10,000 lines of code is 10:1.

However, the benefits of the Software Capability Maturity Model® must be adjusted, by first removing the costs. That is, the costs of inserting the Software Capability Maturity Model® as a SPI method must first be removed from the gross benefits. We will call these the adjusted benefits of the Software Capability Maturity Model®. Subtract $311,433 in Software Capability Maturity Model® costs from $3,023,064 in gross Software Capability Maturity Model® benefits. The result is $2,711,631 in adjusted benefits. Table 23 illustrates the ROI of the Software Capability Maturity Model®.

Now we are ready to determine the ROI of the Software Capability Maturity Model® to help produce 10,000 lines of code. Divide the adjusted benefits of $2,711,631 by the costs of $311,433 for the Software Capability Maturity Model®.

Table 23   ROI of Software Capability Maturity Model®

SPI Method	Benefits/Costs
SW-CMM® Benefits (Gross)	$3,023,064
SW-CMM® Costs	$311,433
SW-CMM® B/CR	10:1
SW-CMM® Benefits (Adjusted)	$2,711,631
ROI	**871%**

Multiply the result by 100%. The ROI of using the Software Capability Maturity Model® to help produce 10,000 lines of code is 871%.

16.5 ISO 9001

The benefits of using ISO 9001 to help produce 10,000 lines of code are $569,841. This was obtained by subtracting $3,940,156 in new total life cycle costs from $4,509,997 in old total life cycle costs.

The special, new, or additional costs that are required to use ISO 9001 consist of process, product, preparation, and audit costs. The specials costs that are necessary to produce 10,000 lines of code are $54,600, $56,000, $26,400, and $36,000, respectively. This totals $173,000 to introduce ISO 9001 as a SPI method.

The development cost of $442,656, testing cost of $667,000, and maintenance cost of $2,830,500 were not included as ISO 9001 costs. The development, testing, and maintenance costs either stayed the same or decreased. Had the development, testing, or maintenance costs increased, the differences or the increases would have been included.

Let's determine the B/CR of ISO 9001 to help produce 10,000 lines of code. Divide the benefits of $569,841 by the costs of $173,000 for ISO 9001. The B/CR of using ISO 9001 to help produce 10,000 lines of code is 3:1.

However, the benefits of ISO 9001 must be adjusted, by first removing the costs. That is, the costs of inserting ISO 9001 as a SPI method must first be removed from the gross ISO 9001 benefits. We will call these the adjusted benefits of ISO 9001. Subtract $173,000 in ISO 9001 costs from $569,841 in gross ISO 9001 benefits, to arrive at $396,841 in adjusted benefits. Table 24 illustrates the ROI of ISO 9001.

Now we are ready to determine the ROI of ISO 9001 to help produce 10,000 lines of code. Divide the adjusted benefits of $396,841 by the costs of $173,000 for ISO 9001. Multiply the result by 100%. The ROI of using ISO 9001 to help produce 10,000 lines of code is 229%.

Table 24   ROI of ISO 9001

SPI Method	Benefits/Costs
ISO 9001 Benefits (Gross)	$569,841
ISO 9001 Costs	$173,000
ISO 9001 B/CR	3:1
ISO 9001 Benefits (Adjusted)	$396,841
ROI	**229%**

Table 25   ROI of Capability Maturity Model Integration®

SPI Method	Benefits/Costs
CMMI® Benefits (Gross)	$3,023,064
CMMI® Costs	$1,108,233
CMMI® B/CR	3:1
CMMI® Benefits (Adjusted)	$1,914,831
ROI	**173%**

16.6 CAPABILITY MATURITY MODEL INTEGRATION®

The benefits of using Capability Maturity Model Integration® to help produce 10,000 lines of code are $3,023,064. This was obtained by subtracting $1,486,933 in new total life cycle costs from $4,509,997 in old total life cycle costs.

The special, new, or additional costs that are required consist of process, product, preparation, assessment, and inspection costs. The special costs to use Capability Maturity Model Integration® are $541,300, $400,400, $48,000, $47,700, and $70,833, respectively. This totals $1,108,233 to introduce Capability Maturity Model Integration® as a SPI method.

The development cost of $254,400, testing cost of $195,000, and maintenance cost of $966,700 were not included as special costs. The development, testing, and maintenance costs either stayed the same or decreased. Had the development, testing, or maintenance costs increased, the differences or the increases would have been included.

Let's determine the B/CR of Capability Maturity Model Integration® to help produce 10,000 lines of code. Divide the benefits of $3,023,064 by the costs of $1,108,233 for Capability Maturity Model Integration®. The B/CR of using Capability Maturity Model Integration® to help produce 10,000 lines of code is 3:1.

However, the benefits of Capability Maturity Model Integration® must be adjusted, by first removing the costs. That is, the costs of inserting Capability Maturity Model Integration® as a SPI method must first be removed from the gross benefits. We will call these the adjusted benefits of Capability Maturity Model Integration®. Subtract $1,108,233 in Capability Maturity Model Integration® costs from $3,023,064 in gross Capability Maturity Model Integration® benefits. The result is $1,914,831 in adjusted benefits. Table 25 illustrates the ROI of Capability Maturity Model Integration®.

Now we're ready to determine the ROI of Capability Maturity Model Integration® to help produce 10,000 lines of code. Divide the adjusted benefits of $1,914,831 by the costs of $1,108,233 for Capability Maturity Model Integration®. Multiply the result by 100%. The ROI of using Capability Maturity Model Integration® to help produce 10,000 lines of code is 173%.

NET PRESENT VALUE

The net present value (NPV) of a software process improvement (SPI) method is what the cash value and economic value of the benefits of a SPI method are worth in the future. In other words, NPV is the economic value less inflation of the benefits. NPV is a realistic measure of how much additional money is gained, saved, or received from use of a SPI method. NPV is a cold, hard, and objective measure of value. It indicates whether the SPI method was worth all of the time, trouble, expense, and investment. There are three inputs, variables, or terms to the simple NPV equation: benefits, inflation rate or rather devaluation rate, and the number of years in which to amortize the benefits. We have already identified the benefits of our chosen SPI methods up to this point. The NPV equation consists of dividing the benefits by the inflation or devaluation rate over time.

However, the NPV model requires that we determine the inflation or devaluation rate of money over time. We must determine the number of years in which to devaluate our benefits. What exactly does NPV do, and why do we need NPV? NPV basically means that money loses its value over time. If we place $10,000 in a safety deposit box and retrieve it some time in the future, it isn't worth $10,000 anymore. Due to inflation, the cost of products and services increases over time. What costs $10,000 today may cost $20,000 a few years from now. Therefore, the estimated benefits of our SPI method may be substantially lower over time, and we need to adjust for the devaluation of our benefits over time. This is especially true for software maintenance or total life cycle benefits. Generally, our benefits occur over a period of many years and must be reduced or devaluated accordingly.

17.1 SOFTWARE INSPECTION PROCESS

The benefits of using the Software Inspection Process to help produce 10,000 lines of code are $2,767,464. This was obtained by subtracting $1,742,533 in new total life cycle costs from $4,509,997 in old total life cycle costs.

The special, new, or additional costs that are required to introduce inspections consist of the training and inspection costs. The training costs to prepare four people to use inspections to help produce 10,000 lines of code are $11,240. The inspection cost for our four trained inspectors to evaluate 10,000 lines of code is $70,833. This amounts to nearly 42 Software Inspection Process runs. That totals $82,073 to introduce the Software Inspection Process as a SPI method.

The development cost of $508,000, testing cost of $195,000, and maintenance cost of $967,900 were not included. The development, testing, and maintenance costs either stayed the same or decreased. Had the development, testing, or maintenance costs increased, the differences or the increases would have been included.

Let's determine the benefit/cost ratio (B/CR) of the Software Inspection Process to help produce 10,000 lines of code. Divide the benefits of $2,767,464 by the costs of $82,073 for the Software Inspection Process. The B/CR of using the Software Inspection Process to help produce 10,000 lines of code is 34:1.

Let's determine the adjusted benefits of the Software Inspection Process to help produce 10,000 lines of code. Subtract $82,073 in Software Inspection Process costs from $2,767,464 in gross Software Inspection Process benefits. The result is $2,685,391 in adjusted benefits.

Let's determine the return on investment (ROI) of the Software Inspection Process to help produce 10,000 lines of code. Divide the adjusted benefits of $2,685,391 by the costs of $82,073 for the Software Inspection Process. Multiply the result by 100%. The ROI of using the Software Inspection Process to help produce 10,000 lines of code is 3,272%. Table 26 illustrates the NPV of the Software Inspection Process.

Now we are ready to determine the NPV of the gross benefits of the Software Inspection Process to produce 10,000 lines of code. Divide the gross benefits of $2,767,464 by the devaluation rate of 1.27628156. The NPV of the gross benefits of using the Software Inspection Process to help produce 10,000 lines of code is $2,168,380.

Now let's determine the B/CR of the Software Inspection Process to produce 10,000 lines of code using NPV of the gross benefits. Divide the NPV of the gross benefits of $2,168,380 by the costs of $82,073 for the Software Inspection Process. The B/CR of using the Software Inspection Process to help produce 10,000 lines of code is 26:1 using the NPV of the gross benefits.

Table 26 NPV of Software Inspection Process

SPI Method	Benefits/Costs
Inspection Benefits (Gross)	$2,767,464
Inspection Costs	$82,073
Inspection B/CR	34:1
Inspection Benefits (Adjusted)	$2,685,391
Inspection ROI	3,272%
Inspection Benefits (NPV)	$2,168,380
Inspection B/CR (NPV)	26:1
Inspection Benefits (Adjusted/NPV)	$2,086,307
Inspection ROI (NPV)	**2,542%**

Now let's determine the adjusted benefits of the Software Inspection Process using the NPV of the gross benefits. Subtract $82,073 in Software Inspection Process costs from $2,168,380, which is the NPV of the gross benefits. The result is $2,086,307 in adjusted benefits.

Finally, let's determine the ROI of the Software Inspection Process to produce 10,000 lines of code using adjusted benefits. Divide the adjusted benefits of $2,086,307 by the costs of $82,073 for the Software Inspection Process. Multiply the result by 100%. The ROI of using the Software Inspection Process to produce 10,000 lines of code is 2,542% using NPV.

17.2 PERSONAL SOFTWARE PROCESS[SM]

The benefits of using the Personal Software Process[SM] to help produce 10,000 lines of code are $4,469,997. This was obtained by subtracting $40,000 in new total life cycle costs from $4,509,997 in old total life cycle costs.

The special, new, or additional costs that are required to introduce the Personal Software Process[SM] consist of only the training cost. The training cost to use the Personal Software Process[SM] to help produce 10,000 lines of code is $105,600.

The development cost of $40,000 was not included as a Personal Software Process[SM] cost. The development cost actually decreased. Had the development cost of the Personal Software Process[SM] increased, the difference or increase would have been included.

Let's determine the B/CR of the Personal Software Process[SM] to help produce 10,000 lines of code. Divide the benefits of $4,469,997 by the costs of $105,600 for the Personal Software Process[SM]. The B/CR of using the Personal Software Process[SM] to help produce 10,000 lines of code is 42:1.

Let's determine the adjusted benefits of the Personal Software Process[SM] to

Table 27 NPV of Personal Software Process^{SM}

SPI Method	Benefits/Costs
PSP^{SM} Benefits (Gross)	$4,469,997
PSP^{SM} Costs	$105,600
PSP^{SM} B/CR	42:1
PSP^{SM} Benefits (Adjusted)	$4,364,397
PSP^{SM} ROI	4,133%
PSP^{SM} Benefits (NPV)	**$3,502,360**
PSP^{SM} B/CR (NPV)	**33:1**
PSP^{SM} Benefits (Adjusted/NPV)	**$3,396,760**
PSP^{SM} ROI (NPV)	**3,217%**

help produce 10,000 lines of code. Subtract $105,600 in Personal Software Process^{SM} costs from $4,469,997 in gross Personal Software Process^{SM} benefits. The result is $4,364,397 in adjusted benefits.

Let's determine the ROI of the Personal Software Process^{SM} to help produce 10,000 lines of code. Divide the adjusted benefits of $4,364,397 by the costs of $105,600 for the Personal Software Process^{SM}. Multiply the result by 100%. The ROI of using the Personal Software Process^{SM} to help produce 10,000 lines of code is 4,133%. Table 27 illustrates the NPV of the Personal Software Process^{SM}.

Now we are ready to determine the NPV of the gross benefits of the Personal Software Process^{SM} to produce 10,000 lines of code. Divide the gross benefits of $4,469,997 by the devaluation rate of 1.27628156. The NPV of the gross benefits of using the Personal Software Process^{SM} to help produce 10,000 lines of code is $3,502,360.

Now let's determine the B/CR of the Personal Software Process^{SM} to produce 10,000 lines of code using NPV of the gross benefits. Divide the NPV of the gross benefits of $3,502,360 by the costs of $105,600 for the Personal Software Process^{SM}. The B/CR of using the Personal Software Process^{SM} to produce 10,000 lines of code is 33:1 using the NPV of the gross benefits.

Now let's determine the adjusted benefits of the Personal Software Process^{SM} using the NPV of the gross benefits. Subtract $105,600 in Personal Software Process^{SM} costs from $3,502,360, which is the NPV of the gross benefits. The result is $3,396,760 in adjusted benefits.

Finally, let's determine the ROI of the Personal Software Process^{SM} to help produce 10,000 lines of code using the adjusted benefits. Divide the adjusted benefits of $3,396,760 by the costs of $105,600 for the Personal Software Process^{SM}. Multiply the result by 100%. The ROI of using the Personal Software Process^{SM} to help produce 10,000 lines of code is 3,217% using NPV.

17.3 TEAM SOFTWARE PROCESS^SM

The benefits of using the Team Software Process^SM to help produce 10,000 lines of code are $4,341,496. This was obtained by subtracting $168,501 in new total life cycle costs from $4,509,997 in old total life cycle costs.

The special, new, or additional costs that are required to introduce the Team Software Process^SM consist of only the training cost. The training cost to use the Team Software Process^SM to help produce 10,000 lines of code is $148,400.

The development cost of $168,501 was not included as a Team Software Process^SM cost. The development cost actually decreased. Had the development cost of using the Team Software Process^SM increased, the difference or increase would have been included.

Let's determine the B/CR of the Team Software Process^SM to help produce 10,000 lines of code. Divide the benefits of $4,341,496 by the costs of $148,400 for the Team Software Process^SM. The B/CR of using the Team Software Process^SM to help produce 10,000 lines of code is 29:1.

Let's determine the adjusted benefits of the Team Software Process^SM to help produce 10,000 lines of code. Subtract $148,400 in Team Software Process^SM costs from $4,341,496 in gross Team Software Process^SM benefits. The result is $4,193,096 in adjusted benefits.

Let's determine the ROI of the Team Software Process^SM to help produce 10,000 lines of code. Divide the adjusted benefits of $4,193,096 by the costs of $148,400 for the Team Software Process^SM. Multiply the result by 100%. The ROI of using the Team Software Process^SM to help produce 10,000 lines of code is 2,826%. Table 28 illustrates the NPV of the Team Software Process^SM.

Now we are ready to determine the NPV of the gross benefits of the Team Software Process^SM to produce 10,000 lines of code. Divide the gross benefits

Table 28 NPV of Team Software Process^SM

SPI Method	Benefits/Costs
TSP^SM Benefits (Gross)	$4,341,496
TSP^SM Costs	$148,400
TSP^SM B/CR	29:1
TSP^SM Benefits (Adjusted)	$4,193,096
TSP^SM ROI	2,826%
TSP^SM Benefits (NPV)	**$3,401,676**
TSP^SM B/CR (NPV)	**23:1**
TSP^SM Benefits (Adjusted/NPV)	**$3,253,276**
TSP^SM ROI (NPV)	**2,192%**

of $4,341,496 by the devaluation rate of 1.27628156. The NPV of the gross benefits of using the Team Software Process[SM] to help produce 10,000 lines of code is $3,401,676.

Now let's determine the B/CR of the Team Software Process[SM] using the NPV of the gross benefits. Divide the NPV of the gross benefits of $3,401,676 by the costs of $148,400 for the Team Software Process[SM]. The B/CR of the Team Software Process[SM] is 23:1 using the NPV of the gross benefits.

Now let's determine the adjusted benefits of the Team Software Process[SM] using the NPV of the gross benefits. Subtract $148,400 in Team Software Process[SM] costs from $3,401,676, which is the NPV of the gross benefits. The result is $3,253,276 in adjusted benefits.

Finally, let's determine the ROI of the Team Software Process[SM] to help produce 10,000 lines of code using the adjusted benefits. Divide the adjusted benefits of $3,253,276 by the costs of $148,400 for the Team Software Process[SM]. Multiply the result by 100%. The ROI of using the Team Software Process[SM] to help produce 10,000 lines of code is 2,192% using NPV.

Since the Team Software Process[SM] is designed for software project teams of up to 150 people, its benefits may be substantially lower.

17.4 SOFTWARE CAPABILITY MATURITY MODEL®

The benefits of using the Software Capability Maturity Model® to help produce 10,000 lines of code are $3,023,064. This was obtained by subtracting $1,486,933 in new total life cycle costs from $4,509,997 in old total life cycle costs.

The special, new, or additional costs that are required consist of process, product, preparation, assessment, and inspection costs. The special costs that are necessary to help produce 10,000 lines of code are $56,100, $117,600, $36,800, $30,100, and $70,833, respectively. This totals $311,433 to introduce the Software Capability Maturity Model® as a SPI method.

The development cost of $254,400, testing cost of $195,000, and maintenance cost of $966,700 were not included as special costs. The development, testing, and maintenance costs either stayed the same or decreased. Had the development, testing, or maintenance costs increased, the differences or the increases would have been included.

Let's determine the B/CR of the Software Capability Maturity Model® to help produce 10,000 lines of code. Divide the benefits of $3,023,064 by the costs of $311,433 for the Software Capability Maturity Model®. The B/CR of using the Software Capability Maturity Model® to help produce 10,000 lines of code is 10:1.

Let's determine the adjusted benefits of the Software Capability Maturity

Table 29   NPV of Software Capability Maturity Model®

SPI Method	Benefits/Costs
SW-CMM® Benefits (Gross)	$3,023,064
SW-CMM® Costs	$311,433
SW-CMM® B/CR	10:1
SW-CMM® Benefits (Adjusted)	$2,711,631
SW-CMM® ROI	871%
SW-CMM® Benefits (NPV)	**$2,368,650**
SW-CMM® B/CR (NPV)	**8:1**
SW-CMM® Benefits (Adjusted/NPV)	**$2,057,216**
SW-CMM® ROI (NPV)	**661%**

Model® to help produce 10,000 lines of code. Subtract $311,433 in Software Capability Maturity Model® costs from $3,023,064 in gross Software Capability Maturity Model® benefits. The result is $2,711,631 in adjusted benefits.

Let's determine the ROI of the Software Capability Maturity Model® to help produce 10,000 lines of code. Divide the adjusted benefits of $2,711,631 by the costs of $311,433 for the Software Capability Maturity Model®. Multiply the result by 100%. The ROI of using the Software Capability Maturity Model® to help produce 10,000 lines of code is 871%. Table 29 illustrates the NPV of the Software Capability Maturity Model®.

Now we are ready to determine the NPV of the gross benefits of the Software Capability Maturity Model® to produce 10,000 lines of code. Divide the gross benefits of $3,023,064 by the devaluation rate of 1.27628156. The NPV of the gross benefits of using the Software Capability Maturity Model® to help produce 10,000 lines of code is $2,368,650.

Now let's determine the B/CR of the Software Capability Maturity Model® using the NPV of the gross benefits. Divide the NPV of the gross benefits of $2,368,650 by the costs of $311,433 for the Software Capability Maturity Model®. The B/CR of the Software Capability Maturity Model® to produce 10,000 lines of code is 8:1 using the NPV of the gross benefits.

Now let's determine the adjusted benefits of the Software Capability Maturity Model® using the NPV of the gross benefits. Subtract $311,433 in Software Capability Maturity Model® costs from $2,368,650, which is the NPV of the gross benefits. The result is $2,057,216 in adjusted benefits.

Finally, let's determine the ROI of the Software Capability Maturity Model® to produce 10,000 lines of code using adjusted benefits. Divide the adjusted benefits of $2,057,216 by the costs of $311,433 for the Software Capability Maturity Model®. Multiply the result by 100%. The ROI of using the Software Capability Maturity Model® to help produce 10,000 lines of code is 661% using NPV.

17.5 ISO 9001

The benefits of using ISO 9001 to help produce 10,000 lines of code are $569,841. This was obtained by subtracting $3,940,156 in new total life cycle costs from $4,509,997 in old total life cycle costs.

The special, new, or additional costs that are required to use ISO 9001 consist of process, product, preparation, and audit costs. The specials costs that are necessary to produce 10,000 lines of code are $54,600, $56,000, $26,400, and $36,000, respectively. This totals $173,000 to introduce ISO 9001 as a SPI method.

The development cost of $442,656, testing cost of $667,000, and maintenance cost of $2,830,500 were not included as ISO 9001 costs. The development, testing, and maintenance costs either stayed the same or decreased. Had the development, testing, or maintenance costs increased, the differences or the increases would have been included.

Let's determine the B/CR of ISO 9001 to help produce 10,000 lines of code. Divide the benefits of $569,841 by the costs of $173,000 for ISO 9001. The B/CR of using ISO 9001 to help produce 10,000 lines of code is 3:1.

Let's determine the adjusted benefits of ISO 9001 to help produce 10,000 lines of code. Subtract $173,000 in ISO 9001 costs from $569,841 in gross ISO 9001 benefits. The result is $396,841 in adjusted benefits.

Let's determine the ROI of ISO 9001 to help produce 10,000 lines of code. Divide the adjusted benefits of $396,841 by the costs of $173,000 for ISO 9001. Multiply the result by 100%. The ROI of using ISO 9001 to help produce 10,000 lines of code is 229%. Table 30 illustrates the NPV of ISO 9001.

Now we are ready to determine the NPV of the gross benefits of using ISO 9001 to help produce 10,000 lines of code. Divide the gross benefits of $569,841 by the devaluation rate of 1.27628156. The NPV of the gross benefits of using ISO 9001 to help produce 10,000 lines of code is $446,485.

Table 30   NPV of ISO 9001

SPI Method	Benefits/Costs
ISO 9001 Benefits (Gross)	$569,841
ISO 9001 Costs	$173,000
ISO 9001 B/CR	3:1
ISO 9001 Benefits (Adjusted)	$396,841
ISO 9001 ROI	229%
ISO 9001 Benefits (NPV)	**$446,485**
ISO 9001 B/CR (NPV)	**3:1**
ISO 9001 Benefits (Adjusted/NPV)	**$273,485**
ISO 9001 ROI (NPV)	**158%**

Now let's determine the B/CR of ISO 9001 to help produce 10,000 lines of code using the NPV of the gross benefits. Divide the NPV of the gross benefits of $446,485 by the costs of $173,000 for ISO 9001. The B/CR of using ISO 9001 to help produce 10,000 lines of code is 3:1 using the NPV of the gross benefits.

Now let's determine the adjusted benefits of ISO 9001 to produce 10,000 lines of code using the NPV of the gross benefits. Subtract $173,000 in ISO 9001 costs from $446,485, which is the NPV of the gross benefits. The result is $273,485 in adjusted benefits.

Finally, let's determine the ROI of ISO 9001 to help produce 10,000 lines of code using the adjusted benefits. Divide the adjusted benefits of $273,485 by the costs of $173,000 for ISO 9001. Multiply the result by 100%. The ROI of using ISO 9001 to help produce 10,000 lines of code is 158% using NPV. (This indicates that for every dollar spent, 58 cents is returned.)

17.6 CAPABILITY MATURITY MODEL INTEGRATION®

The benefits of using Capability Maturity Model Integration® to help produce 10,000 lines of code are $3,023,064. This was obtained by subtracting $1,486,933 in new total life cycle costs from $4,509,997 in old total life cycle costs.

The special, new, or additional costs that are required consist of process, product, preparation, assessment, and inspection costs. The special costs to use Capability Maturity Model Integration® are $541,300, $400,400, $48,000, $47,700, and $70,833, respectively. This totals $1,108,233 to introduce Capability Maturity Model Integration® as a SPI method.

The development cost of $254,400, testing cost of $195,000, and maintenance cost of $966,700 were not included as special costs. The development, testing, and maintenance costs either stayed the same or decreased. Had the development, testing, or maintenance costs increased, the differences or the increases would have been included.

Let's determine the B/CR of Capability Maturity Model Integration® to help produce 10,000 lines of code. Divide the benefits of $3,023,064 by the costs of $1,108,233 for Capability Maturity Model Integration®. The B/CR of using Capability Maturity Model Integration® to help produce 10,000 lines of code is 3:1.

Let's determine the adjusted benefits of Capability Maturity Model Integration® to help produce 10,000 lines of code. Subtract $1,108,233 in Capability Maturity Model Integration® costs from $3,023,064 in gross Capability Maturity Model Integration® benefits. The result is $1,914,831 in adjusted benefits.

Let's determine the ROI of Capability Maturity Model Integration® to help

Table 31   NPV of Capability Maturity Model Integration®

SPI Method	Benefits/Costs
CMMI® Benefits (Gross)	$3,023,064
CMMI® Costs	$1,108,233
CMMI® B/CR	3:1
CMMI® Benefits (Adjusted)	$1,914,831
CMMI® ROI	173%
CMMI® Benefits (NPV)	**$2,368,650**
CMMI® B/CR (NPV)	**2:1**
CMMI® Benefits (Adjusted/NPV)	**$1,260,416**
CMMI® ROI (NPV)	**114%**

produce 10,000 lines of code. Divide the adjusted benefits of $1,914,831 by the costs of $1,108,233 for Capability Maturity Model Integration®. Multiply the result by 100%. The ROI of using Capability Maturity Model Integration® to help produce 10,000 lines of code is 173%. Table 31 illustrates the NPV of Capability Maturity Model Integration®.

Now we are ready to determine the NPV of the gross benefits of Capability Maturity Model Integration® to produce 10,000 lines of code. Divide the gross benefits of $3,023,064 by the devaluation rate of 1.27628156. The NPV of the gross benefits of using Capability Maturity Model Integration® to help produce 10,000 lines of code is $2,368,650.

Now let's determine the B/CR of Capability Maturity Model Integration® using the NPV of the gross benefits. Divide the NPV of the gross benefits of $2,368,650 by the costs of $1,108,233 for Capability Maturity Model Integration®. The B/CR of using Capability Maturity Model Integration® is 2:1 using the NPV of the gross benefits.

Now let's determine the adjusted benefits of Capability Maturity Model Integration® using the NPV of the gross benefits. Subtract $1,108,233 in Capability Maturity Model Integration® costs from $2,368,650, which is the NPV of the gross benefits. The result is $1,260,416 in adjusted benefits.

Finally, let's determine the ROI of Capability Maturity Model Integration® to produce 10,000 lines of code using adjusted benefits. Divide the adjusted benefits of $1,260,416 by the costs of $1,108,233 for Capability Maturity Model Integration®. Multiply the result by 100%. The ROI of using Capability Maturity Model Integration® to help produce 10,000 lines of code is 114% using NPV.

18

BREAKEVEN POINT

The breakeven point of software process improvement (SPI) methods is the economic value at which the benefits overtake and exceed the costs. This is the profit of the SPI methods. Breakeven point is a useful measure of how far out into the future the benefits of SPI methods will be achieved. Breakeven point indicates in numeric terms when the benefits of SPI methods can be expected, achieved, and obtained. There are three basic inputs, variables, or terms to the breakeven point equation: cost, old productivity, and new productivity. The breakeven point equation consists of dividing the costs of the SPI methods by one less the productivity of the old process. The result is divided by the productivity of the new process.

However, the breakeven point model requires that we determine the sources of the costs, old productivity, and new productivity. The breakeven point inherently and implicitly indicates when the investment cost of the new SPI method is recovered. Therefore, only the special costs of the SPI methods will be used. The special costs include training, process, product, preparation, assessment, and inspection costs.

Now we just have to determine the sources of the old and new productivity of the SPI methods. We have been comparing the costs and benefits of the SPI methods against the costs and benefits of using only the testing process. Therefore, the old productivity is the software size divided by the total life cycle costs of using software testing alone. The new productivity is the software size divided by the total life cycle cost of the SPI method.

18.1 SOFTWARE INSPECTION PROCESS

Let's use our total life cycle cost model to determine the cost of developing 10,000 lines of code using software testing. The formula is software size multiplied by 10.51, less the test hours times nine. Our total life cycle cost for using software testing alone is 45,100 hours.

Let's use our productivity model to determine the old productivity of using testing. The formula is software size divided by the total life cycle costs of testing. Divide 10,000 by 45,100, and the old productivity of testing is 0.22.

Let's use our total life cycle cost model to determine the cost of developing 10,000 lines of code using inspections. The formula is software size multiplied by 10.51, less the inspection hours times 99 and less the test hours times 9. Our total life cycle cost for using the Software Inspection Process is 17,425 hours.

Let's use our productivity model to determine the new productivity of using the Software Inspection Process. The formula is software size divided by the total life cycle costs of the Software Inspection Process. Divide 10,000 by 17,425, and the new productivity of the Software Inspection Process is 0.57.

Let's determine the difference between the old productivity of software testing and the new productivity of inspections. The formula is old productivity of software testing divided by new productivity of the Software Inspection Process. Divide 0.22 by 0.57. The difference between the old productivity of testing and the new productivity of the Software Inspection Process is 0.39.

The special, new, or additional costs that are required to introduce inspections consist of the training and inspection costs. The training costs to prepare four people to use inspections to help produce 10,000 lines of code are $11,240. The inspection cost for our four trained inspectors to evaluate 10,000 lines of code is $70,833. This amounts to nearly 42 Software Inspection Process runs. That totals $82,073 to introduce the Software Inspection Process as a SPI method. Table 32 illustrates the breakeven point of the Software Inspection Process.

Now we are ready to determine the breakeven point of using the Software Inspection Process to produce 10,000 lines of code. Divide the special costs of

Table 32   Breakeven Point of Software Inspection Process

SPI Method	Benefits/Costs
Software Size	10,000
Total Life Cycle Cost Hours (Testing)	45,100
Old Productivity (Testing)	0.22
Total Life Cycle Cost (Inspection)	17,425
New Productivity (Inspection)	0.57
Productivity Difference (Testing/Inspection)	0.39
Special Costs (Inspection)	$82,073
Breakeven Point (Inspection)	$133,751
Breakeven Point After Project Start (Inspection)	129 Hours

$82,073 by one less the productivity difference of 0.39. The breakeven point of using the Software Inspection Process to help produce 10,000 lines of code is $133,751.

Finally, let's put the breakeven point of the Software Inspection Process into proper perspective. Subtract the special costs of $82,073 from the breakeven point of $133,751, and divide the results by 400. (Divide by 100, which converts dollars into hours, and then divide by 4, which converts staff hours into elapsed or calendar time). This final manipulation tells us that the special costs of $82,073 will be recovered in 129 hours after project start. This is less than one calendar month.

18.2   PERSONAL SOFTWARE PROCESS[SM]

Let's use our total life cycle cost model to determine the cost of developing 10,000 lines of code using software testing. The formula is software size multiplied by 10.51, less the test hours times nine. Our total life cycle cost for using software testing alone is 45,100 hours.

Let's use our productivity model to determine the old productivity of using testing. The formula is software size divided by the total life cycle costs of testing. Divide 10,000 by 45,100, and the old productivity of testing is 0.22.

Let's determine the total life cycle cost of developing 10,000 lines of code using the Personal Software Process[SM]. The formula is software size divided by 25. Our total life cycle cost for using the Personal Software Process[SM] is 400 hours.

Let's use our productivity model to determine the new productivity of using the Personal Software Process[SM]. The formula is software size divided by the total life cycle costs of the Personal Software Process[SM]. Divide 10,000 by 400, and the new productivity of the Personal Software Process[SM] is 25.00.

Let's determine the difference between the old productivity of testing and the new productivity of the Personal Software Process[SM]. The formula is old productivity of software testing divided by new productivity of the Personal Software Process[SM]. Divide 0.22 by 25.00. The difference between the old productivity of testing and the new productivity of the Personal Software Process[SM] is 0.01.

The special, new, or additional costs that are required to introduce the Personal Software Process[SM] consist of only the training cost. The training cost to use the Personal Software Process[SM] to help produce 10,000 lines of code is $105,600. Table 33 illustrates the breakeven point of the Personal Software Process[SM].

Table 33 Breakeven Point of Personal Software Process^{SM}

SPI Method	Benefits/Costs
Software Size	10,000
Total Life Cycle Cost Hours (Testing)	45,100
Old Productivity (Testing)	0.22
Total Life Cycle Cost (PSP^{SM})	400
New Productivity (PSP^{SM})	25.00
Productivity Difference (Testing/PSP^{SM})	0.01
Special Costs (PSP^{SM})	$105,600
Breakeven Point (PSP^{SM})	$106,545
Breakeven Point After Project Start (PSP^{SM})	2 Hours

Now we are ready to determine the breakeven point of using the Personal Software Process^{SM} to help produce 10,000 lines of code. Divide the special costs of $105,600 by one less the productivity difference of 0.01. The breakeven point of using the Personal Software Process^{SM} to produce 10,000 lines of code is $106,545.

Finally, let's put the breakeven point of the Personal Software Process^{SM} into proper perspective. Subtract the special costs of $105,600 from the breakeven point of $106,545, and divide the results by 400. (First divide by 100, which converts dollars into hours, and then divide by 4, which converts staff hours into elapsed or calendar time). This final manipulation tells us that the special costs of $105,600 will be recovered in two hours after project start. This is less than one day.

18.3 TEAM SOFTWARE PROCESS^{SM}

Let's use our total life cycle cost model to determine the cost of developing 10,000 lines of code using software testing. The formula is software size multiplied by 10.51, less the test hours times nine. Our total life cycle cost for using software testing alone is 45,100 hours.

Let's use our productivity model to determine the old productivity of using testing. The formula is software size divided by the total life cycle costs of testing. Divide 10,000 by 45,100, and the old productivity of testing is 0.22.

Let's determine the total life cycle cost of developing 10,000 lines of code using the Team Software Process^{SM}. The formula is software size divided by 5.9347. Our total life cycle cost for using the Team Software Process^{SM} is 1,685 hours.

Let's use our productivity model to determine the new productivity of using

Table 34   Breakeven Point of Team Software Process[SM]

SPI Method	Benefits/Costs
Software Size	10,000
Total Life Cycle Cost Hours (Testing)	45,100
Old Productivity (Testing)	0.22
Total Life Cycle Cost (TSP[SM])	1,685
New Productivity (TSP[SM])	5.93
Productivity Difference (Testing/TSP[SM])	0.04
Special Costs (TSP[SM])	$148,400
Breakeven Point (TSP[SM])	$154,160
Breakeven Point After Project Start (TSP[SM])	14 Hours

the Team Software Process[SM]. The formula is software size divided by the total life cycle costs of the Team Software Process[SM]. Divide 10,000 by 1,685, and the new productivity of the Team Software Process[SM] is 5.93.

Let's determine the difference between the old productivity of testing and the new productivity of the Team Software Process[SM]. The formula is old productivity of software testing divided by new productivity of the Team Software Process[SM]. Divide 0.22 by 5.93. The difference between the old productivity of software testing and the new productivity of the Team Software Process[SM] is 0.04.

The special, new, or additional costs that are required to introduce the Team Software Process[SM] consist of only the training cost. The training cost to use the Team Software Process[SM] to help produce 10,000 lines of code is $148,400. Table 34 illustrates the breakeven point of the Team Software Process[SM].

Now we're ready to determine the breakeven point of using the Team Software Process[SM] to help produce 10,000 lines of code. Divide the special costs of $148,400 by one less the productivity difference of 0.04. The breakeven point of using Team Software Process[SM] to help produce 10,000 lines of code is $154,160.

Finally, let's put the breakeven point of the Team Software Process[SM] into proper perspective. Subtract the special costs of $148,400 from the breakeven point of $154,160, and divide the results by 400. (First divide by 100, which converts dollars into hours, and then divide by 4, which converts staff hours into elapsed or calendar time). This final manipulation tells us that the special costs of $148,400 will be recovered in 14 hours after project start. This is less than two days.

The breakeven point of using the Team Software Process[SM] can be much farther out into the future. There are half a dozen or more ancillary training courses that drive the costs up much higher.

18.4 SOFTWARE CAPABILITY MATURITY MODEL®

Let's use our total life cycle cost model to determine the cost of developing 10,000 lines of code using software testing. The formula is software size multiplied by 10.51, less the test hours times nine. Our total life cycle cost for using software testing alone is 45,100 hours.

Let's use our productivity model to determine the old productivity of using testing. The formula is software size divided by the total life cycle costs of testing. Divide 10,000 by 45,100, and the old productivity of testing is 0.22.

Let's determine the total life cycle cost of developing 10,000 lines of code using the Software Capability Maturity Model®. The formula is software size multiplied by 10.2544, less the inspection hours times 99 and less the test hours times 9. (0.2544 is 50% of 0.5088, which is due to a 100% productivity increase associated with Level 3 compliance.) Our total life cycle cost for using the Software Capability Maturity Model® is 14,869 hours.

Let's use our productivity model to determine the new productivity of using the Software Capability Maturity Model®. The formula is software size divided by the total life cycle costs of the Software Capability Maturity Model®. Divide 10,000 by 14,869, and the new productivity of the Software Capability Maturity Model® is 0.67.

Let's determine the difference between the productivity of testing and the productivity of the Software Capability Maturity Model®. The formula is old productivity of software testing divided by new productivity of the Software Capability Maturity Model®. Divide 0.22 by 0.67. The difference between the productivity of testing and the new productivity of the Software Capability Maturity Model® is 0.33.

The special, new, or additional costs that are required consist of process, product, preparation, assessment, and inspection costs. The special costs that are necessary to help produce 10,000 lines of code are $56,100, $117,600, $36,800, $30,100, and $70,833, respectively. This totals $311,433 to introduce the Software Capability Maturity Model® as a SPI method. Table 35 illustrates the breakeven point of the Software Capability Maturity Model®.

Now we are ready to determine the breakeven point of using the Software Capability Maturity Model® to produce 10,000 lines of code. Divide the special costs of $311,433 by one less the productivity difference of 0.33. The breakeven point of using the Software Capability Maturity Model® is $464,616.

Finally, let's put the breakeven point of the Software Capability Maturity Model® into proper perspective. Subtract the special costs of $311,433 from the breakeven point of $464,616, and divide the results by 400. (First divide by 100, which converts dollars into hours, and then divide by 4, which converts staff

Table 35   Breakeven Point of Software Capability Maturity Model®

SPI Method	Benefits/Costs
Software Size	10,000
Total Life Cycle Cost Hours (Testing)	45,100
Old Productivity (Testing)	0.22
Total Life Cycle Cost (SW-CMM®)	14,869
New Productivity (SW-CMM®)	0.67
Productivity Difference (Testing/SW-CMM®)	0.33
Special Costs (SW-CMM®)	$311,433
Breakeven Point (SW-CMM®)	$464,616
Breakeven Point After Project Start (SW-CMM®)	383 Hours

hours into elapsed or calendar time). This final manipulation tells us that the special costs of $311,433 will be recovered in 383 hours after project start. This is less than three months.

18.5 ISO 9001

Let's use our total life cycle cost model to determine the cost of developing 10,000 lines of code using testing. The formula is software size divided by 10.51, less the test hours times nine. Our total life cycle cost for using software testing alone is 45,100 hours.

Let's use our productivity model to determine the old productivity of using testing. The formula is software size divided by the total life cycle costs of testing. Divide 10,000 by 45,100, and the old productivity of testing is 0.22.

Let's determine the total life cycle cost of analyzing, designing, and developing 10,000 lines of code using ISO 9001. The formula is software size multiplied by 10.442656, less the test hours times nine. (0.442656 is 87% of 0.5088, which is due to a 13% productivity increase associated with using ISO 9001.) Our total life cycle cost for using ISO 9001 is 44,397 hours. However, there is also a 15% increase in software quality due to using ISO 9001. This lowers our software maintenance hours by 4,995. So, our adjusted total life cycle cost for using ISO 9001 is 39,402 hours.

Let's use our productivity model to determine the new productivity of using ISO 9001. The formula is software size divided by the total life cycle costs of ISO 9001. Divide 10,000 by 39,402, and the new productivity of ISO 9001 is 0.25.

Let's determine the difference between the old productivity of software testing and the new productivity of ISO 9001. The formula is old productivity

Table 36   Breakeven Point of ISO 9001

SPI Method	Benefits/Costs
Software Size	10,000
Total Life Cycle Cost Hours (Testing)	45,100
Old Productivity (Testing)	0.22
Total Life Cycle Cost (ISO 9001)	39,402
New Productivity (ISO 9001)	0.25
Productivity Difference (Testing/ISO 9001)	0.87
Special Costs (ISO 9001)	$173,000
Breakeven Point (ISO 9001)	$1,369,206
Breakeven Point After Project Start (ISO 9001)	2,991 Hours

of software testing divided by new productivity of ISO 9001. Divide 0.22 by 0.25. The difference between the old productivity of software testing and the new productivity of ISO 9001 is 0.87.

The special, new, or additional costs that are required to use ISO 9001 consist of process, product, preparation, and audit costs. The specials costs that are necessary to produce 10,000 lines of code are $54,600, $56,000, $26,400, and $36,000, respectively. This totals $173,000 to introduce ISO 9001 as a SPI method. Table 36 illustrates the breakeven point of ISO 9001.

Now we are ready to determine the breakeven point of using ISO 9001 to help produce 10,000 lines of code. Divide the special costs of $173,000 by one less the productivity difference of 0.87. The breakeven point of using ISO 9001 to help produce 10,000 lines of code is $1,369,206.

Finally, let's put the breakeven point of ISO 9001 into proper perspective. Subtract the special costs of $173,000 from the breakeven point of $1,369,206, and divide the results by 400. (First divide by 100, which converts dollars into hours, and then divide by 4, which converts staff hours into elapsed or calendar time). This final manipulation tells us that the special costs of $173,000 will be recovered in 2,991 hours after project start. This is 1.5 years.

18.6 CAPABILITY MATURITY MODEL INTEGRATION®

Let's use our total life cycle cost model to determine the cost of developing 10,000 lines of code using testing. The formula is software size multiplied by 10.51, less the test hours times nine. Our total life cycle cost for using software testing alone is 45,100 hours.

Let's use our productivity model to determine the old productivity of using testing. The formula is software size divided by the total life cycle costs of testing. Divide 10,000 by 45,100, and the old productivity of testing is 0.22.

Let's determine the total life cycle cost of developing 10,000 lines of code using Capability Maturity Model Integration®. The formula is software size multiplied by 10.2544, less the inspection hours times 99 and less the test hours times 9. (0.2544 is 50% of 0.5088, which is due to a 100% productivity increase associated with Level 3 compliance.) Our total life cycle cost for using Capability Maturity Model Integration® is 14,869 hours.

Let's use our productivity model to determine the new productivity of using Capability Maturity Model Integration®. The formula is software size divided by the total life cycle costs of Capability Maturity Model Integration®. Divide 10,000 by 14,869, and the new productivity of Capability Maturity Model Integration® is 0.67.

Let's determine the difference between the productivity of testing and the new productivity of Capability Maturity Model Integration®. The formula is old productivity of software testing divided by new productivity of Capability Maturity Model Integration®. Divide 0.22 by 0.67. The difference between the old productivity and the new productivity of Capability Maturity Model Integration® is 0.33.

The special, new, or additional costs that are required consist of process, product, preparation, assessment, and inspection costs. The special costs to use Capability Maturity Model Integration® are $541,300, $400,400, $48,000, $47,700, and $70,833, respectively. This totals $1,108,233 to introduce Capability Maturity Model Integration® as a SPI method. Table 37 illustrates the breakeven point of Capability Maturity Model Integration®.

Now we are ready to determine the breakeven point of Capability Maturity Model Integration® to produce 10,000 lines of code. Divide the special costs of $1,108,233 by one less the productivity difference of 0.33. The breakeven point of using Capability Maturity Model Integration® to help produce 10,000 lines of code is $1,653,332.

Table 37   Breakeven Point of Capability Maturity Model Integration®

SPI Method	Benefits/Costs
Software Size	10,000
Total Life Cycle Cost Hours (Testing)	45,100
Old Productivity (Testing)	0.22
Total Life Cycle Cost (CMMI®)	14,869
New Productivity (CMMI®)	0.67
Productivity Difference (Testing/CMMI®)	0.33
Special Costs (CMMI®)	$1,108,233
Breakeven Point (CMMI®)	$1,653,332
Breakeven Point After Project Start (CMMI®)	1,363 Hours

Finally, let's put the breakeven point of Capability Maturity Model Integration® into proper perspective. Subtract the special costs of $1,108,233 from the breakeven point of $1,653,332, and divide the results by 400. (First divide by 100, which converts dollars into hours, and then divide by 4, which converts staff hours into elapsed or calendar time). This final manipulation tells us that the special costs of $1,108,233 will be recovered in 1,363 hours after project start. This is less than eight months.

19

ANALYSIS OF RETURN ON INVESTMENT

Analysis of return on investment (ROI) involves using a set, group, or portfolio of metrics and models to count, quantify, and evaluate software process improvement (SPI) economics. Analysis of ROI involves much more than the use or exploitation of but a single metric or model, cost or benefit, or ROI equation. Instead, analysis of ROI involves a wide, broad, and expansive suite of metrics and models. Using several metrics and models helps quantify the economic consequences of a SPI method. There are many cost, benefit, and ROI metrics, models, and values to consider when quantifying the economics of SPI.

Some of the fundamental metrics and models to consider include complete costs, total life cycle costs, and special costs. Important metrics are benefits, benefit/cost ratio (B/CR), adjusted benefits, ROI, net present value (NPV) benefits, NPV B/CR, NPV adjusted benefits, and NPV ROI. Productivity, productivity difference, breakeven point, and breakeven point after project start cannot be ignored. The point is that analysis of ROI consists of evaluating many metrics, models, and measurements, not just one. These models are readily identifiable, simple, and powerful indicators of SPI economics.

For the sake of simplicity, we will focus only on the most basic metrics, models, and measurements for analyzing ROI. These include costs, benefits, B/CR, ROI, NPV, and breakeven point. We will do this to strike a balance between simplicity and objectivity, without introducing unnecessary complexity.

19.1 ANALYSIS OF COSTS

The special, new, or additional costs required use the Software Inspection Process to produce 10,000 lines of code are $82,073. This is obtained by adding the training and inspection costs of $11,240 and $70,833.

The special, new, or additional costs required use the Personal Software Process[SM] to produce 10,000 lines of code are $105,600. This is obtained by using only the training cost of $105,600.

The special, new, or additional costs required use the Team Software Process[SM] to produce 10,000 lines of code are $148,400. This is obtained by using only the training cost of $148,400.

The special, new, or additional costs required to use the Software Capability Maturity Model[®] to produce 10,000 lines are $311,433. This is obtained by adding the process, product, preparation, assessment, and inspection costs. The costs are $56,100, $117,600, $36,800, $30,100, and $70,833, respectively.

The special, new, or additional costs required use ISO 9001 to produce 10,000 lines of code are $173,000. This is obtained by adding the process, product, preparation, and audit costs. The costs are $54,600, $56,000, $26,400, and $36,000, respectively.

The special, new, or additional costs required to use Capability Maturity Model Integration[®] to produce 10,000 lines of code are $1,108,233. This is obtained by adding the process, product, preparation, assessment, and inspection costs. The costs are $541,300, $400,400, $48,000, $47,700, and $70,833, respectively. (The assessment costs are for one four-person software project.) Table 38 illustrates the analysis of costs.

The least expensive SPI method is the Software Inspection Process at $82,073. The most expensive SPI method is Capability Maturity Model Integration[®] at $1,108,233. Cost per person ranges from $20,518 for the Software Inspection Process to $277,058 for Capability Maturity Model Integration[®].

The Software Inspection Process, Personal Software Process[SM], Team Soft-

Table 38 Analysis of Costs

SPI Method	Cost	Cost/Person	Normalized
Inspection	$82,073	$20,518	1.00
Personal Software Process[SM]	$105,600	$26,400	0.98
Team Software Process[SM]	$148,400	$37,100	0.94
Software Capability Maturity Model[®]	$311,433	$77,858	0.79
ISO 9001	$173,000	$43,250	0.92
Capability Maturity Model Integration[®]	$1,108,233	$277,058	0.07

ware Process^SM, and ISO 9001 have the lowest special costs. This is on a normalized scale. Capability Maturity Model Integration® has the highest special cost on a normalized scale.

19.2 ANALYSIS OF BENEFITS

The benefits of using the Software Inspection Process to help produce 10,000 lines of code are $2,767,464. This is obtained by subtracting $1,742,533 in new total life cycle costs from $4,509,997 in old total life cycle costs.

The benefits of using the Personal Software Process^SM to help produce 10,000 lines of code are $4,469,997. This is obtained by subtracting $40,000 in new total life cycle costs from $4,509,997 in old total life cycle costs.

The benefits of using the Team Software Process^SM to help produce 10,000 lines of code are $4,341,496. This is obtained by subtracting $168,501 in new total life cycle costs from $4,509,997 in old total life cycle costs.

The benefits of using the Software Capability Maturity Model® to help produce 10,000 lines of code are $3,023,064. This is obtained by subtracting $1,486,933 in new total life cycle costs from $4,509,997 in old total life cycle costs.

The benefits of using ISO 9001 to help produce 10,000 lines of code are $569,841. This is obtained by subtracting $3,940,156 in new total life cycle costs from $4,509,997 in old total life cycle costs.

The benefits of using Capability Maturity Model Integration® to help produce 10,000 lines of code are $3,023,064. This is obtained by subtracting $1,486,933 in new total life cycle costs from $4,509,997 in old total life cycle costs. Table 39 illustrates the analysis of benefits.

The most beneficial SPI method is the Personal Software Process^SM at $4,469,997. The least beneficial SPI method is ISO 9001 at $569,841. Benefit per person ranges from $142,460 for ISO 9001 to $1,117,499 for the Personal Software Process^SM.

Table 39   Analysis of Benefits

SPI Method	Benefit	Benefit/Person	Normalized
Inspection	$2,767,464	$691,866	0.62
Personal Software Process^SM	$4,469,997	$1,117,499	1.00
Team Software Process^SM	$4,341,496	$1,085,374	0.97
Software Capability Maturity Model®	$3,023,064	$755,766	0.68
ISO 9001	$569,841	$142,460	0.13
Capability Maturity Model Integration®	$3,023,064	$755,766	0.68

On a normalized scale, the Personal Software Process^{SM} and Team Software Process^{SM} have the highest benefits. ISO 9001 has the lowest benefits on a normalized scale.

19.3 ANALYSIS OF BENEFIT/COST RATIO

The B/CR of the Software Inspection Process to help produce 10,000 lines of code is 34:1. This is obtained by dividing the benefits of $2,767,464 by the costs of $82,073 for the Software Inspection Process.

The B/CR of using the Personal Software Process^{SM} to help produce 10,000 lines of code is 42:1. This is obtained by dividing the benefits of $4,469,997 by the costs of $105,600 for the Personal Software Process^{SM}.

The B/CR of using the Team Software Process^{SM} to help produce 10,000 lines of code is 29:1. This is obtained by dividing the benefits of $4,341,496 by the costs of $148,400 for the Team Software Process^{SM}.

The B/CR of using the Software Capability Maturity Model® to help produce 10,000 lines of code is 10:1. This is obtained by dividing the benefits of $3,023,064 by the costs of $311,433 for the Software Capability Maturity Model®.

The B/CR of using ISO 9001 to help produce 10,000 lines of code is 3:1. This is obtained by dividing the benefits of $569,841 by the costs of $173,000 for ISO 9001.

The B/CR of using Capability Maturity Model Integration® to help produce 10,000 lines of code is 3:1. This is obtained by dividing the benefits of $3,023,064 by the costs of $1,108,233 for Capability Maturity Model Integration®. Table 40 illustrates the analysis of B/CR.

The SPI method with the highest B/CR is the Personal Software Process^{SM} at 42:1. The SPI methods with the lowest B/CR are Capability Maturity Model Integration® and ISO 9001 at 3:1. All of the SPI methods had a B/CR above 1:1. The Personal Software Process^{SM}, Software Inspection Process, and Team Software Process^{SM} have a B/CR of 42:1, 34:1, and 29:1, respectively.

Table 40   Analysis of Benefit/Cost Ratio

SPI Method	B/CR	Normalized
Inspection	34:1	0.80
Personal Software Process^{SM}	42:1	1.00
Team Software Process^{SM}	29:1	0.69
Software Capability Maturity Model®	10:1	0.23
ISO 9001	3:1	0.08
Capability Maturity Model Integration®	3:1	0.06

On a normalized scale, the Personal Software Process℠ has the highest B/CR. ISO 9001 and Capability Maturity Model Integration® have the lowest B/CR on a normalized scale.

A low B/CR may indicate high costs or low benefits or a combination of the two. A high B/CR may indicate low costs and high benefits or very high benefits and high costs.

19.4 ANALYSIS OF RETURN ON INVESTMENT

The ROI of using the Software Inspection Process to help produce 10,000 lines of code is 3,272%. This is obtained by dividing the adjusted benefits of $2,685,391 by the costs of $82,073 and multiplying the result by 100%.

The ROI of using the Personal Software Process℠ to help produce 10,000 lines of code is 4,133%. This is obtained by dividing the adjusted benefits of $4,364,397 by the costs of $105,600 and multiplying the result by 100%.

The ROI of using the Team Software Process℠ to help produce 10,000 lines of code is 2,826%. This is obtained by dividing the adjusted benefits of $4,193,096 by the costs of $148,400 and multiplying the result by 100%.

The ROI of using the Software Capability Maturity Model® to help produce 10,000 lines of code is 871%. This is obtained by dividing the adjusted benefits of $2,711,631 by the costs of $311,433 and multiplying the result by 100%.

The ROI of using ISO 9001 to produce 10,000 lines of code is 229%. This is obtained by dividing the adjusted benefits of $396,841 by the costs of $173,000 and multiplying the result by 100%.

The ROI of using Capability Maturity Model Integration® to help produce 10,000 lines of code is 173%. This is obtained by dividing the adjusted benefits of $1,914,831 by the costs of $1,108,233 and multiplying the result by 100%. (This assumes that the benefits are no greater than the Software Capability Maturity Model®.) Table 41 illustrates the analysis of ROI.

Table 41   Analysis of Return on Investment

SPI Method	ROI	Normalized
Inspection	3,272%	0.79
Personal Software Process℠	4,133%	1.00
Team Software Process℠	2,826%	0.68
Software Capability Maturity Model®	871%	0.21
ISO 9001	229%	0.06
Capability Maturity Model Integration®	173%	0.04

The SPI method with the highest ROI is the Personal Software Process^{SM} at 4,133%. The SPI method with the lowest ROI is Capability Maturity Model Integration® at 173%. All of the SPI methods had an ROI above 100%, topping out with the Personal Software Process^{SM}, Software Inspection Process, and Team Software Process^{SM} at 4,133, 3,272, and 2,826%, respectively.

On a normalized scale, the Personal Software Process^{SM} has the highest ROI. ISO 9001 and Capability Maturity Model Integration® have the lowest ROI on a normalized scale.

19.5 ANALYSIS OF NET PRESENT VALUE

The ROI of using the Software Inspection Process to produce 10,000 lines of code is 2,542% using NPV. This is obtained by dividing the benefits of $2,767,464 by the devaluation rate of 1.27628156. The special costs of $82,073 are subtracted, and the adjusted NPV benefits of $2,086,307 are divided by the special costs of $82,073. The result is multiplied by 100%.

The ROI of using the Personal Software Process^{SM} to help produce 10,000 lines of code is 3,217% using NPV. This is obtained by dividing the benefits of $4,469,997 by the devaluation rate of 1.27628156. The special costs of $105,600 are subtracted. The adjusted NPV benefits of $3,396,760 are divided by the special costs of $105,600. The result is multiplied by 100%.

The ROI of using the Team Software Process^{SM} to help produce 10,000 lines of code is 2,192% using NPV. This is obtained by dividing the benefits of $4,341,496 by the devaluation rate of 1.27628156. The special costs of $148,400 are subtracted. The adjusted NPV benefits of $3,253,276 are divided by the special costs of $148,400. The result is multiplied by 100%.

The ROI of using the Software Capability Maturity Model® to help produce 10,000 lines of code is 661% using NPV. This is obtained by dividing the benefits of $3,023,064 by the devaluation rate of 1.27628156. The special costs of $311,433 are subtracted. The adjusted NPV benefits of $2,057,216 are divided by the special costs of $311,433. The result is multiplied by 100%.

The ROI of using ISO 9001 to help produce 10,000 lines of code is 158% using NPV. This is obtained by dividing the benefits of $569,841 by the devaluation rate of 1.27628156. The special costs of $173,000 are subtracted. The adjusted NPV benefits of $273,485 are divided by the special costs of $173,000. The result is multiplied by 100%.

The ROI of using Capability Maturity Model Integration® to help produce 10,000 lines of code is 114% using NPV. This is obtained by dividing the benefits of $3,023,064 by the devaluation rate of 1.27628156. The special costs of $1,108,233 are subtracted. The adjusted NPV benefits of $1,260,416 are

Table 42   Analysis of Net Present Value

SPI Method	NPV	Normalized
Inspection	2,542%	0.79
Personal Software Process[SM]	3,217%	1.00
Team Software Process[SM]	2,192%	0.68
Software Capability Maturity Model®	661%	0.21
ISO 9001	158%	0.05
Capability Maturity Model Integration®	114%	0.04

divided by the special costs of $1,108,233. The result is multiplied by 100%. Table 42 illustrates the analysis of NPV.

The SPI method with the highest NPV is the Personal Software Process[SM] at 3,217%. The SPI method with the lowest NPV is Capability Maturity Model Integration® at 114%. All of the SPI methods have an NPV above 100%. The Personal Software Process[SM], Software Inspection Process, and Team Software Process[SM] have an NPV of 3,217, 2,542, and 2,192%, respectively. On a normalized scale, the Personal Software Process[SM] has the highest NPV. ISO 9001 and Capability Maturity Model Integration® have the lowest NPV on a normalized scale.

19.6 ANALYSIS OF BREAKEVEN POINT

The breakeven point of using the Software Inspection Process to help produce 10,000 lines of code is $133,751. This is obtained by dividing the special costs of $82,073 by one less the total life cycle cost of 17,425 hours. The result is divided by 45,100 hours.

The breakeven point of using the Personal Software Process[SM] to help produce 10,000 lines of code is $106,545. This is obtained by dividing the special costs of $105,600 by one less the total life cycle cost of 400 hours. The result is divided by 45,100 hours.

The breakeven point of using the Team Software Process[SM] to help produce 10,000 lines of code is $154,160. This is obtained by dividing the special costs of $148,400 by one less the total life cycle cost of 1,685 hours. The result is divided by 45,100 hours.

The breakeven point of using the Software Capability Maturity Model® is $464,616. This is obtained by dividing the special costs of $311,433 by one less the total life cycle cost of 14,869 hours. The result is divided by 45,100 hours.

The breakeven point of using ISO 9001 to help produce 10,000 lines of code is $1,369,206. This is obtained by dividing the special costs of $173,000 by one

Table 43 Analysis of Breakeven Point

SPI Method	Breakeven Point	Normalized
Inspection	$133,751	0.98
Personal Software Process[SM]	$106,545	1.00
Team Software Process[SM]	$154,160	0.97
Software Capability Maturity Model®	$464,616	0.78
ISO 9001	$1,369,206	0.24
Capability Maturity Model Integration®	$1,653,332	0.06

less the total life cycle cost of 39,402 hours. The result is divided by 45,100 hours.

The breakeven point of using Capability Maturity Model Integration® to help produce 10,000 lines of code is $1,653,332. This is obtained by dividing the special costs of $1,108,233 by one less the total life cycle cost of 14,869 hours. The result is divided by 45,100 hours. Table 43 illustrates the analysis of breakeven point.

The SPI method with the lowest breakeven point is the Personal Software Process[SM] at $106,545. The SPI method with the highest breakeven point is Capability Maturity Model Integration® at $1,653,332. The Personal Software Process[SM], Software Inspection Process, and Team Software Process[SM] have the lowest breakeven points. They are $106,545, $133,751, and $154,160, respectively.

On a normalized scale, the Personal Software Process[SM] has the lowest breakeven point. The Software Inspection Process and Team Software Process[SM] have low breakeven points too. Capability Maturity Model Integration® has the highest breakeven point on a normalized scale.

20

OPTIMIZING RETURN ON INVESTMENT

Optimizing return on investment (ROI) involves creating a vision, strategy, and process for maximizing the amount of money that is gained from software process improvement (SPI). In other words, it is best to maximize the amount of money that is returned or earned above the resources that are spent on SPI. Optimizing ROI essentially means choosing, designing, or using a SPI method with the largest number of benefits. Optimizing ROI means something for large, nonprofit organizations as well. It involves maximizing the value of their investments and expenditures.

There are two fundamental scenarios to consider when optimizing ROI. The first is the commercial operation or firm that wishes to make a profit. In this scenario, the commercial firm wishes to invest in a SPI method. However, the firm actually wants to recoup its investment in the SPI method. That is what SPI methods are all about. Commercial firms do not invest in SPI methods for the sake of SPI. Commercial firms invest in SPI methods to make more money than they are currently making. SPI is not a philosophical exercise or an exercise in philanthropy for commercial software firms. For the commercial firm, SPI is a means to fix a problem, optimize the production line, and produce more units at a lower price. SPI is used by commercial firms to increase the yield of the production line. You may be in the wrong business if you are part of a commercial firm and you are not trying to increase its profitability and performance.

Optimizing ROI is a tool not only for the profit-driven commercial firm. Optimizing ROI is just as well suited for a large, nonprofit organization. Why?

Isn't the job of a large, nonprofit organization to spend money, not make money? The answer is often a resounding "yes." If your job is to spend money, then it is your job to optimize the value of your investments. Oftentimes, large, nonprofit organizations are given budgets of $10 million, $100 million, or even $1 billion to spend.

Why not get the greatest number of products and services for every dollar spent? Large, nonprofit organizations are notorious for spending $10 or even $100 for every single dollar of products and services. Why not increase the value of the nonprofit dollar beyond a single penny or dime? Large, nonprofit organizations can increase their spending power significantly by optimizing the ROI of SPI. They can extend the value of their budgets by using basic ROI tools to identify, quantify, evaluate, and choose wise investments. Instead of buying one product or service this year, why not buy 10, 100, or 1,000 products or services by optimizing ROI?

20.1 LOW COSTS

Low cost means selecting SPI methods that are not very expensive to implement. Low cost means selecting inexpensive SPI methods and reserving investment capital for other opportunities. Low cost means buying the largest number of SPI methods possible for the amount of money that it is possible to spend.

The lowest priced SPI method examined here is the Software Inspection Process at $20,518 a person. The Personal Software Process^{SM} is a close second at $26,400 a person, and it offers many more helpful tools and techniques. The highest priced SPI method examined here is Capability Maturity Model Integration® at $277,058 per person. The Software Capability Maturity Model® is not far behind at a cost of $77,858 a person.

All of these numbers far exceed the amount of money that most organizations are willing or even able to invest in SPI. Only the largest organizations can afford the Software Capability Maturity Model® or Capability Maturity Model Integration®. The smaller organizations could never afford even the Software Inspection Process or Personal Software Process^{SM}. The risk of investing in expensive SPI methods is too great, and the probability of being successful with them is very low. ROI can be used as a method for quantifying the value of your investments in SPI methods. It makes sense to identify methods that will earn large profits or maximize your spending dollars versus using SPI methods that do not have a high ROI. Why invest in SPI methods that will drain your budgets or SPI methods that will waste your spending dollars?

20.2 HIGH BENEFITS

High benefits means selecting SPI methods with the largest number of benefits. High benefits means wading through the plethora of SPI methods that are available and discarding SPI methods with low ROI. Instead, select SPI methods that yield the maximum number of benefits. High benefits involves choosing great value. For profit-driven commercial firms, this is intuitively obvious. The basic goal and objective of the commercial firm are to make money, make more money, and then make even more money. Commercial firms intuitively use ROI tools to select, use, and apply SPI methods that yield the greatest number of benefits.

However, even the large, nonprofit firm is interested in using SPI methods with the largest possible ROI. The large, nonprofit organization uses SPI methods with high ROI in order to optimize its SPI budget. Doing so reduces its SPI budget to a manageable level, and the organization receives the greatest number of products and services per fiscal year. Benevolent donors bestow a large number of resources upon large, nonprofit organizations. They must satisfy their donors by providing the highest possible quality products and services at the lowest possible cost. Yes, large, nonprofit organizations are interested in the highest number of benefits and largest ROI too.

However, it is important not to evaluate benefits independent of costs. For instance, the Personal Software Process^{SM} offers the highest number of benefits at $1,117,499 per person, but these benefits come at a high price of $26,400 per person. Consider the benefits of Capability Maturity Model Integration®, which amount to $3,023,064. However, Capability Maturity Model Integration® comes at a steep price of $277,058 per person. High benefits with high costs are simply unattainable for the average commercial firm or large, nonprofit organization. Identify and apply SPI methods with large benefits, but not at the expense of the future of the organization.

SPI is funded by an organization's revenues or profits, whether commercial or nonprofit. This money can go to shareholders, bonuses, capital improvements, or it can even be donated to charities. Now that executives are getting used to the idea of SPI, monies for SPI are easier to obtain than ever before. We have the basic responsibility to maximize the value of our expenditures, make more money, and increase our revenues.

20.3 GOOD BENEFIT/COST RATIO

A good benefit/cost ratio (B/CR) consists of comparing the benefits of a SPI method to its cost. In other words, a good B/CR begins to take into consideration some of the ideas that have been discussed here. A good B/CR is a ratio of benefits to cost for a particular SPI method. For instance, a B/CR of 1:1 means that for every dollar a SPI method costs, one dollar is returned. That's pretty good. Look for SPI methods with a good B/CR.

What does a good B/CR mean? Is 0.1:1, 0.5:1, or 0.9:1 a good B/CR? Perhaps a return of 10, 50, or 90 cents on the dollar is a good B/CR. However, why use a SPI method with a B/CR in single digits? There are SPI methods with a double- and even triple-digit B/CR. It is the fundamental objective of commercial firms to look for a good B/CR, and it is the fundamental responsibility of large, nonprofit organizations to use SPI methods with a very good B/CR.

Attempt to achieve a high B/CR by design. Estimate the costs of using the various SPI methods. Estimate their benefits, and then calculate the simple ratio of benefits to costs. It is an intuitive model that anyone can use. Also, begin to gravitate or steward your SPI resources and investments toward SPI methods with at least a double-digit B/CR. Remember that a promising B/CR may never justify SPI methods with high costs for commercial or nonprofit organizations. This holds true for organizations of any type, size, or kind.

Don't believe the myth that economic analysis is only for high-maturity organizations. Use of economic analysis is why high-maturity organizations have reached that plateau — and ignorance of economic analysis is why low-maturity organizations stay low.

20.4 HIGH RETURN ON INVESTMENT

High ROI consists of identifying, evaluating, and selecting SPI methods with the greatest number of economic benefits. High ROI also involves choosing SPI methods at the least possible cost. ROI is a ratio of benefits to cost. However, ROI involves subtracting the costs from the benefits before declaring them as benefits. This subtraction validates the benefits and marginalizes SPI methods with high costs.

ROI is superior to the individual assessment of the costs, benefits, and B/CR of SPI methods. ROI no longer analyzes and evaluates the costs and benefits independently of one another. Instead, ROI treats costs and benefits as inseparable variables which must be considered together as a whole. Thus, costs and benefits are no longer evaluated in a vacuum, but are evaluated together along with their impacts on one another. For instance, a SPI method with high benefits and low cost has a high ROI. This SPI method is certainly worthy of consideration. On the other hand, a SPI method with low benefits and high costs has a low ROI. This SPI method is worthy of further analysis and justification.

Sometimes even ROI alone does not tell the whole story. For example, some SPI methods have admirable ROI values. The Personal Software Process[SM], Software Inspection Process, and Team Software Process[SM] have high ROI values. The Software Capability Maturity Model[®], ISO 9001, and Capability Maturity Model Integration[®] have high ROI values as well. The ROI values amount to 4,133, 3,272, 2,826, 871, 229, and 173%, respectively.

Let's take Capability Maturity Model Integration[®] as an example. Its ROI is 173%. This alone may be the only justification necessary to convince a software executive that it is the right SPI method to pursue. However, when you consider the costs of these SPI methods, they lose their attraction. Their costs are $26,400, $20,518, $37,100, $77,858, $43,250, and $277,058 per person, respectively. What piece of evidence would you show your software executive: an ROI of 173% or a cost per person of $277,058?

Think of ROI as more than just an objective ratio of benefits to costs that is considered in isolation. Think of ROI as an evaluation of multiple factors involving costs and benefits. At some point, the costs must be identified, counted, and validated. Use ROI as a tool, but do not ignore the other indicators of economic performance along the way, such as costs.

20.5 HIGH NET PRESENT VALUE

High net present value (NPV) is a way to select SPI methods whose benefits and ROI have been accurately portrayed in future economic terms. It is a simple technique to account for future economic inflation, inflated benefits, and inflated ROI. High NPV is a means to remove the hype from the benefits and remove the hype from the ROI of a SPI method. NPV is used to test the economic validity of a SPI method in terms software executives can believe.

For instance, an eager SPI analyst might proclaim that a SPI method will save a firm $1 million over the next 10 years. After NPV analysis, it turns out that the savings is not actually $1 million but merely $700,000. The cost of implementing the SPI method is $350,000, so the NPV is only 100%. It is best to qualify or validate your benefits and ROI using NPV. Do so before approaching your company's executives with your proposition for investment in one or more SPI methods.

For example, some SPI methods have high ROI values. These values remain high even if we assume an organization already has institutionalized software testing at world-class levels. In other words, the ROI would be even higher had we realistically assumed most organizations do not perform any testing at all. The ROI of the Personal Software Process[SM], Software Inspection Process, and Team Software Process[SM] is quite high. The ROI of the Software

Capability Maturity Model®, ISO 9001, and Capability Maturity Model Integration® is high too. The ROI values are 4,133, 3,272, 2,826, 871, 229, and 173%, respectively.

The first question your financial officer will ask is, "What's the NPV of these SPI methods?" You can astutely answer 3,217, 2,542, 2,192, 661, 158, and 114%. Notice that the NPV for these SPI methods is 28.49, 28.72, 28.89, 31.81, 45.11, and 51.92% lower than the gross ROI. Yet, all of the SPI methods continue to have an ROI above 100%. These are figures your financial officer is willing to consider. However, remember that even these NPV figures obscure the high costs of these SPI methods. Your chief executive officer will not ignore the budget you are requesting in isolation, based on ROI or NPV figures.

20.6 NEAR BREAKEVEN POINT

Near breakeven point means selecting a SPI method that will yield benefits in the shortest period of time. Near breakeven point means evaluating whether the benefits of a SPI method will come in the short, medium, or long term. Near breakeven point means gravitating toward SPI methods with a short breakeven point, and it means shying away from SPI methods with a long breakeven point.

We have all heard the same old rhetoric: SPI is a long journey. We must do SPI for the sake of doing SPI. It's not the outcome that matters, but the lessons we learn along the way. These philosophical arguments are okay for some people.

However, these arguments are meaningless to the profit-driven commercial firm. Commercial firms must repair the process now, increase the yields tomorrow, and draw a profit in the near term. These arguments also do nothing for large, nonprofit organizations. They are often charged with creating a five-year budget to effectively manage from fiscal year to fiscal year.

Large, nonprofit organizations, like profit-driven commercial firms, need to maximize the value of their investments. They must maximize the power of every spending dollar. They must responsibly purchase the largest number of products and services for their spending dollars.

Some may argue that the benefits, B/CR, ROI, and NPV are the most attractive features of the top-performing SPI methods. The top performers may seem like the Personal Software Process℠, Software Inspection Process, and Team Software Process℠, or the Software Capability Maturity Model®, ISO 9001, and Capability Maturity Model Integration® may seem like the top performers.

Their breakeven points are even more interesting, however. Their breakeven points are $106,545, $133,751, $154,160, $464,616, $1,369,206, and $1,653,332, respectively. These numbers begin to make sense only when we examine what they mean in practical terms. These SPI methods begin to yield their benefits within 2, 129, 14, 383, 2,991, 1,363 hours after project start.

The Personal Software Process^{SM}, Software Inspection Process, and Team Software Process^{SM} yield their benefits within a month of project start. Wouldn't your organization's executives like to know that? The Personal Software Process^{SM} and Team Software Process^{SM} begin to yield their benefits in less than two days.

The breakeven points of these methods are probably the most interesting results of performing ROI-related analyses. Why? Well, for many of us, SPI is merely a long and noble journey whose breakeven point lies far out into the distant future. It is commonly believed that only the most visionary commercial firms and large, nonprofit organizations embark on such SPI journeys.

It is clear from these ROI-related analyses that even small, fast-moving commercial firms and organizations can succeed with SPI. If well orchestrated, they may even do so in days.

21

FUTURE OF SOFTWARE PROCESS IMPROVEMENT

What is the future of software process improvement (SPI)? Which SPI methods boldly embrace the future? Is the future of SPI the Software Inspection Process, Personal Software Process^{SM}, and Team Software Process^{SM}? Is the future of SPI the Software Capability Maturity Model®, ISO 9001, or Capability Maturity Model Integration®? Does the return on investment (ROI) of SPI reveal the future of SPI? Do ROI values of 3,272, 4,133, 2,826, 871, 229, and 173% tell the future of SPI?

The future of SPI is embodied by SPI methods with low costs, high benefits, and good benefit/cost ratio. High ROI, high net present value, and near breakeven points are the characteristics of SPI methods that embrace the future of SPI. Indeed, some SPI methods score well on many of these criteria and some do not. The lesson is not to get caught up investing in an expensive SPI method. Rather, seek SPI methods that yield cost-effective benefits.

The most telltale indicator of the future of SPI is cost. The Software Inspection Process, Personal Software Process^{SM}, Team Software Process^{SM}, Software Capability Maturity Model®, ISO 9001, and Capability Maturity Model Integration® cost $20,518, $26,400, $37,100, $77,858, $43,250, and $277,058 per person. A small engineering firm with 100 software engineers has to pay $2,051,800 for the least expensive of these SPI methods. A medium-sized organization of 500 software engineers has to pay $13,200,000 for the SPI method with the highest benefits. A large, nonprofit organization of 1,500

213

software engineers has to pay $415,587,000 for the newest of these SPI methods.

It is safe to say that $2,051,800 is completely out of the question for a small software organization. For a medium-sized software organization, $13,200,000 is a nonstarter. For a large, nonprofit organization, $415,587,000 is simply out of the question. The marketplace is very resilient. Like a river flowing through a great valley, it follows the path of least resistance and flows gently around the obstacles, namely cost.

21.1 TRAININGLESS METHODS

SPI methods that require little or no training are the future of SPI. Two of our SPI methods, the Personal Software Process[SM] and Team Software Process[SM], cost $26,400 and $37,100 per person. The future of SPI is in methods that can be quickly grasped, utilized, and exploited to begin yielding benefits. The future of SPI is not in pouring tens of thousands of dollars into individuals. Most likely, they have already spent tens of thousands of dollars on education in order to get their jobs.

The future of SPI is in methods that any software engineer, in any domain and at any skill level, can immediately and intuitively grasp. This must occur without requiring tens or hundreds of thousands of dollars in training. The benefit of SPI methods that require little or no training is enjoyed not only by the software engineer. This is also good news for the commercial software firm as well as the large, nonprofit organization.

Do organizations need to spend millions of dollars hiring scientists and formulating expensive strategies? Must they spend tens of thousands of dollars training already highly qualified people in the latest SPI method? Or can software organizations focus on their business goals and objectives and minimize the concentration of profits on SPI? Can they rest easy knowing their software engineers are producing the best possible software at the least possible cost?

The answer is obvious. The marketplace is already gravitating toward SPI methods that do not require expensive training and implementation costs. In fact, it is these low-cost market leaders that represent the greatest threat to the leading cost-intensive SPI methods. However, just as the marketplace is resilient to the obstacle of cost, researchers are resilient to the forces of the marketplace. SPI researchers are already creating SPI methods that require little or no training, at little or no cost. ROI analysis can be used to objectively evaluate the alternatives and choose the most effective approach.

21.2 AUTOMATED WORKFLOW METHODS

The SPI methods of the future are largely automated workflow methods. This means that computers and software will automate and perform most of the software management and engineering tasks. Two of the SPI methods, the Personal Software Process[SM] and Team Software Process[SM], cost $26,400 and $37,100 per person to convince humans to perform sound software engineering. Automated workflow methods perform most of these tasks without the associated investment of $26,400 and $37,100 per person. Automated workflow methods effortlessly perform the tasks of estimation, planning, replanning, and analysis support. Design support, code generation, testing, verification, validation, and, most importantly, documentation are also performed by these tools. Documentation is a painstaking process that absolutely no one wants to perform. Most people don't have the slightest idea how to document their work, are bad at documentation, and do it inconsistently. The first question people ask about SPI is, "Can we hire technical writers to document our work?"

21.3 LOW-COST COMMERCIAL TOOLS

The greatest innovations always seem to come out of the blue. Low-cost commercial tools abound. They usually come from small software firms attempting to do the impossible. They often automate complex scientific tasks and algorithms and their authors give away their solutions for next to nothing.

The future of SPI is in low-cost commercial tools. Low-cost commercial tools are already emerging to automate complex software management and engineering tasks. They often automate the SPI methods themselves.

It is the fundamental responsibility of SPI analysts and executives to create a powerful vision for SPI. This vision must consist of garnering high benefits at the least possible cost, through the use of low-cost commercial tools. Don't forget to consider the power, flexibility, and role of low-cost automated tools in your ROI analysis. This holds true when you use ROI to evaluate the myriad of extremely expensive and manually intensive SPI methods.

Don't confuse extremely expensive tools with low-cost commercial tools. Expensive tools also abound. Expensive tools will drain your SPI budget faster than an expensive, manually intensive SPI method.

Automated static analyzers are a perfect example of low-cost commercial tools. They range in cost from a few hundred dollars to hundreds of thousands of dollars. Aim your resources at automated tools that cost hundreds or thousands of dollars, not hundreds of thousands of dollars. There are many to choose from and their population is growing rapidly.

Automated static analyzers embody the best techniques of the most expensive and manually intensive SPI methods. The question is whether to train all of your software engineers in the latest manually intensive SPI method at $37,100 per person or to buy an automated static analyzer for hundreds of dollars instead.

21.4 NONINVASIVE MEASUREMENT

The future of SPI is in noninvasive software measurement, modeling, prediction, tracking, and project replanning. Software measurement is a discipline that persistently eludes and evades the most qualified SPI analysts in industry.

Noninvasive software measurement alleviates this burden today. Noninvasive software measurement technologies produce software estimations and predict costs, quality, and reliability. They build software project plans, track project status, and replan software projects if necessary.

The World Wide Web is currently the best example of the ability of noninvasive measurement to overcome human weakness. Web hosting services collect millions of data points, report these statistics transparently, and predict future Web site performance.

The weakness of SPI methods that cost $26,400 and $37,100 per person is that humans must manually record thousands of data points. Humans must furthermore conduct complex statistical analyses using these manually-recorded data points. Unfortunately, it turns out that many if not most of the data points are in error, thus rendering further statistical analyses ineffective.

21.5 EXPERT SYSTEM WORKFLOW TOOLS

Expert system workflow tools are perhaps the brightest spot in the future of SPI. Expert system workflow tools are similar to automated workflow tools. However, they use artificial intelligence, expert system engines, and fuzzy logic. They also use knowledge management to manage the software process.

Expert system workflow tools plan projects, document them, and balance and track project budgets and personnel resources. They assign tasks, direct workflow, measure progress, and enact contingency plans when humans fails to meet expectations.

There are already tools on the market that fall into the class of expert system workflow tools for SPI and software engineering. These tools do more than collect measurements, automate complex algorithms, and predict project and product performance.

Expert system workflow tools currently on the market have databases of design alternatives. Furthermore, they correlate design alternatives to project costs. They also construct complex program and project scenarios that humans would be utterly confounded to do manually.

21.6 SELF-DOCUMENTING APPROACHES

Self-documenting approaches to SPI go hand in hand with automated workflow methods and expert system workflow tools. The heart of most popular SPI methods is manual documentation. That is, popular SPI methods call for documented customer requirements, specifications, project plans, code, and tests. This seems relatively innocuous on the surface, but when we look deeper, we see dozens of documents hundreds of pages thick.

Take, for example, a popular international standard for software engineering. It has five major clauses or types of software processes. However, its software development life cycle alone calls for 27 documents. Many of these documents must be produced for every major system function of a single application or software project. A good software system specification requires over two weeks of labor to perform, at a very minimum. Multiply this by 27 or more, and the economic burden becomes apparent.

Also consider the fact that most people hate the documentation task. They aren't good at it and they don't have the slightest idea how to conform to a software engineering standard. A court of law couldn't make some people conform to the requirements of a software engineering standard.

Self-documenting approaches are the antithesis of popular SPI methods which require people to produce dozens of documents. Manually intensive SPI methods seem to have as a fundamental necessity making humans do what they simply will not do. Self-documenting approaches consist of automating the creation of software documentation.

Software documentation, apart from training in a SPI method, is the single largest source of SPI costs. This holds true for popular approaches to SPI. Once again, software engineering life cycle standards call for the creation of dozens if not hundreds of software documents, and that's only for a single software project which only adds marginal value at best. Documentation requirements of SPI methods are the source of resistance from project managers, engineers, and programmers. Automating documentation production may be the linchpin of successful SPI.

21.7 BOUNDARYLESS VIRTUAL TEAMS

Boundaryless virtual teams are more of a state of things to come rather than a SPI method itself. However, they do represent both a challenge and even affirmation of traditional SPI methods. Most traditional SPI methods consist of managing tightly knit, co-located teams of people. The theory is that people can't be managed unless they can be seen. It is also theorized that people can't be managed effectively unless they sit together.

The economics of bringing people together under one roof are prohibitive. This industrial age principle not only is fading but must be eliminated altogether as a matter of principle. Telecommuting is the future. People must work out of their homes, their regional preferences, and even their national preferences.

With that in mind, SPI methods of the future must embrace the boundaryless virtual team. Does this mean that traditional software project management methods no longer apply? Absolutely not!

Software project management is the key enabler to boundaryless virtual teams. Boundaryless virtual teams cannot function without carefully orchestrated project plans and precisely organized resources. Furthermore, they cannot function without rigorous resource management and tracking. The future of telecommuting will not marginalize software project planning-driven SPI methods, but rather will validate them.

Boundaryless virtual teams are realized by combining all of the best features of traditional and future SPI methods. This includes sound software project and quality management together with trainingless methods and automated workflow methods.

Low-cost commercial tools, noninvasive measurement, expert system workflow tools, and self-documenting approaches are keys to success. In fact, they are the future.

It is ironic that the prevailing SPI methods seem to stand in opposition to boundaryless virtual teams. Do not limit your ROI analysis to the study of 20th century SPI methods. Instead, open your eyes to the bold possibilities of the 21st century.